Inner-City Schools, Multiculturalism, and Teacher Education

D0147563

CRITICAL EDUCATION PRACTICE
VOLUME 8
GARLAND REFERENCE LIBRARY OF SOCIAL SCIENCE
VOLUME 916

CRITICAL EDUCATION PRACTICE

SHIRLEY R. STEINBERG AND JOE L. KINCHELOE, *SERIES EDITORS*

Inner-City Schools, Multiculturalism, and Teacher Education
A Professional Journey

Frederick L. Yeo

Garland Publishing, Inc.
New York and London
1997

Library of Congress Cataloging-in-Publication Data

Yeo, Frederick L.
    Inner-city schools, multiculturalism, and teacher education : a professional
journey / by Frederick L. Yeo.
        p.   cm. — (Garland reference library of social science ; v. 916.
Critical education practice ; v. 8)
    Includes bibliographical references (p.) and index.
    ISBN 0-8153-1434-5 (hc.) — ISBN 0-8153-2311-5 (pbk.)
    1. Education, Urban—Social aspects—United States. 2. Minorities—Edu-
cation—Social aspects—United States. 3. Multicultural education—United
States. 4. Teachers—Training of—United States. I. Title. II. Series: Garland
reference library of social science ; v. 916. III. Series: Garland reference library
of social science. Critical education practice ; vol. 8.
LC5131.Y46   1997
371.96'7—dc20   96–34476
                                                                    CIP

Cover photograph by Tony Donovan, The Ivoryton Studio.
Paperback cover design by Robert Vankeirsbilck.

This book is expressly dedicated to the children of a middle school in Compton, California, for what we taught each other and for their taking me into their lives; for the tears of frustration and the tears of laughter and love. Also to my wife, Nancy for her patience and caring through this struggle. And lastly, to Doug and Jessica for their forbearance and willingness to never take Padre too seriously.

Contents

Acknowledgments

In my struggle to write this book and come to some beginning of an understanding of the intense experiences of teaching in the inner city, I received a great deal of support from special friends, not the least of whom were the kids in my classes and the teachers without whom I would have been lost. They were and are special people who took me into their lives, and mine is the richer for it.

I want to especially express my gratitude to my wife, Nancy, for keeping the faith and supporting this effort through gallons of coffee, and my own children, Doug and Jessica, who kept me from taking myself too seriously.

I have also received significant insight, intellectual and personal, from three teachers who shared my struggle to understand and added their own special intensity—my deep thanks to Svi Shapiro, David Purpel and Fritz Mengert of UNCG for their help, support, inspiration and tolerance. None of this effort nor any alternative vision in education or philosophy would have been possible without the long-time urging, intellectual stimulation, and continued friendship of Barry Kanpol, to whom I owe a career and a voice.

I also want to express my thanks to Joe Kincheloe and Shirley Steinberg for their willingness to acknowledge the struggle in this form, their patience, and especially their friendship. Lastly, it is difficult to thank all of the people who have touched me through their own struggles to make this a better world, even though they were not aware of it; but in particular, I must acknowledge Peter McLaren whose book, *Life in Schools*, first brought clarity into confusion and set the path.

Introduction

Contrary to popular opinion, the state of minority education, communities, and lives in this country is increasingly segregated, impoverished, and marginalized. The United States ranks first among the industrialized nations in the poverty in which one-fourth of America's children live, and 80% percent of them live in our ghettos and barrios (Marable, 1992). The statistics representing racial minority alienation in the United States are both depressing and shameful.[1] Particularly for Native and black Americans, the living conditions of racial minorities are worsening at an accelerating rate when measured by such indicators as infant mortality, life spans, families in poverty, and the statistics that describe renewed segregation, increasing joblessness, and profound educational failure. This information is to a great extent not unknown to the American public or politicians; indeed it has been well publicized. In spite of which, the American populace remains callous about the situation of blacks and other racial minorities. Worse, in a conservative climate there seems to be a new mood of "social meanness pervading the U.S." (Omi & Winant, 1986)

Compounding the problem, the racial demographics of this country are permanently changing with rapidly increasing immigrant and domestic populations of racial minorities and a consequent broadening of diversity. Diversity and race, perhaps more often masked than faced in our history, will be one of the major issues configuring all levels of politics, culture, education and business in the United States as we move into the next century. The twenty-first century will be marked by the struggles of people of color for position, credibility and respect within this and other Western societies (Gordon, 1992).

Historically, we in this country have not performed well as a purported democratic society in the matter of racial minorities. Despite our rhetoric of the "golden door" and Horatio Alger stories of immigrant success, the U.S. has confronted each racially defined minority with a unique form of despotism and degradation. The examples are all too familiar; Native Americans faced genocide, blacks were subjected to racial slavery and segregation, Mexicans were invaded and colonized and Asians faced labor exploitation and exclusion (Omi & Winant, 1986).

Contrary to the dominant culture's successful portrayal of the United States as the "melting pot," the U.S. is not the triumphant accomplishment of a "nation of Immigrants"; instead the white-male-Euro-American version of our own constructed history fosters understandings and social beliefs that have long fueled group and individual stratification and oppression (King & Wilson, 1990). That ethnicity and diversity are seen as problems of social engineering and assimilation of differences is the principle governing U.S. social, economic, political and educational policies at all institutional and governmental levels (Omi & Winant, 1986).

Both a victim and instrument in the cultural and ideological maintenance of these policies is American education. American schools as an institution are in general bewildered both by the increased diversity itself and the persistence of minority failure and alienation as evidenced by the high rate of dropouts and relegation to special education programs of racial minority students (Fine, 1991; Nieto, 1995; Sleeter, 1989; Banks, 1991; Gollnick & Chinn, 1990; McLaren, 1991, hooks & West, 1991). Schools and teachers are often demoralized by increasing difference (where the consequent questions and issues are not simply ignored) despite a plethora of mainstream compensatory programs aimed at ameliorating racial differences in education (McCarthy, 1992). The irony of these intolerable levels of minority underachievement is in their occurrence precisely at a time when school populations in the U.S. are becoming more ethnically diverse. The even greater irony is the use of the word "intolerable"; because what we have been doing through the course of our educational history is, in fact, tolerating endemic minority schooling losses and constructing ever-more-refined processes and educational programs to facilitate the tolerance and rationalize the losses through explanations that thrust the responsibility for failure on the victims. The schools themselves are heavily implicated in the process by providing explanations of racial minority "underachievement" situated within pathological constructions of minority cognitive capacities, family structures, linguistic styles, etc.

> Curriculum practices and interventions predicated on these
> approaches attempt to influence positive changes in minority
> school performance through the manipulation of specific school
> variables, such as teacher behavior, testing, placement counseling
> and so forth. (McCarthy, 1992, p.5)

Contrary to what mainstream and/or conservative spokespersons would have us believe, the social and educational hemorrhaging in minority education is not the result of standardized test results and teaching rote memorized facts (Nieto, 1995; Kincheloe & Steinberg, 1992), nor in the representation that school failure is either the fault of the students, who are inferentially inferior, or of the social characteristics of their communities (Nieto, 1995). Instead it is derived from the continuous playing out of social, economic, and political constructs of difference and race, class and gender with little regard for the public well-being. Witness the tragic plight of one of two black and two out of five Hispanic children living in poverty in the U.S. today and attending predominantly racially segregated schools typified by dwindling resources and increasing frustration and irrelevance.

The schools and education, with their assertion of moral, ideological, and political neutrality, are inseparably linked to the crisis of urban America's cultural and social life. The whole educational paraphernalia of objectivity, standardized testing, instrumental pedagogy, stratified bureaucracy and ethical and political disengagement reinforces and replicates the forms of cultural/moral hegemony which elicits increasing levels of alienation, cynicism and dwindling levels of public legitimacy (Shapiro, 1992). As Cornel West charges in his 1993 book, *Beyond Eurocentrism and Multiculturalism*, "white America has been historically weak-willed in insuring racial justice . . . we must acknowledge that as a people—we are on a slippery slope toward economic strife, social turmoil and cultural chaos" (West, 1993a, p.15).

Educators at all levels are realizing that the demographic changes in our society are requiring people who never had to deal with each other to seriously work together. Schools are being required to respond to the challenge of educating different groups of students and to confront issues of racism, sexism, and classism that to a large part have been previously ignored and are hounding the educational community with increasing intensity (Grant, 1992). Within the established hierarchy of education, the increasing panacea for social and educational diversity problems has become the various formulations and practices of multiculturalism, albeit truncated and/or irrelevant to its clientele.

Presently, multicultural education is receiving significant national and state bureaucratic attention; hardly a state has not incorporated some formalized statement as to multiculturalism. As student populations have become increasingly racially and culturally diverse and the teacher force increasingly white, interest in training teachers, establishing new curricula, and revising pedagogy within some construction of multiculturalism has grown (Sleeter, 1994).

What has become increasingly apparent to those who have worked intensely with racial minority students is that the mainstream incorporation of the principles of even the least radical approach to multicultural education has led to more of the same failure as did the traditional mainstream approaches. Both liberal and conservative variations of multicultural education are seriously flawed in their failure to address moral, social and political issues, thereby perpetuating the marginalization of minority schools and youth. What is needed in order to construct significant changes in education is a triumvirate of anti-racist policies, emancipatory pedagogy and cultural consciousness that involves political action at both school and community levels (Gordon, 1992).

One of the intrinsic problems of multicultural education has been that it arises from the social and educational margins, from the conceptual, epistemic and ethical hinterlands of our polity. Its origination and absorption by the schools has come about due directly to minority demands for equality, cultural inclusion and democratic participation (Carlson, 1992). The issues of multicultural education are often and unfortunately perceived by mainstream educators as divisive, particularistic, and alien, as are the students whom mainstream education is currently failing. One of the reasons for this state of affairs is that the literature on multicultural education in this country reveals few theoretical models to guide classroom implementation of an education that is truly multicultural (Gordon, 1992). In addition, the few models, texts, and "how-to" books on multiculturalism are generally replicative of mainstream and/or liberal paradigms lacking any deep probing of the profound moral and/or social issues implicating education or the incorporation of concepts such as the nonsynchronous nature of race, class, and gender (McCarthy, 1992; Sleeter & Grant, 1987) or the need to connect multiculturalist issues with political issues of the urban community and/or the greater society (Weiner, 1993; Yeo, 1995). The general approach to multicultural education in schools, textbooks, and the great percentage of educational literature is assimilatory, denigrating the cultures of non-white Americans and giving rise to deculturalization, alienation, and ultimately the rejection of education's methods and content by non-whites (Banks, 1991), which is concomitantly perceived and labelled as educational failure. Where it intends a more emancipatory effort, multiculturalism often founders on misassumptions about how urban students form identity, individually and collectively, and/or the failure to allow space for the conflicting historical perspectives of its clientele and/or the intrinsic basal logic of its liberatory project (Weiner, 1993; Yeo, 1995).

Worse for the future of minority educational prospects in this country has been the almost total lack of understanding of any of the foregoing within teacher education. Although teacher education programs have in general incorporated at least minimal attention to multiculturalism, they are usually grounded in the assimilation mode which continues a pattern of irrelevance to urban education (Grant, 1992; Sleeter, 1991). Most teacher education programs in this country are guilty of poorly preparing pre-service teachers for inner-city service, or worse, suggesting that urban schools are only a temporal aberration and derailing any serious discussion by denigrating references to urban schools' practices of hiring alternatively certified teachers as if those schools had any choice in the matter—a thinly disguised racist construction of pre-service teachers' understanding of urban schools and children.

The purpose of this text is to address both experientially and theoretically the nature of contemporary urban education, particularly in terms of teaching and pedagogy, to connect central principles (paradigms) of our culture in general and in education specifically to urban schools, and to connect both themes to the specifics of teacher education. It is framed by my personal experiences teaching in the Los Angeles inner city and my angst at the human tragedy seemingly so easily tolerated by our society and the irrelevance and failure of institutional education's response.

In significant part, this book derives out of my own experience as a new teacher with a first assignment in an inner-city middle school. I believe it reflects the profound failure of teacher education in urban schools, the impoverished resources imposed by educational jurisdictions, and the effects of social triaging and marginalization on both the inner city and the schools and those I came to think of as "my children."

This book is intended to address the problems raised by McCarthy and Gordon, as well as others whose concerns and anxieties about our future and the direction of education appear within the explicit and implicit boundaries of this text. The primary themes are: (1) the current manner in which pedagogical and curricular theorization of urban education is disconnected from the exigencies of the urban community; i.e., its profound irrelevance; (2) the extent and depth to which the social ideology of racism constructs and frames the rationales, politics and economics of urban education; (3) the lack of understanding of the relations between the dominant ideologies and practices of teacher education and the lives, cultures, and personal experiences of racial minorities; (4) the theories and manifestations of multicultural education as it has been inculcated within urban schools as a panacea for diversity and failure and the reasons for its continuation of that failure; and (5) for me most importantly, the postulation of how these understandings can be implicated in the construction of praxes for teacher education within the specific topical frame of inner-city schools.

Although this text is not intended as a "how-to" primer on teaching in the inner city, I will periodically make suggestions or represent models of teaching and/or curriculum as to both teaching in urban schools and as to teacher education. However, given the limitations of such deriving out of my own experience and the fact that all things are different, my intent is to pose the context for others to practice their own experiential understandings.

In Chapter One, I will introduce the reader briefly and descriptively to the inner-city school as an institution, the societal and cultural ideologies that ground the rationales for its actualities, and the impact of national history and thinking that sets the context for the theoretical formulations in which this book is framed. This will include specific discussion of differing concepts of ethnicity, race, and racial identity with perspectives on how these have played out in urban education. Since I believe that we cannot know where we are without some idea of from whence we come, I will briefly discuss the history of the segregated urban centers in this country from within the perspectives of minority understandings. Lastly, this chapter will link that history with the endemic ideology and sociology of racism that has provided and does provide connective frameworks for whites in this country to rationalize and facilitate continued marginalization of those who have the ill luck to be described as people of color.

Chapter Two will investigate the conditions and forces, both sociological and educational, that demark the inner-city school. This will include presenting analytically the economic and environmental (communal) issues pertinent to these schools, particularly those demanded and maintained by the continued curricular and pedagogical dominance of mandated compensatory programs, the history of funding and resources, and the understandings of what constitutes the teaching and learning that teachers, students and parents bring to the school site. The intent of this chapter is to bring together, as much as possible, current anthropological and educational research on inner-city schools and their constituencies within the frame of the variegated conflicts between classrooms and streets. This chapter will introduce and analyze (critique) the approaches to actual curriculum and pedagogical styles used by teachers and administrators in inner-city schools. It will provide an in-depth presentation of the primary mode of teaching; the "Basic Skills Program," its rationale(s) and its results in terms of how its ideologies and practices have influenced styles of discipline, pedagogy, and relationships in these schools.

Chapter Three will attempt to enlist the reader vicariously in exploring one teacher's experiences at a predominantly African American South Los Angeles middle school. Although recognizing the egocentricity of such a narrative, the intent is to as candidly as possible describe one teacher's expectations, frustrations, adaptations, failures, and successes within the boundaries formed by the identities of others whose relationships are delineated by the institution. I have tried as gently and lovingly as possible to convey a picture (admittedly partial and fractured) of the school in total, including other teachers, students, and administrators whose realities and epistemes impinged on mine and those of my children. Lastly, this chapter will relate through a critical narrative style how the ideologies, assumptions and practices discussed in Chapter Two played out within the boundaries of real hopes and despairs. It will also set the stage for more specific references to be made in later chapters to the connections between urban schools, institutional teacher preparation and multicultural pedagogy.

Chapter Four will analyze the current reforms within education (specifically as they are directed toward inner-city schools and, to a lesser extent, teacher education) rhetorically constructed to solve the problems of growing demographic difference and to "celebrate" the burgeoning diversity within the nation. Although I intend to sketch the multicultural approaches typologized by others for understanding of the different rationales and purposes to multiculturalism, my main object will be a critique of multicultural education as typified within urban education and how it has played out in the actualities of urban teaching and teacher education, specifically within those spaces that purport to speak to preparing teachers to work in urban schools. Although multicultural education cannot escape general critique, I will concentrate the analysis on urban schools and their cross-connections within teacher education as played out through current promulgations of multiculturalism.

Chapter Five moves away from the inner-city school to the arena of institutionalized teacher education in general, emphasizing its impact on teachers' understandings of minority students in and out of urban schools. Although teacher education will be discussed in terms of its overarching ideologies and enabling paradigms, the goal is to tease out those strands of teacher preparation applicable to preparing (or not) predominantly white, middle-class pre-service teachers to become (or not) urban educators. This chapter will connect with Chapters Two and Three to illustrate and critique the dysfunctionalism of educational preparation with reference to the environment of urban schools and with Chapter Four to investigate the connections between inner-city schools and teacher pre-service preparation.

Finally, in Chapter Six, the text will present a critical interrogation of the missing linkages between urban schools, institutional teacher education, and multicultural education. With some acknowledged sense of hubris I will sketch what I believe to be meaningful alternatives so as to propound synergistic connectivities between the three themes. Admittedly the hubris lies in the assumption that what seemed to emerge at one school site may not emerge at others, but, given the profound failure of educational efforts in the preponderance of inner-city schools and the utter meaninglessness of teacher education in relation to those schools, this book represents a personal choice for educational improvement conditioned by the knowledge that within the context of the greater society and its understandings of race perhaps little effect may occur. Yet, I will propose change within a sense of guarded hope that at least the lives of my children and the teachers who work with them may be bettered in some small way. Lastly, this chapter represents an attempt to make sense out of personal experience and thereby perhaps politicize it.

Limitations

> Scholars who write about an ethnic group to which they do not belong rarely discuss in the introductions the ethical issues of their race privilege, or what motivates them, or why they feel their perspective is important. (hooks, 1989, p. 44)

As in every text there are silences, so too as this is written and read, there are embedded intrinsic limitations derived from my own focus and interests. For example, although referencing issues of the state, ethnicity, class and gender, and individual and collective identity as terrains of struggle and nonsynchrony, I have chosen the boundaries of ethnicity and culture, albeit they are admittedly osmotic. This is not to imply or assert that these issues are any less momentous, specifically as to gender; however, time and space impose their own silencing.

Another limitation is the *ethical* danger of writing about the experiences of a group to which I do not and cannot belong. Since I proceed to do so, there is the concern that it will be used to reinforce the very domination I critique. There is a risk entailed with being a white, male "authority" writing about groups to which I cannot claim membership, since as bell hooks has so trenchantly noted, as long as my authority is constituted by either the absence of the voices of the individuals whose experiences I seek to address, or the dismissal of those voices as unimportant, the subject-object dichotomy is maintained and domination is reinforced (hooks, 1989).

In the manner akin to "witnessing," this text-cum-narrative is being written to represent anger and frustration at the conditions in which urban students, their families and teachers are mired and socially triaged. It derives of the subjective and the understanding of those who are silent within its borders. However, the assertion is made herein that their voices are interwoven between the lines of text; one need only listen. The primary framework of this "work" is an unconditional caring and love for those who took me into their lives and in so doing, irrevocably changed mine.

Lastly, in organizing this text, I have tried to keep in mind Abraham Heschel's admonitions that reverse mainstream, and often radical, spins on "celebrating diversity." That is, assimilation (i.e., masking and deculturalization of difference) is not celebratory;

celebration is a confrontation, giving attention to the meaning of one's actions (Heschel, 1965). Celebration without appreciation is artificial and impersonal; the inability to celebrate in this sense is a sign of social insolvency and means according to Heschel that the man of our time is losing the power of celebration: "Instead of celebrating, he seeks to be amused or entertained, while celebration is an active state, . . . To be entertained is a passive state . . . [it] is to share in a greater joy, to participate in an eternal drama." (Heschel, 1965, p. 116)

Quintessentially, celebration is an act of expressing respect or reverence for that which another person needs or honors (Heschel, 1965).

This book is thusly intended as an act of "celebration," of confrontation with our social and racial insolvency and its attendant educational moments within an inner-city school.

Notes

1. By the year 2000, one in three Americans will be from groups currently designated as "minority"; five states and 53 major cities will have a majority of minority populations.

At least 40 percent of Hispanics and 60 percent of blacks drop out by 10th grade; 56 percent of Hispanics and 44 percent of blacks are functional illiterates. Forty percent of U.S. immigrants are Asian, and 40 percent of those are on welfare and 27 percent of the students drop out of school. In Los Angeles, over 80 languages are spoken in the schools; Chicago school statistics evidence that 75 percent of blacks in that city's schools drop out of high school.

See also: Schensul, J. and Carroll, T. (1990). "Visions of America in the 1990's and Beyond: Negotiating Cultural Diversity and Educational Change," *Education and Urban Society*, 22:4, Aug. 1990; Berry, G. & J. Asamen. (1989). *Black Students*, Newbury Park: Sage Publications; Fine, Michelle. (1991). *Framing Drop-Outs*, Albany, NY: SUNY Press; Weiner, Lois. (1993). *Preparing Teachers for Urban Schools: Lessons from Thirty Years of School Reform*, NY: Teachers College Press; Comer, J. & N. Haynes. (1990). "Helping Black Children Succeed: The Significance of Social Factors," in *Going to School: the African American Experience* (K. Lomotey, Ed.), Albany: SUNY Press; and Coontz, Stephanie, "The American Family and the

Nostalgia Trap," Kappan Special Report, *Phi Delta Kappan*, March 1995, pp. K1-K20.

Inner-City Schools, Multiculturalism, and Teacher Education

CHAPTER ONE

Connecting Inner Cities and Urban Schools: Racism's "Slippery Slope"

That Justice is a blind goddess
Is a thing to which we black are wise:
Her bandage hides two festering sores
That once perhaps were eyes. (L. Hughes [1])

Introduction

A short drive up Martin Luther King Boulevard in South Los Angeles presents a stark contrast to the usual images of the city; white beaches, palm trees, and Beverly Hills—this is the zone—a terrain of black, nightmarish, kaleidoscopic images of blackened husks of buildings, black wrought-iron bars on store windows and doors, black roving police cars and helicopters, and black blank faces inhabiting one of America's urban centers. Its atmosphere of ugly xenophobia, palpable tension and violence bears witness to the consequences of the lethal linkage of economic decline, cultural decay, and political lethargy in American life (Bell, 1992).

As we approach the end of the twentieth century, still struggling with the dramatic changes that have taken place in the cultural and socioeconomic fabric of this society, evidence of continued, if not exacerbated, racial inequality ought to be viewed as alarming evidence of a potential lethality within the commons. The racism that supported nineteenth-century slavery is far from dead, and the civil rights gains of the 1960s are being steadily eroded (Bell, 1992).

Nowhere is this more true than in America's urban centers,

populated in increasing numbers and diversity by those people particularly burdened with life-long poverty and soul-devastating despair, who live beyond the pale of the American Dream (Bell, 1992). As William Glasgow noted in his 1980 research of the Watts ghetto after the '65 riots; "No fanciful detention centers 'secretly' being built to house niggers could be worse than the reality of the modern ghetto trap. . . . No one is spared the destructive consequences of ghetto living" (Glasgow, p. 154).

Scattered within America's urban ghettos and barrios are those sites euphemistically termed "inner-city" schools, learning centers for those destined to become members of America's "underclass."

As noted in the Introduction, this book intends to describe, analyze, and struggle with possible changes in the practices and underlying theoretical interpretations of urban education and its connectivity to teacher education in the United States, specifically that form of teacher preparation housed in institutional sites such as colleges and universities. Currently, much of the educational literature attempts to explain the experiences and structures of urban education in such a way that the schools and their occupants are disconnected from their very environment, as if they could be analyzed *in absentia* from their community. That literature (indicative of how much of the educational community views the world outside of schools) reflects the pervasive ideologies of this country wherein loss, failure, and personal devastation are seen as the failures of the victim.

As will be discussed in Chapter Two, urban education's curriculum, the teachers' pedagogy, the availability of resources, the defining and labeling of urban students as "at risk" and the restrictive isolated physicalities of the schools themselves all illustrate the plethora of state and federal compensatory programs aimed at rhetorically "curing" the problem of minority educational failure and simultaneously maintaining the racialized understandings of most white Americans.

Urban schools, particularly the inner-city variety, do not exist outside of society, however much the majority of the populace would desire it. Instead, they represent the educational portion of a society that as Heath & McLaughlin (1993) have commented has had a love-hate relationship with cultural diversity. In what is perhaps one of the most divisive contradictions of our society, the public seems to want on one hand to discern and label any possible source of ethnicity or cultural diversity while on the other hand to claim to promote integration and cultural homogenization to deny differences (Heath & McLaughlin, 1993).

In order to understand to any extent the students and the schools in an urban environment, it is incumbent upon us to be able to contextualize their surroundings demographically, economically, socially, and, certainly, historically. Although the sociality of an urban minority community might seem to be a good place to initiate our exploration of urban schools, it actually is not. No community, no matter how marginalized within the overall main society (or maybe because of it), exists outside of the dominant cultural and ideologic influences of that social, political and cultural milieu. Its very status as marginalized derives from the common sense understandings of the dominant hegemonic culture (Giroux, 1991a; Geertz, 1983; Eagleton, 1991). This is certainly no less true for America's urban ghettos and barrios.

Therefore in this chapter, we will begin examining those ideologic paradigms by which the larger American society views its minority members as well as the social effects on those people(s) that white, middle-class and working-class Americans mean when they speak of diversity, "them," or some more familiar racial pejorative. This chapter will examine within the frame of those common understandings the demographic, economic, and educational results of America's conflict with diversity and the resulting configuration of what is regarded by Americans, according to Stephen Haymes (1995), as our own jungle, the inner city. The balance of this book is configured by the open assertion that much of what passes for urban education, the forces that socioculturally constructed the urban minority communities that radiate frustration, violence, and nihilism (Bell, 1992; West, 1993), and the demographic statistics that reflect the profound failure of a democratic society are all inescapably and directly related to the ebb and flow of a basal ideological, quasireligious belief in the rightness and righteousness of white superiority.

As I often suggest to my introductory education classes, the social triaging and human defeat statistics we discuss so cavalierly are relatively easy to decipher in the sense of determining their source. They are the result of a belief in the intrinsic inferiority of minorities (whether through nature or nurture, genetics or environment, does not matter). To accept that premise is to accept that people whose characteristics have not been socially constructed as "white" are genetically and/or culturally less intelligent, less capable, less productive, etc. Of course, if that is true, it begs the question of the rationale for so much white fear, particularly as to black sexuality (hooks, 1992). Very few students will own up to such open bias, and most vehemently deny believing in that scenario. Secondly, we can postulate that the statistics are the fault of education and teachers; that somehow teachers target minorities for poorer education. Students find that it does not make much sense to blame teachers when they have little empowerment themselves. This only leaves the source of social, economic and political power as the possible villain; that is, the State which represents the majority, or at least a plurality, in a democracy. It is the State which represents the cumulative sense of the dominant culture. Granted that the logic seems simplistic, but through the ensuing dialogue students begin to understand that Pogo was correct; we have met the enemy and he is us, which constitutes a fitting starting point to an analysis of urban education.

Thus, in order to comprehend the "why" of inner city schools and in order to offer for discussion any amelioration of their conditions, practices, and failures, we must confront the consummatory social ideology of our culture; the defining of the "Other," the alien stranger, and the subsequent dehumanization of those so labelled on the basis of race, not ethnicity, meritocracy or distorted individualism. To understand what passes for education in urban schools, the State mandates that position the funding, the curriculum and/or pedagogy, and the ongoing urban travesty against democratic ideals is to confront what Derrick Bell (1992) calls the "faces at the bottom of the well; the maintenance in American society of racism" which is deeply and inextricably embedded in the psychology, economics, politics, religion, education and culture of our society. This is specifically not to argue that economics, other ideologies of the American scene (individualism, competition, elitism, etc.), and extracts of Euro-Western culture and philosophy (Positivism, Rationalism and Empiricism) are not important in forming American society. However, the issue I will address herein is their synchronicity within the penumbra of racism and the historical development of inner cities.

The Inner City: The Economic and Social Evolution of the Urban Community and the "Underclass"

The current environment of the inner city evolved to its present visage through a complex history of economic and demographic changes, increased migration of peoples traditionally marginalized in our society (blacks, Hispanics, Native Americans and Asians), and the gradual impoverishment of the cities through an eroding tax and industrial base. Some of the worst urban areas in the country today were working class, predominantly white neighborhoods in the early 1960s. However, over the next ten years, as racial barriers to housing collapsed in these communities, often due to civil rights legislation, and the familiar 70s syndrome of "white flight" (where black families moved in and whites moved out to newly built "white" suburbs), these communities underwent drastic and debilitating changes (Wilson, 1987; West, 1993).

As the country's economic infrastructure changed through the 1960s and 70s, the types of industry historically found in urban centers either relocated (sometimes out of the country entirely) or closed down permanently (Wilson, 1987). In this period of demographic and economic flux, many of the middle-class black families, churches, businesses and social organizations also relocated to suburbia. "White flight" was joined by "black flight" removing mainstream and minority social and support systems from the now increasingly poor, unemployed, and traumatized inner-city ghetto (Wilson, 1987; Glasgow, 1980) and creating what Cornel West (1993) refers to as "chocolate cities and vanilla suburbs"; wherein the former is "colored" by devastating unemployment, homelessness, and rage-borne crime that typifies these existential wastelands (West, 1993):

> We have always had to deal with traumatization, but we had buffers. We had Black civil society, Black family, Black churches, Black schools, and so forth. What market forces have done in the last twenty-five years is to thoroughly weaken and/or remove entirely those institutions of Black civil society . . . from the cities. (hooks & West, 1991, p. 97)

The current economic straits of the inner cities has several primary sources as described in a book by W. Wilson (*The Truly Disadvantaged*, 1987) and by other anthropological researchers:

First, black middle and working classes moved to the suburbs, taking community infrastructures and social support institutions with them, e.g., churches, small businesses that often buffered economic hard times by serving as employer of last resort for urban denizens, stores and service agencies (Wilson, 1987; Massey & Denton, 1993; West, 1993).

Second, industry jobs that traditionally did not require high school education moved out of the ghettos to rural areas, such as the South or out of the country altogether (Wilson, 1987).

Third, the mid-city zones went from centers of production to high-tech information and financial centers, causing an increase in service-sector jobs requiring higher literacy and educational skills (Wilson, 1987).

Fourth, schools provided an increasingly skills-based state mandated education preparatory for the very jobs that were at the same time disappearing from the cities; i.e., the urban schools' education became increasingly extraneous to the type and number of jobs available for graduates (Carlson, 1992b; Wilson, 1987).

Fifth, at the same time, federal and state fiscal policies decreased per capita (and total) expenditures providing social, educational and welfare support (Wilson, 1987).

These structural changes in the urban economy, massive joblessness, and concurrent out-migration of working- & middle-class blacks from metropolitan centers from 1970 to 1980 progressively worked to unravel the social fabric of the inner cities (Young & Melnick, 1988).

One indicator of these changes has been the dramatic increase in unemployment and poverty in the inner cities. From 1975-1985, in the five largest U.S. cities, the number of poverty areas increased by 161% (Wilson, 1987). The jobless or unemployment rate for black males in the inner cities rose to around 75% (Glasgow, 1980; Massey & Denton, 1993). The apartheid-like economics of the ghetto translate into high crime (50 percent of black males will have been arrested at least once by age fifteen), unremitting poverty, dilapidated housing projects, mostly female-headed single parent families, rampant alcohol and drug addiction, proliferating liquor stores and crack houses, graffiti and gangs. "Crime and crack have become the new urban slavery" (Marable, 1992).

At the highest level of underdevelopment, the daily life of urban dwellers becomes a continuous problematic, an unresolvable set of dilemmas which confronts everyone caught in this existence. The patterns of degradation are unrelenting, destroying many efforts to create social stability and/or any level of collective political integrity (Marable, 1983).

A report by the National Research Council (1989) summarizes these patterns:

1. Black poverty rates are two to three times higher than white rates.
2. Residential segregation patterns have remained relatively unchanged since the 1960s.
3. Blacks are disproportionately victims of crime.
4. Approximately 50 percent of the prison population is black, with more blacks per capita in prison in the United States than in South Africa.
5. The majority of black children live in families headed by mothers, as is the case for only one in five for white children (Council Report cited in Jaynes & Williams, 1989).

Although Wilson frames his analysis in the language of economics, it is not difficult to note that most of the residents of these urban areas are predominantly black or Hispanic; very few are poor whites. This should suggest that underlying the economic explanations is another analysis taking into account the racialized segregation contemporaneous with the economic dissolution of urban communities.

As noted by Massey & Denton (1993) in *American Apartheid*, most Americans (particularly white Americans) realize that urban centers are peopled by racial minorities for the most part but few appreciate the depth of black segregation or the degree to which it is maintained by ongoing institutional arrangements and contemporary individual actions (Massey & Denton, 1993). The assumption sponsored by mainstream political, economic and cultural leaders (including educators) and maintained by educational institutions is that segregation is to be found in only a few places in the South and a few of the larger cities. Even textbooks for educational introduction courses posit that segregation has been cured by busing, civil rights laws, and affirmative action (giving rise to the current political calls for the removal of the same) (Hessong & Weeks, 1991). Perhaps a brief glimpse of the underseam of America in the inner city was afforded us during the Los Angeles riots in April 1992, but it was quickly buried under normalcy. Massey & Denton (1993) argue that there is little recent data to suggest in fact that racial segregation has been moderated over the last decade, nor is there anything in the political or social climate of the country to suggest that it will. They contend that Wilson's theories, while substantially correct, did not go far enough in determining the causes of inner-city devastation by failing to note the way racial segregation concentrates poverty spatially: that it was segregation that confined the increased deprivation to a small number of densely packed and geographically isolated areas (Massey & Denton, 1993).

> Our fundamental argument is that racial segregation—and its characteristic institutional form, the black ghetto—are the key structural factors responsible for the perpetuation of black poverty in the United States. Residential segregation is the principal organizational feature of American society that is responsible for the creation of the urban underclass (Massey & Denton, 1993, p. 9).

The key argument here, one in line with the construction assertion as to racism above, is that segregation (in whatever form, including that of Native American reservations) functions institutionally to link other racialized inequities by the synergistic concentration of effect in an isolated spatial/urban area. As Stephen Haymes charges in *Race, Culture and the City*, urban areas represent spatially racialized social values in the urban realization of the ideology of apartheid (Haymes, 1995). Or, put more specifically, Haymes suggests that our way of seeing cities and thinking about cities is deeply racialized. It is in this racialized urbanism that blackness is the urban Other, the disordered and the dangerous (Haymes, 1995).

Although typically whites respond to this argument that white ethnicities have suffered ghettoization (e.g., Jews, Irish, Polish, Italian), that rationale confuses ethnicity with raciality, and, as Massey & Denton (1993) maintain, none of the white ethnic groups has ever experienced the sustained segregation of racial minorities. White society has defined the issues of urban-ness as technical, negating the issues of race and segregation and promulgating policies within the mediated image of the city as alien, foreign, a place to fear; i.e., the urban has become a metaphor for race and more specifically for black, for the jungle (Haymes, 1995). More pointed, however, is the charge that the maintenance of racial segregation is intrinsic and rooted in American culture. The minority enclaves of the inner city, ghetto and barrio are part of modern American society. They are maintained by a set of institutions, attitudes, and practices that are deeply embedded in the structure of American life. As conditions in the ghetto have worsened and as poor blacks have adapted socially and culturally to this deteriorating environment, the ghetto has assumed even greater importance as an institutional tool for isolating the by-products of racial oppression: crime, drugs, violence, illiteracy, poverty, despair, and their growing social and economic costs (Massey & Denton, 1993).

Although Massey & Denton's explication of the role of systemic segregation in the creation and sustaining of the racialized inner city supports and extends Wilson's more economic thesis, the issue of the ideologic rationale for segregation still remains. The question of what social and/or cultural thinking rationalizes for the greater population, the existence of segregation, was not dealt with by Massey & Denton, but others have done so in an attempt to understand how in a democratic society a substantial portion of the population can be marginalized by the rest over long periods of time, under dehumanizing conditions and justified by public and private rhetoric that places responsibility on the very people the society has oppressed.

In conjunction with Wilson's predominantly economic approach, there are two cultural theories that seem cogent to explain the occurrence and perpetuation of the inner city condition: first, the "cultural ecology" thesis developed and argued by John Ogbu (an educational and cultural anthropologist at the University of California), and, second, the argument that urban conditions and racialization arise out of endemic societal and institutional racism within the dominant white Euro-American culture, which is aimed specifically at deculturalizing people of color.

Ogbu's "Caste" or "Cultural Ecology" Theory

One theory attempting to explain the current existence and conditions of the inner city is that of "cultural ecology" or "caste stratification" formulated by J. Ogbu (1978, 1988, 1989, 1990). Ogbu differentiates minority groups as primarily cultural and/or political and as racially derived, and then distinguishes "subordinate" minorities from those groups that do not share similar social problems. Ogbu suggests that all subordinate minorities (those in oppressive power relations) can be classified into three categories autonomous, immigrant and caste-like (Ogbu, 1990, 1988).

The "autonomous" minorities are often part of the dominant culture who suffer some prejudice, but are not truly subordinated (usually racially white, such as the Irish, Italians, etc.), and any separateness is not based on specialized denigrated economic, political, or socio-ritual roles. Nor is any separateness maintained by institutionalized actions of law, finance, education or public policy making. They are predominantly assimilated and maintain ethnic minority status usually as a result of historical or religious consciousnesses; i.e., Jews, national groups, etc. (Ogbu, 1988).

The "immigrant" minorities are those who have come to the United States generally voluntarily and, although subject to discrimination and/or social subordination (which may or may not be based on racism), have not internalized the effects, particularly as a group (Ogbu, 1988; Levinson, 1992). They tend to measure individual and/or social success against conditions of their respective homelands and believe fervently in the "American Dream." Although aware collectively of discrimination against them, there often tends to be a sense that they match previous immigrant assimilatory patterns and succeeding generations will blend and thereby escape the current oppressive conditions. Often they are portrayed as being more conservative than most minority groups, and although they may well be, they are also used as a stalking horse on behalf of the Right's rhetoric against minorities (Nieto, 1995). Examples of this group might include Cubans, Eastern Europeans, and some Central and South American groups. This particular grouping may seem somewhat problematic when we examine the recent experiences of groups such as Jamaicans, Grenadeans, Haitians, and other Caribbean islanders, who because of skin coloration often find themselves considered to be blacks.

The "caste-like" minority characterization is assigned their grouping by virtue of ascribed racial/ethnic attributes and have few or no options for escape. They are involuntarily structured within the society through slavery or conquest and have internalized their relegation to permanent inferiority (Ogbu, 1988, 1990); e.g., blacks, Hispanics and Native Americans. Ogbu (1988, 1990) contends that this grouping is almost entirely racially defined and delineated and that these minority groups face what none of the other minority category groups does, a "job ceiling," which circumscribes occupational, educational and economic opportunities (individually and collectively). Social barriers constructed and practiced within the endemic racism and discrimination consign them to jobs at the lowest level of status, power, and income (or the ubiquitous labor surplus pool) if not to public welfare dependency (Ogbu, 1990, 1978).

Ogbu extends his "cultural" theory further by arguing that the "job ceiling's" existence has caused the social evolution of "survival strategies" or patterns of behavior to effect "survival" by these particular minorities (Ogbu, 1990, 1978), such as seeking (as does the black middle class) to comply with dominant ideologies in conventional society and jobs or in oppositional strategies seen in every inner city as in the "street economy," the nonconventional economic and cultural adaptations to the job ceiling. Ogbu argues that some blacks consciously disassociate themselves from black collective identity and from a black cultural frame of reference and prefer to "assimilate" or follow white ways (Ogbu, 1988). However, he also suggests that there exists a distinct black cultural frame of reference that guides their relationship with whites and that guides their behavior, especially in white controlled or modelled institutions (Ogbu, 1988).

Ogbu believes that many of the behaviors and understandings evident in black and Hispanic children (and parents) in urban schools are derived from these survival strategies; they are part of that collective and learned identity that all "caste-like" minorities develop in opposition to the dominant white culture. Ogbu, in conjunction with other researchers (e.g., Weis, 1988; Solomon, 1988, 1992; Weiner, 1993), argues that black culture, in particular, has developed contradictory patterns of behavior with reference to education that are specifically configured by such survival strategies. Black culture, since (if not before) slavery, has regarded education as a vital method of generational and group improvement, however, at the same time being suspicious and oppositional to what are often perceived as "white" schools (Ogbu, 1988, 1993; Nieto, 1995). In proof of this position, one might cite data that show high levels of absenteeism in predominantly white colleges for black students versus the reverse at historically black colleges (Hacker, 1992). Ogbu argues that much of black and Hispanic children's behavior in schools is understandable if viewed from this perspective.

However, Ogbu's theory, specifically as to education, is too structural; it fails to take into account those who actively seek (and gain to some extent) assimilation into the dominant culture. Additionally, Levinson (1992) maintains that Ogbu's theory positions students too passively and fails to take into account their active cultural production in opposition to teachers, school, and parents that is irrepresentative of racial or "caste" meanings. Ogbu does not take into account issues of ideology or the effect of the State as a mediative or struggled-over site of social production (Levinson, 1992; Fordham, 1991).

Another problem with Ogbu's theory is the lack of any correlation between the social stratification in his archetype "ecology" and issues of race, racial formations, and/or societal structural racism. The theory fails to connect generationally as to the "immigrant" groups. While the first generation is accepting of status and discrimination, what happens from there? Obviously, their descendants do not have their perspective and have suffered from racial discrimination, so is there a fourth group, do they assimilate to the level of the "autonomous" minorities or become relegated to the "caste-like" groups? Ogbu does not attempt that analysis and therein fails to theorize as to the long-term effects of either racism or minority group cultural production. While Ogbu does not analyze racism within this country, other theorists have attempted to do so.

Theories and Practices of Racial Formation in the United States

In attempts to explain and/or understand the continued existence in the United States of racialized groups, racial discrimination and segregation, racism and the impact of these factors on urban communities and schools, cultural theorists have argued that racism is a fundamental social construct that pervasively frames social relations, economics, education, etc. in the United States. Institutionalized racism, which is both subtle and endemic in this society, connects to the development and maintenance of the conditions of inner cities. For example, Yetman in *Majority and Minority: The Dynamics of Racial and Ethnic Relations* (1988) argues that institutional discrimination refers to the effects of inequalities that are rooted in the system-wide operation of a society and involves policies and practices which appear to be neutral in their effect on minority individuals or groups but actually disproportionately impact upon them in harmful ways.

Although the State has legitimated actions to eliminate racial discrimination, and claims are made that equal treatment and opportunity abound, this ignores the fact that minority groups in the inner cities quite simply do not have access to the "equal" job market and are thus outside of that equal treatment, affirmative action, and opportunity. As Glasgow (1980) argued, escaping underclass entrapment is not determined simply by having a job or income. The underclass entrapment of poor blacks is furthered by their lack of connections with institutions that act as feeder systems to the labor market (Glasgow, 1980).

These limitations are evidence of institutional racism in many cases. For example, "red-lining" (the pernicious practice of denying mortgages, insurance, allowing usury by merchants within certain demarked urban zones, which although illegal, is still ignored or rationalized by authorities) is endemic in inner cities. As will be described in Chapter Two, curriculum and pedagogy in urban schools are explicitly stated in both State and school "mission statements" as existing to prepare students for jobs that patently do not exist in urban communities, yet the practice is continued by State mandate. Although it is difficult and expensive to procure a liquor store license in suburban areas, it is relatively easy and cheap to do so in the ghetto.

Usury and "bait & switch" sales tactics are illegal but rampant in urban areas. One of the factors fueling the anti-Korean violence in Los Angeles in April 1992 was the continued (and government condoned) existence and imposition on the populace of usury rates approaching 100 percent in some cases. Another example from Los Angeles: it is no secret in California that unemployment runs approximately 75 percent in South Los Angeles, but when contracts for rebuilding were granted by the City of Los Angeles, they uniformly went to Japanese or suburban contractors, and the contract provisions for the most part did not require hiring of indigenous workers (West, 1990).

A last example is educational funding. Again using Los Angeles as an example, California law requires the State to provide equal funding for all schools, which the State of California does. However it appropriates the same amount per student to every school district, ignoring the fact that many school districts have far wealthier tax bases than do the inner cities and provide resources for their schools that outstrip what an inner-city district has to spend. The argument that the State guarantees equal school financing is simply fallacious. Additionally, in many cases, "high-tech" or defense industries located in urban areas are granted property tax exemptions or special zoning exemptions (for an example, see Kozol, *Savage Inequalities*, 1991), effectively removing them as tax sources for education. Thus even in the face of widespread media reporting of school poverty in the urban communities, neither the State or any other governmental (or business) agency acts to correct the school funding imbalance. Lest we surmise that this condition is restricted to Los Angeles, both Kozol (1991) and Hacker (1992) reported similar school funding distortions in cities such as Chicago, East St. Louis, Houston, San Antonio, New York City, etc.

Although it could be and is argued that these conditions exist because of the faults of the inner-city residents or some other rationale, it seems substantive that these conditions and limitations are primarily restricted to communities that are urban and inhabited by racial minorities. Yet, agencies and businesses facetiously continue to maintain that these conditions are not correlative to race, that government and the market are neutral. Perhaps in essence they are, but they are actualized by men with racist ideologies rationalizing what actions they take, and any argument that either government or business is neutral is simply specious.

In opposition to this politically mediated ideological notion that the United States is a "color-blind" society where no special significance, right or privilege should attach to "race" is the historical acknowledgment that this society has always been extremely "color-conscious," never less so than in the 1990s. As pointed out by Omi and Winant (1986), race has been a major determinant of political rights, location and strata in the labor market, and personal and/or social identity from the very beginnings of the nation to the present. The critical theme of American history has been racism, in one form or another, not the abstract ethos of liberty and equality. While there have been incidences of differential treatment of various racial minority groups, each is a witness to the results of racial oppression (Omi & Winant, 1986).

As Stephanie Coontz wrote in a recent *Phi Delta Kappan* "Special Report" (March 1995), the conservatives have increasingly argued in their propounding of a new Social Darwinism that urban ills are the result of disintegrating families and related "values." Mainstream liberal politicians and the media have over the past several years supported a similar proposition rather than acknowledge the racially structured dysfunctioning institutions in this country.

Although granting that the face and/or practices of racism have changed historically, it is argued that underlying the economic and demographic conditions of minorities, particularly in urban ghettos, are the political dynamics of racial formation (Omi & Winant, 1986). The economic, cultural, etc. constructs with which we as a society contend are nuanced by current conflicts and tensions revolving around racial identity and formation: "the presence of a system of racial meanings and stereotypes, of racial ideology, seems to be a permanent feature of U.S. culture" (Omi & Winant, 1986, p. 63).

Omi & Winant (1986) argue that racial meanings are organized by a continuity of tensions between racial beliefs combined with the reciprocity of change and stability between the two levels of social relations, the individual and the collective. However, these levels are not distinct; racial discrimination, racism and formulation of racial identities (both for "self" and the "other") occur continually and reciprocally in a complex system of social understandings. They suggest that currently the dominant ideology mediates a perception, an understanding, that race is an "essence," something biological, fixed, and objective. In contrast, they argue that *race* is an "unstable and decentered complex of social meanings constantly being transformed by political and cultural struggle" (Omi & Winant, p. 68).

In the pragmatic sense this has implications for how we as a society identify "who" is and/or belongs to a race, thereby conferring certain identity and social benefits to a particular group. Conversely, the reciprocity of change and stability which delineates racial formation refers to how a group defines itself in consort with or in opposition to socially imposed definition, thus the process of racial formation is always in flux.

> The term *racial formation* refers to the process by which social, economic and political forces determine the content and importance of racial categories . . . race is a *central axis* of social relations which cannot be subsumed or reduced to a broader category. (Omi & Winant, 1986, p. 62)

Since "race" has historical trajectories of understandings and commitments, it has undergone at various times differential interpretations, both constructing and re-constructing its definitional meanings and its rationales. In this country understandings of race have patterned a dominant "racial etiquette," which exists as a set of interpretative codes and consciousness formulations that operate throughout the interactions of daily life and formulate dynamic tensions between the "mainstream" and the values and beliefs of subordinate groups in contestation with the dominant (Omi & Winant, 1986).

Omi & Winant (1986) contend that 'race' is a pervasive, dynamic concern in this society and that at no point or time has this culture ever been color-blind or neutral; i.e., "race" as a cultural issue was and is omnipresent. Further, that definitions of racial inclusion carry connotations of entitlement, both positively (in the sense of "deserving") and negatively (as in "not-deserving"). The "deserving" has to do with economic, political, *and* educational resources as in urban versus suburban schools. The dynamism is in the constant cultural attempts to articulate and/or re-articulate social understandings of racial definition ("racial formation"), which is struggled over at all social levels: national and local, community and individual.

For example, one definition of the dominant view of raciality is that of a pluralistic, liberal set of meanings primarily focused on ethnicity and assimilation of difference. Within this interpretive construct, race is subsumed as a parameter within the concept of ethnicity (Omi & Winant, 1986). Since ethnicity has historically been more fluid and subject to assimilatory social and educational efforts, the inclusion of race within ethnicity suggests that racial minorities should be (and in this view, are) equally capable of absorption. By focussing on ethnicity and thereby perceiving racial minorities as ethnic minorities, responses to minority demands for a share in societal assets are capable of being reduced to compensatory programs (historically perceived as "successful" in similar situations with white "ethnics"), and masking racial formations and the impact of racism in society.

However, there are other interpretations that have bitterly contested the above to argue for outright racial exclusion and/or domination, often openly acknowledging that the issue is race or the need for domination over defined racial minorities.

In particular is the political and ideological Right's articulation of race as definitive of human nature, wherein a *natural* racial hierarchy is presupposed and grounds a political context of privilege accrual to specific racial groups, based on a fixed, particularly historical identification of race. Their contentions stem from a specific "racial" understanding connected to a current sense of social dislocation (Omi & Winant, p. 113). While such a sense may have a real basis given the social contortions of the last two decades, it has also become politically and ideologically bound within the framework of a conservative rearticulation of the meaning of race within American value systems. The target, besides the minorities themselves, is often the State, and the rhetoric, usually couched within individualistic traditional authoritarian values, describes an impoverishment of traditional Americana by the State and racial minorities.

The Right's effort at re-racialization of mainstream paradigms is an attempt to create an authoritarian, right-wing popularism fueled by resentment and racial angst (Omi & Winant, 1986; Hacker, 1992; hooks & West, 1991; Purpel, 1989). The Right is politically and culturally responding to perceptions of the transformations and dislocations in the society over the last several decades, changes that for some engender fear of both balkanization and mongrelization of the Republic (Omi & Winant, 1986). The objective is to dismantle the perceived political gains of racial minorities by a rearticulation of the "racial etiquette" (Omi & Winant, p. 120). The key device used by the right in its effort to limit the political gains of racial minority movements has been the incorporation into political and educational speech of what has been termed as "coded" language. These are phrases and symbols which refer directly to racial themes, but do not directly challenge popular democratic or egalitarian ideals; e.g., justice, equality (Omi & Winant, 1986).

These rearticulation efforts by the Right emphasize in education such notions as (1) an end to state-sponsored preferences for minorities ("affirmative action") (Bloom, 1987); (2) an end to curriculum dilution by ethnic studies and a "return" to a rigorous core-curriculum stressing "Euro-western" cultural, aesthetic, epistemological, and social values (Bloom, 1987; Hirsch, 1987); (3) an increase in accountability and "effectiveness" in education emphasizing linkage to the economy (McCarthy, 1990). According to McCarthy (1990) and others:

> These conservative currents within government policies have directly influenced the drive for greater "accountability" in education, for state mandates directed at "raising standards and competence," and for an approach that privileges the needs of the economy over minority demands for equality. (Apple & Beyer, 1988; cited in McCarthy, 1990, p. 107)

Within the context of education, the Right has gained political and cultural credence through the articulation of ideological messages of "common-sense" racialism within a system of "codedness" (McCarthy, 1990). Although in the media the Right's debate is often contexted within issues such as busing, textbooks and other nonracial issues (i.e., sex education, family values), this effectively masks the more insidious effects of the racial rearticulation efforts of the Right that impact curriculum, school testing, funding and pedagogy, particularly in urban schools.

As noted earlier, the dominant, "mainstream," paradigm of race and its social consequences in this country has been primarily articulated through *ethnicity theory* (Omi & Winant, 1986; Hacker, 1992), which configures liberal and mainstream understandings as to race and racial minorities in this country. This theory acknowledges racial differences but does so within the contradictory notion of attempting to forge a "color-blind" society, with the color dominating the "blindness" being, of course, white. The interpretative basis of ethnicity theory as an ideology is derived from a combination of themes: a quest for conditional minority membership in favor of assimilation, a reliance on a peculiar rationale based on the perceived "melting-pot" experience of *white* immigrants, and presumed categories of individuals and groups in terms of ethnicity, not race. Additionally, there is the emphasis on the individual which configures this "theory" to the derogation of groups so as to avoid their consideration.

A significant premise within ethnicity theory is that racial minority cultures, particularly black, are deficient sociologically and are thus inherently "pathological" (Omi & Winant, 1986, p. 18), a condition that individually and socially can be cured through assimilation. Unfortunately, by basing its argument on the historical perception of white immigrant assimilation, the liberal paradigm ignores experiential specificities that have affected different *racial* experiences in this country, not ethnic ones. The liberal view is that race is subsumed within ethnicity, and, since the latter is cultural, it is ameliorable through social, political, and educational efforts. This plays itself out through a host of compensatory programs targeting socially perceived "deprived" groups, generally defined in racial terms, although masked as ethnicity. More about these programs as they impact on urban schools will be discussed in Chapter Two.

The inherent misunderstandings occur when what are perceived as ethnic groups, instead of racial groups, fail to quantitatively or qualitatively accede to the dominant predictions. Instead of perceiving either a problem with the paradigm or seeing that there are deeper, more complex understandings necessitated by minority "failure," the liberal interpretation can only perceive that cultural aberrations or deficiencies are the cause and fall back into a "blame the victim" syndrome (Omi & Winant, 1986; Hacker, 1992; Nieto, 1995).

A Rationale for Educational Programs' Failure: "Blaming the Victim"

Blaming the victim for social inequities not within the victim's power to ameliorate has a sordid history in this country. Beginning with the racial interpretation of genetic inhumanness and/or deficiency to the current concept of *cultural deprivation*, the generic process of blaming the victim is applied to almost every American problem. For example, the miserable health care of the poor is explained by asserting that the victim has poor motivation. The problems of slum housing are traced to tenants who are labelled as migrants or have poor communal or personal values. The poor, it is claimed, suffer the psychological effects of impoverishment, the "culture of poverty" and the deviant value system of lower classes; they cause their own problems. The growing number of families on welfare are fallaciously linked with the increased number of illegitimate children as twin results of promiscuity and sexual abandon among lower classes. Every important social problem, such as crime, mental illness, civil disorder, has been analyzed within the framework of the victim-blaming ideology (Ryan, 1992).

This ideology, with its racist undergirding, justifies a perverse form of social action designed to change not society, but rather the victim of society's acts. It attributes defect and inadequacy (failure) to the nature of the individual and/or group who is suffering, although the emphasis is on the individual as cause and target of resolution. The stigma that marks the victim and accounts for his/her victimization is acquired; it is a stigma of social origin (Ryan, 1992). The formula for action becomes simple, change the victim, not society. A routinized process has developed. First, identify a social problem. Second, study those affected and determine the ways they are different. Third, define the differences as the cause of the social problem, and fourth, invent a bureaucratic compensatory program to correct the victim's differences (Ryan, 1992), which has the bad habit of becoming a permanent institution.

This ideologized social and educational process of *blaming the victim* depends on a process of identification whereby the victim of the social problem(s) is typified as strange, different, i.e., the Other. This is generally done through research aimed at demonstrating that the poor, blacks, Hispanics, the elderly, the jobless are different, alien; that they think, value, live and learn differently from us. Many of the educational practices found in the urban school are directly related to compensatory programs instituted to reform the perceived victims, not the environment that victimizes.

Cultural scholars have argued that the current formulation of racism stems from recent, and still oscillating, changes in the dominant ideology that aligns itself with particular capitalistic virtues, such as meritocracy and individualism:

> The dominant white ideology is that of free will; anyone can better himself if he is not too lazy to make the effort. Such an ideology refuses to acknowledge the impact of the oppressive socioeconomic conditions on subordinate groups. It places the responsibility for the disadvantage on the group itself. The emphasis implies that members of the minority group must be inferior to whites, or they would be doing as well. (Gollnick & Chinn, 1990, p. 92)

The result has been to hegemonize the changes in racism toward meritocratic paradigms, resulting in a racially oriented underclass segregation delineated by supposedly individual failings, such as poverty, crime, teen-age pregnancies, educational and job failure, etc. This includes the promulgation of cultural or racial minority group deficiency rationales for minority problems and the State-mandated compensatory programs that target "at-risk" individuals, instead of impoverished institutions such as schools.

The overall problem of each of these theories, particularly those based solely on an historical interpretation of ethnicity, is the missing ingredient, the masked social interpretation of racism. The argument is that racism is the ideology, the learned interpretation of difference that configures and correlates the other social and religious-based ideologies of this society. Endemic, pervasive racism ultimately contributes to the continuation of urban impoverishment, oppression, and alienation in this country resulting in the increasing growth of the American urban "underclass" and the wretched conditions of urban schools. As many scholars, in and out of education, have noted (although I think it bears repeating) racism is an ideological poison that is learned. It is a historical and social understanding that seeps into social practices, the unconscious, and our very common sense construction of the world and others. Mainstream American culture seems indifferent or even hostile to the deepening poverty and despair affecting a growing population of African Americans in the underclass in our nation's cities; the growing dropout rate among African American students is explained by political diatribes and the refusal to engage the racism prevalent in our nation's schools; racial hatred is erupting into racist terror (Giroux, 1992).

The Underclass: America's Newest Racial Formation

The residents of these Third World American cities and their children who attend urban schools have come increasingly to be labelled and stereotyped by sociologists, politicians, and economists as the underclass. They have been collectively described as the long-term poor, the hostile street gangs, the hustlers and con-men and the traumatized (homeless, the drunks, and the mentally ill) (Gollnick & Chinn, 1990). This urban mix is leavened with the hard-core unemployed, school dropouts, the aged and disabled, recent Hispanic immigrants and the rest of the socially isolated (Wilson, 1987). Coincident with the blame-the-victim ideology pervading dominant cultural understandings, the underclass is blamed for its own condition, as if human beings would voluntarily choose such a life for themselves and their children. To be poor in the United States is to be stigmatized as lazy, dishonest, morally loose and criminally aggressive (Gollnick & Chinn, 1990).

Douglas Glasgow, in his 1980 text, *The Black Underclass*, examined the inner-city youth of Los Angeles from the year of the Watts riots (1965) to the late 1970s, and documented the evolution of the underclass in that area and its effects on young black males. Glasgow characterizes this volatile group as having a common condition of being jobless and lacking salable skills, as well as the opportunities to obtain them. Glasgow described the young men he worked with as being consistently labelled as social problems by the police, the schools, the employment and welfare agencies. They sought other options for economic survival ranging from private schemes to working the welfare system. Hustling, pimping, drug sales, and other extra-legal activities were alternatives to working the jobs that didn't exist for them (Marable, 1983; citing Glasgow, 1980).

Glasgow (1980) suggests that the urban underclass is typified by an absence of generational socioeconomic upward mobility, the lack of real opportunities to legitimately succeed, and widespread despair and anger at the mainstream institutions that reject them. This interpretation is widely shared by urban ethnographers, although ignored generally by white America (hooks & West, 1991).

The urban ecology of the underclass is argued to be the culmination of the social and/or political process of black ghettoization, economic exploitation and urban decay (Marable, 1983). It has effectively eliminated millions of blacks from working class jobs and lifestyles, in the process eroding and destroying the social institutions of black culture in this country. The extension of permanent penury to broad segments of the black majority provokes the disruption of black families; increase the number of black-on-black murders, rapes, suicides and assaults; and makes terror a way of life for all blacks of every class who live in the inner city (Marable, 1983).

The terrible scenes of April 1992 in Los Angeles demonstrate the profound anger of ghetto residents at what they see as their betrayal by white America. As Cornel West argues, what happened in Los Angeles this past April was neither a race riot nor a class rebellion; rather the monumental upheaval was a multiracial, trans-class and largely male display of justified social rage. It signified the sense of powerlessness in American society (West, 1993a). This sense of powerlessness is framed within a searing interpretation by ghetto residents that believes that white society is deeply implicated in the ghetto: white institutions created it, white institutions maintain it, and white society condones it. Further, Marable has pointed out that the direction of America's political economy and social hierarchy is veering toward a subtle apocalypse which promises to obliterate the lowest stratum of the black and Latino poor (Marable, 1983, 1988).

West's sense of the rage of hopelessness and Marable's charge of white implication is all too often disavowed by white society in this country. This is, of course, to deny an everyday reality, that to be black is to be consigned to the margins of American life (also true for Hispanics and certainly for Native Americans) (Hacker, 1992). To be black in the United States is to wonder if the nation has an unstated policy for annihilation. How else can one explain the incidence of death and debilitation from drugs and disease, the incarceration of much of a generation of young men, the consignment of millions of women and children to half-lives of poverty (Hacker, 1992). The statistics of racially constructed discrimination suggest such a pervasive inequality in our society that most whites *must* be aware of it, yet little is done to ameliorate the results or the causes. Even if unintentional, it is a negligence that borders on criminality. If intentional, then the intent, the understandings that formulate the intent and the resultant actions (all of which constitute racism) must be confronted, denounced, and combated.

Within the boundaries of America's inner cities exist human beings whose lives consist of pain, hunger, poverty, crime, and misery relieved only periodically by glimpses of the "Dream," often contextualized within the historic black hope of education. Nowhere in the ghetto is this more problematic than in the urban schools, where hopes and dreams of generational and racial betterment meet the "peculiar institution" of urban education.

Change and Diversity: A Nation Divided by Difference

While we will examine the terrain of urban schools more specifically in the next chapter, some description of the demographics of those schools as well as the communities in which they reside would seem appropriate at this point. Equally trenchant for our discussion is the question of the increasing destabilization of difference in this country; a condition brought about by a marked change in both the numbers and nature of immigrants to the United States over the last decade and a half. From the prospective of the average white American, the country is darkening; people of color are both more visible and more intrusive. This has resulted in a decided upswing of reactionary forces and polemics in political, economic and social debates in the United States. For example, more politicians have begun to use political language aimed at and coded for white middle- and working-class Americans that is self-assuredly racist. States have begun to pass laws through the popular ballot (e.g., California's recent Proposition 187) limiting racial immigrants' access to social welfare and education, legislating English-only classrooms (notwithstanding the increasing numbers of LEP children whose home language is other than English) and increasingly attacking educational attempts under the rubric of multicultural education to come to grips with the increasing diversity of students.

Be that as it may, there can be no denying that the population of this country is fundamentally changing. Immigration is having a profound effect on who Americans are, how they speak, and how they look, act, and think. During the past decade, approximately 7.3 million people came to the U.S., an increase of 63 percent over the period from 1971 to 1980. By far the largest group were from Mexico, with the

Philippines, China, Korea, and Vietnam following in order (*U.S. Census Bureau Reports* cited in Figueroa & Garcia, 1994). The U.S. Hispanic population is growing approximately five times faster than the general population; the Asian population will double by the year 2000 (Banks, 1991). The American Council of Education reported in 1988 that by that same year, one-third of the U.S. population will consist of non-whites (Banks, 1991).

The impact on the nation's schools cannot be denied; over the next 30 years classrooms will undergo an inversion of the white-minority ratio. In 1994-95, the non-white student population was estimated at 13.7 million (or 34 percent while whites represent 66 percent). However, extrapolating demographic trends suggests that by 2026 non-white students will number some 45 million or 75 percent of total student population (Figueroa & Garcia, 1994). Perhaps closer to home, it is estimated that by 2000, 20 million Hispanic and 30 million African Americans will comprise at least 30 percent of U.S. school enrollment (Grossman, 1995). Non-white students are already in the majority in the 25 largest school districts, and in some constitute 95 percent or more.

Equally significant because of the profound effect on learning and school are the rising income disparities and poverty and hunger demographics in this country. Although I will provide more detail on the latter's effect in Chapter Two as to urban schools, poverty, particularly in its racialized form, is a cancer, a malignancy on the body politic of our society. It is estimated that approximately 30 million Americans or 12.5 percent of the population go hungry on a daily basis (Coontz, 1995), and 1 in 5 children live in poverty.

The racialized nature of poverty in America should not be surprising to anyone who has read this far. Three times as many African American children and 2.5 times as many Hispanic children as whites live their school years in poverty. Infant mortality in the U.S. is the worst in the industrialized world, and for African Americans it ranks with such places as Costa Rica, Malaysia, and Liberia. Even the very expectancy of life is affected as there is a widening gap between white life expectancy and those of minorities, with Native Americans falling even further behind.

The amazing irony of this litany of human social triaging is its toleration by the mainstream of American society. The Right trumpets that it points unfailingly to the intrinsic deficiency of minorities in their lack of appropriate values, their poor character, deficient cultures and/or even their genetic flaws. The liberal mainstream, while unsure if the Right isn't correct, argues that individuals need more self-esteem, more modes of meritocracy, more standardized tests in schools, and more paternalistic institutional programs:

> One side thinks we can reverse undesirable social trends through discipline and moral exhortation; the other side thinks that therapy and sensitivity will do the trick. Both sides ignore the long-term structural changes that underlie many of the problems. (Coontz, 1995, p. K2)

The truly incredible absurdity is that both sides seem to have increasingly convinced the American public that we can raise middle-class income by attacking the poor and different, who account for only 3.9 percent of total income, including the cash value of food stamps, AFDC, and other entitlements (Coontz, 1995). As Henry Giroux comments:

> There is a tragic irony at work when a government can raise $500 billion to bail out corrupt bankers and $50 billion to fight a war in Iraq, while at the same time cutting back food stamp and school lunch programs in a country in which nearly one out of every four children under six live in poverty . . . the imperatives of privatization and the profit margin become more important than issues of human suffering and social justice. (Giroux, 1995, p. 111)

At issue here is the profound and deeply inscribed belief in this society that individuals are the sum of their individual efforts, that corporations are neutral and difference is a threat. More succinctly, the racialization of American attitudes, beliefs and organizations has resulted in the ghettoization of peoples declared marginal within those beliefs and attitudes. This is rationalized through a "blame the victim" philosophy that ignores history, justice and the very heart of a democracy. It derives from a notion of deserving that hierarchializes people to the level of expendability (Purpel, 1995).

Nowhere is this more evident, more a part of daily life than in the urban centers of America, those racialized zones of space where human beings live their lives on the edge of survival, despair, and frustration of hope. Yet they do have hope, especially for their children, whom they send to urban schools in increasing numbers, across gang boundaries, into classrooms of routinized instruction, incoherent curricula, and diminished resources and returns. The next chapter will move us into those schools with an analysis of who attends, who sends, and what they find.

Notes

1. "Justice" by Langston Hughes, cited in Marable, M. (1983).

CHAPTER TWO

When and Where They Enter:
Going to School in Urban America

> Being broke, hustling, jiving,
> stealing, rapping, balling;
> a fight, a bust, some time;
> no job, lost job, a no-paying job;
> a lady, a baby, some weight;
> some wine, some grass, a pill;
> no pride, no ride, lost pride;
> man going down, slipping fast, can't see where to make it;
> I've tried, almost died, ready now (from Glasgow[1])

Introduction

Within the geographical and political enclaves of urban zones exist the inner-city schools, whose dehumanizing conditions should be a national embarrassment except that they exist within a national concord of silence. These schools bear witness to the national response (or lack of one) to the increasing diversification and impoverishment of this country's ethnic minority populations and nurture the seeds of potential social disorder as the urban racial minority population is increasing at a faster rate than the general population (Banks, 1991). That increase, however, is hardly benign, given the conditions and nihilism of inner-city communities (West, 1993).

American urban schools are increasingly populated by a clientele that is "of color," predominantly black and Hispanic, poor, non-English speaking and educationally demarked by profound racialized differences in achievement scores, drop-out rates and illiteracy (Nieto, 1995; Grossman, 1995). Racial minorities, particularly blacks, Hispanics and Native Americans, have historically not done well in American schools (McCarthy, 1992) and have been largely written off by the rest of the country.

The schools of America's urban centers are appalling: bankrupt districts, burgeoning populations of minorities and immigrants, classrooms empty of materials but packed with children, pandemic drug and alcohol abuse, gang violence, situated in impoverished communities malignant with anger and frustration. The national drop-out percentile for secondary schools is in the low 20's, but it is 65 to 75 percent in urban schools (Fine, 1991). In Chicago's ghetto schools, only 8 percent of a 9th grade class will graduate reading at grade level, only 15 percent will even graduate (Fine, 1991). Many urban children come to school hungry, abused and/or poorly clothed. They come to school from communities distinguished by empty buildings, boarded-up shops, proliferating liquor stores, random violence, pent-up anger and dehumanizing marginalization, poverty, and self-inflicted crime. They constitute

> a complex of deterritorialized realities of nightmare metropolises and small towns that have lost their soul, where everyday life consists of living narratives of exile and victimage. . . . (McLaren, 1992, p. 24)

As Michelle Fine so cogently points out, urban youths who begin their lives at the greatest risks of class, racial or ethnic or gender exploitation, who have the least to begin with in terms of community and educational resources, attend the most traumatized schools in the country and receive the poorest and most impoverished educations (Fine, 1991, p. 23-24).

Their overwhelming school experience is demarked by educational failure; among black and Hispanic students in the five largest U.S. cities, the dropout rate exceeds 55 percent, and for black males it approximates 75 percent nationwide (Comer & Haynes, 1990). African American children are three times as likely as whites to be placed in special education classes (McLaren, 1988b; Nieto, 1995) and subsequently drop out; Latino students drop out of school at a rate higher than any other group, in some areas, nearly 80 percent (Nieto, 1995).

The pressures on urban youth to drop out of school and risk life on the streets are immense, as Fine (1986) states:

> The incidence of parental and sibling death from illness, accident, homicide, or suicide; drug overdoses and drug-related arrests; harassment by welfare agents, banks, immigration officials and police; and domestic and street violence is indeed astonishing to any observer. . . . These adolescents leave school because they live surrounded by unemployment and poverty, have experienced failure in school . . . feel terrible about themselves, and see little hope. (Fine, 1986, p. 119)

Other research reports similar figures representing social and educational failure; that 50 percent to 80 percent of all inner-city students drop out by the second year of high school; one million urban teenagers cannot read above the third grade level and almost one-fourth are functionally illiterate. This same report cites that in New York alone, 66 percent of all high school students fail to graduate; for Hispanics the rate is over 80 percent, for blacks, 72 percent, and for other non-whites, the statistics are around 70 percent. The fastest growing minority, Hispanics, has been particularly damaged; 40 percent of all Hispanic students drop out before the 10th grade, 35 percent are systematically tracked into vocational education and/or special education (McLaren, 1988b).

The tragic result of these kinds of school experiences in the inner city is evident in the continued reproductive cycles of student and school failure and the prophesy-fulfilling dropping out of adolescents; they understand that school can't ensure a job, so they drop out and ensure joblessness. The irrelevance of the curriculum, the turnover in teachers, the burdensome pedagogy, and the discordance of school rhetoric juxtaposed to student experiential knowledge results in large numbers (many times in excess of 50 percent) of students choosing to make their own way in the more familiar and seemingly affirming world of the streets and gangs (Yeo, 1992; Fine, 1986, 1991).

In part this can be understood from the standpoint of the children themselves who attend urban schools in communities terrorized by the crack cocaine epidemic, violence, and the alcoholism devastating an entire generation of urban blacks and Hispanics. One author refers to this as the result of the "brutal bite of poverty":

> Our children are found with their backs to the wall . . . the street

gangs who traffic in drugs present a serious threat to the welfare and future of our children who are stalked and surrounded by the gangs and forced through violent intimidation, actual physical beatings, and outright murders to succumb to drug use and trafficking. (King & Wilson, 1990)

In the 1988 report ("Barriers to Excellence: Our Children at Risk") numerous indicators of racial discrimination in education were described. Only 33 percent of the estimated 2.7 million limited-English-proficient (referred to in educational jargon as *LEP* students) students receive any form of special programming to compensate; only 10 percent of Hispanic LEP students were in bilingual programs. Nearly 55 percent of all public school classrooms have LEP students, but fewer than 3.2 percent of teachers have received any training to assist these students. The report's conclusion is that:

> Minority children do not matter as much as non-minority children. Non-English speaking children still face language and cultural barriers throughout America . . . . The failure to educate millions of children is creating an enormous social deficit for which the bill *will* come due. (National Coalition Report, 1988)

To put the statistics in more human terms, racial segregation and racialized education of children is bad enough, but when the hellish conditions of inner city schools are added, travesty and tragedy become the order of the day. Jonathan Kozol, in his 1991 book, *Savage Inequalities*, after visiting about thirty school districts around the country noted not only the remarkable degree of racial segregation but that urban schools were generally always 95% to 99% non-white. He observes that national reports cite concern with passing and achievement scores, literacy rates and dropout rates but not inequality and segregation. In fact, most students of color in this country are currently to be found in predominantly minority schools (Nieto, 1995; Children's Defense Fund Report, 1990). Segregation has become reinstituted in this country, both in the cities and in urban schools. For the first time since the Supreme Court's ruling in *Brown v. Board of Education* took effect, racial and ethnic segregation, among cities, suburbs, schools, and classrooms, is growing worse (Miller, 1995).

The "blame the victim" syndrome plays out in urban schools through the mandates of federal and state compensatory programs as well as in the so-called educational failure of the schools. What is not questioned are the conditions, instead "cultural deprivation" becomes an omnibus explanation for the educational disaster area known as the inner-city school (Ryan, 1992):

> No one asks about the collapsing buildings and torn textbooks, the frightened and/or insensitive teachers, the 15 additional desks in the room, the blustering harried principals, the remorseless segregation, the irrelevant curriculum, the greedy or disinterested school board, the insulting history, the stingy taxpayers or the self-serving faculty of the local teacher's college. We are to confine our attention to the child and his alleged defects as the reason for *all* of this! (Ryan, 1992, p. 364-5).

As Kozol documents, children do not at first realize that they are either defective or being cheated of education and opportunity. As is so often the case, inner-city children come to school with a degree of faith and optimism and seem to thrive in the first few years. By fifth or sixth grade, many children demonstrate their loss of faith by staying out of school (Kozol, 1991).

Kozol argues, as have others herein, that this cheating is actually condoned and augmented by the State, since the State mandates and assigns people to schools. Thus by requiring attendance but refusing to require equity, the State effectively requires inequity.

Kozol describes in depth the brutality of urban school conditions, the irrelevance of an education taught within tattered excuses for schoolrooms, classes packed with 40-plus children and a teacher often without a credential, perhaps not even speaking the same language. The innocence and incredible exuberance of students is contrasted with husks of rooms, broken chalkboards, no school nurse, guns and knives, schoolyards ribboned with barbed wire fences, and teachers floundering with classes rife with anger, hostility, and hopelessness.

In a recent study, Heath and McLaughlin (1993) found that inner-city youth feel disconnected from the larger society, including schools, churches and workplaces. In this context, in the fierce communion of the streets and the barren economic life of the inner-city neighborhoods the deep pessimism, low self-esteem, and destructive behavior are not surprising. The street becomes the refuge for youth who can no longer bear a sense of invisibility in their family, school or community (Heath & McLaughlin, 1993, p. 54-55).

This is not an isolated, rhetorically satisfying description meant to tug at liberal heartstrings; it represents the daily school lives of millions of urban children. These places, along with the rest of the urban zones in which they exist, spawn lives cheapened by poverty, violence, and the racism of an uncaring society that blames them for the very conditions it imposes:

> Something violent hits almost every young person living in America's inner cities. The flagrant violence of street crime, the concealed violence within families, and the silent violence of emotional neglect and absence of nurture are commonplace in urban neighborhoods . . . the violence that is part of their lives disables or deflects any positive sense of future or even the conviction that they have a future. . . . "Ain't no makin it" in legitimate or mainstream society becomes the perceived reality of most inner city youngsters. (Heath & McLaughlin, 1993, p. 37)

However, it is not enough to document the numbers, the losses, nor is it enough to simply empathize with the hurt, the failure, the anger that resonates through the corridors and classrooms of urban schools as will be sketched experientially in Chapter Three. There are unequivocally reasons, understandings, and choices, groups and individuals that formulate the texture of inner-city education. These connections between people, institutions, and cultural differences do not arise by accident. The actors' beliefs, cultural consciousnesses and identities (both individual and collective) come together synergistically within urban schools and classrooms to form and drive the particular educational practices of inner-city education.

The purpose of this chapter is to situate urban education, not as some isolated happenstance bereft of connectivity, but as conceptually and ideologically grounded within our society's dominant cultural, political and economic value systems. The aim is an analysis of those curricular and pedagogical interpretations and choices of practice constructed by those value systems that go to make up urban education. These I have divided into three general categories for purposes of discussion.

First, there are the more general social and educational paradigms, the cultural ideologies, that underlie many of the interpretations and rationales for the programmatic practices that occur in urban schools.

Second, there is the context, content, and praxis of the actual curriculum and pedagogy, including attempts to deal with issues of diversity (which will be discussed in Chapter Five).

Third, there are the experiences, histories and ways of knowing that students and parents (the community) bring to the classrooms and the interactions with the school and staff.

It is my intent to sequentially and critically investigate each of the three respective categories to extract the dominant rationales that frame the practices of education in urban schools and their concomitant failure. The sequence will move from social interpretations and educational paradigms to the classroom construction of teaching and content to the experiences and understandings that the actors themselves bring to the school site as a framework for analysis. However, it should be kept in mind that these categories are not completely discrete nor are they nonsynchronous.

As a caveat, there are undoubtedly other rationales and/or ideological points that impact on urban education that may not be cited or analyzed herein. However, the mainstream cultural paradigms (that, in attempting to explain the tragedy and failure of urban education maintain it through compensatory programs, the impact of State-mandated programs arising from those paradigms, and the experiences, cultural understandings, and knowledge of the people themselves) form collectively the "constructive" factors of urban education.

Therefore, we will look first to positioning and analyzing the cultural and social verities that frame the educational conditions within urban schools and from which derive the teaching and management practices designed to "educate" and control urban youth.

I. Deficit Theories, Deculturalization and Ethnocentrism: Social and Educational "Truths"

The primary cultural values that construct much of the ideologically based rationales that impact upon urban schools arise out of a number of deeply embedded American social and/or cultural understandings or what can be termed as dominant, mainstream, middle-class "truths." These frame the primary rationales for State and local programs, mandated curriculum and pedagogical "Frameworks,"[2] and even the language by which urban educational research and evaluative statistics are interpreted (McCarthy, 1992).

Although there is significant interplay and influence of each by the others, these interpretive understandings can be grouped in terms of their respective emphasis. First, targeting the students and/or their community, lifestyles and even their communicative abilities, are those explanations of educational failure termed as "deficit theories."

Traditionally, the educational community has tended to view culturally diverse students as coming from a deficit model. There is a perspective that somehow these students lack the "right stuff." Rarely have schools and educational institutions viewed culturally diverse students as being culture "rich" and not "at risk" (Pang & Barba, 1995, p. 341). These so-termed explanations for minority disadvantagement derive differentially from both liberal and conservative views; however, they posit the same project (compensatory programs) to "correct" perceived faults within marginalized social groups. Although these deficit theories can be and are applied by mainstream discourse to women, the aged, the poor, the disabled, gays, as well as racial minorities, it is the latter in terms of urban schools that we will interrogate in this chapter.

The *second* understanding is more cultural in its configuration and perceives racial minority cultural and/or linguistic differences with their underlying values and behaviors as threatening to the mainstream (i.e., white, Eurocentric, middle-class) (McCarthy, 1992; King & Wilson, 1990). They are anathematic to those empowered to maintain a Euro-western, positivistic, ethnocentric standard, whose institutions and practices for maintenance of this standard give rise to numerous curricular and pedagogical practices aimed at deculturizing children of color and imposing an assimilatory educational regime.

This is not to imply that these regimes of "truth" are always successful; however, success is a relative term. It may be defined by failure and dropping out (being relegated to the margins and silence) as well as by assimilation (being silenced through co-option). Although these rationales and their collective practices are resisted (and assimilated) by students, parents and community, they do constitute the dominant rationales for urban educational themes and praxis, the primary justificatory rhetoric both within and without urban schools, and the daily efforts of administrators and staff.

In this section, I will discuss first the concept of deficit theories and how they impact urban education and then follow with the same analysis of deculturalization.

A. *Deficit Theories*

The disadvantagement of minority groups in this country, particularly those defined by various notions of race, has a long history of argument between the more conservative who claim the deficiencies are genetic or cultural within racial minorities and the more liberal who argue that perceived deficiencies derive from minority environment and can be "cured" through compensatory programs (Darder, 1991; Sleeter & Grant, 1994; West, 1993; Nieto, 1995).

Christine Sleeter (1995, 1993) paraphrasing Cornel West, suggests that there is an additional complexity: there are conservatives who maintain a "sociobiology" explanation that relies on a genetic determination for social inequality. Others rely on a culturalist explanation that blames the quality and context of African American culture, giving rise to programs to assimilate and deculturalize African Americans to extract that culture. Lastly, some conservatives (and mainstream liberals), including many black conservatives such as Thomas Sowell, believe in what West (Sleeter, 1994) terms a "market" explanation whereby changing consumer preferences will alleviate discrimination if blacks are educated into the dominant value systems of consumer capitalism. Liberals, on the other hand, tend to believe that there is social and/or individual discrimination at work, but it is not part of the structure of the society or institutions. Therefore, they argue for governmental intervention to ensure that individuals are treated equitably and for massive governmental compensatory programs in minority schools, communities, etc., which they have argued for relatively successfully. However, the success of the programs themselves is another issue entirely.

Much of what passes for education in urban schools falls under the heading of *self-fulfilling prophesy*; educators and sociological researchers document the educational failures (dropouts, unemployed, etc.) and prescribe compensatory programs based on hegemonic under-standings of urban residents, schools, and culture (Carlson, 1992b). These "programs" are incorporated into the schools by mandate where they generally fail to some degree (always determined by empirical studies by professionals from outside the urban milieu). The program initiators usually blame the urban schools and/or the students, or their culture, language, or morality for program failure and thereby justify the generation of additional studies from whence more programs to compensate for "new" conceptualizations for urban failure are advocated.

The mainstream-determined social and educational perception and/or "reality" is unequivocally that the urban student, culture, language, home life, etc. is at fault; not the school as an institution nor the curriculum or pedagogical styles nor the social understandings of the researchers themselves.

The result is a circle of self-fulfilling prophesies that are manifested in a plethora of compensatory programs to "cure" the perceived "deficits." Historically, the deficits were argued as being genetically derived; today the deficit is cultural, environmental or linguistic. The key assumption within these schemes is that there is always some form of "deficiency" which only the mainstream from within its particular framework of values, understandings and social practices can "cure."

Deficit theories of culture and education have framed for some time the liberal mainstream responses to urban problems (Nieto, 1995; Carlson, 1989). These responses are usually couched within a "blame the victim" typology and generally result in some form of State compensatory program. The rationale for the programs is that students from "deprived" homes need to be compensated for their deprivation, be it genetic, cultural, or linguistic and brought up to the mainstream norm (Nieto, 1995). Urban schools are particularly demarked by this process, with much of their funding, programs, curriculum, hiring, etc. set within a complex mix of federal and state "reform" programs, which are justified as being beneficent and meant to assist the designated "victims." All too often the process merely maintains the status quo of the perceived disablement (Sleeter, 1991), due to the underlying cultural misunderstandings or faulty assumptions about the very people they are meant to benefit.

Sleeter (1991) defines four styles of these "benevolent" relationships, differentiated on the basis of who is believed responsible (by the benefacting institution) for causing the problem and who should take responsibility for the solution:

1. The *moral model*: blames the victim as responsible for the problems, absolves society for any complicity and advocates the "bootstrap" approach to solutions.

2. The *medical model*: blames victim's environment and/or society for the problems; poses solutions to be determined by outside "experts" with professional power and knowledge.

3. The *enlightenment model*: blames the victim for the problems but assumes a "curable" ignorance; also sees

resolution at the direction of "experts."

4. The *empowerment model*: views society as responsible for the victim's plight, but posits the resolutions as a partnership between victim and society, with the victim as own "expert." (Sleeter, 1991, p. 3-4)

Sleeter notes that in general *only* the first three models are active within urban schools (Sleeter, 1991). The *moral model* is familiar to any student or teacher in an urban school; it consists of both the exhortations to students to "be responsible," "try harder," "stay on task," "work hard," "follow the rules" and the beliefs grounding them. It ignores or denigrates student racial experiences, "painting a picture of American society as an equal opportunity enterprise in which anyone can get ahead through hard work" (Sleeter, 1991, p. 4; Solomon, 1992). The model tends to perceive low-income parents as both disinterested in student achievement and responsible for student failure, and ignores the exigencies of adult lives in urban communities and frames the negative manner in which most parents are perceived and treated in urban schools.

The *medical model* underwrites and/or justifies special programs (e.g., "at risk," GATE, etc.) where students are placed at the behest and control of "experts," who diagnose and remediate perceived deficiencies, be they physical, intellectual, or educational. Special Education and ESL programs are classic examples of this style of approach. Within urban schools, there are a plethora of these expert programs, and there is a constant tension between teachers and "experts" for student attention and time.

The *enlightenment model* arises out of its understanding of the urban student as deficient but places the blame within a schema that the urban student is merely ameliorably ignorant as opposed to culturally or ethnically deficient and attempts (again through the "expert") to provide compensatory instruction.

> The assumption is that students from "disadvantaged" groups need special instruction to "catch them up" with everyone else, and once they have the information or skills they had lacked, they will learn and behave "appropriately" and thus succeed. (Sleeter, 1991, p. 4)

These programs range from justifying the dominant curriculum and pedagogical style (i.e., "Basic Skills") to State-mandated special tutoring, transitional bilingual programs, and an enormous number of special instructional programs offered by public and private groups to the urban schools. These programs structure, however, their own failure by propounding instructional or motivational messages in opposition to students' own experiences, thereby lessening their effect, one example of which is the "motivational" assembly cited in Chapter Three. Also, many of the funds granted by these agencies (e.g., Title I) and designated for special program entitlement are siphoned off by districts and/or school administrators,[3] in order to meet the requirements of other mandated programs, thereby diluting or at least diverting the intentions of the first or underfunded programs.

Nieto (1995) notes that under these "models," urban schools and their administrators (as well as state and local bureaucratic officials) believe that they need to reduce students of color to a *tabula rasa* state. For most curriculum approaches used in urban schools, this means to "tear down the building blocks the children already have in order to start from a middle-class foundation" (Nieto, 1995, p. 194). Worse, in some instances, particularly with students identified as learning disabled or ESL, it means to demean and destroy the fabric of the child's prior experience and knowledge so as to replace it with western, white, middle-class understandings and culture (Sleeter, 1991). Teachers are often educated to believe that the first step in education is to convert all children to replicas of white, middle-class suburban children. A "Euro-American-centered" consciousness has therefore remained the basis of curriculum development and instruction in the public school system (Boateng, 1990).

School failure is usually explained in terms of these models and assorted deficiencies, never from the standpoint that it might be the school's racialized and institutionalized perceptions of the students, including their race, language and culture, that is deficient and inadequate (Nieto, 1995).

The language and terms used in current educational literature continue to exemplify a pervasive deficit model mentality (Soto, 1992; Grant, 1992). For example, the term LEP (Limited English Proficient) in use in numerous states applies almost unequivocally to non-whites. This implies an inherent limitation in the second-language learner, as opposed to an enriching attribute, and corrective (or compensatory) programs are exclusively targeted at ethnic minority students.

We rarely read about fluent Spanish speakers; fluent Hmong speakers; proficient multilingual speakers. Children continue to

be viewed as deficient language receptacles instead of potentially
enriched individuals; the "half empty glass syndrome" as opposed
to the "half full" philosophy prevails. (Soto, 1992)

In the sections that follow (specifically Section II, which deals
with curriculum, pedagogy, and classroom practices), it must be
understood that virtually *all* in-situ educational practices are derived and
justified within a deficit theory rationale constructed out of perceptions
engendered by notions exemplified by and/or reflective of Sleeter's
models. Many of the practices discussed result directly from
compensatory programs designed to alleviate the presupposedly deficient
cultural, linguistic and epistemological characteristics of urban students
as well as to effect a deculturalization process.

B. Deculturalization and Ethnocentrism in the Urban Curriculum

The second social or cultural imperative directly affecting curriculum
and pedagogy in inner-city schools is that of deculturalization, the
perceived need to "correct" "deficient" minority cultures by and through
a process of acculturation to the mainstream or dominant culture
(Boateng, 1990). The educational basis is that students of color need to
be *reculturalized* through the imposition of a "correct" curriculum that
emphasizes western Euro-American history, language, and knowledge.
The basic rationale is that urban students' ambient culture causes
educational failure. Deculturalization is a process by which the
individual is conditioned to other cultural values. "To deculturalize
African-American children is to deprive them of that which determines
the way they think, feel and behave" (Boateng, 1990, p. 73).
   Any curriculum used in educational settings is replete with choices,
decisions about what is thought to be important as to knowledge,
experience and values (Nieto, 1995). These decisions accord preference
and truth-status to particular choices of knowledge and experience
(Nieto, 1995); however, non-mainstream (minority) knowledge and
experience are rejected as tainted "non-truth."
   Unfortunately, the children of the inner cities, who are usually
from non-mainstream cultures, confront a curriculum that ignores their
cultural capital in favor of the dominant, western Euro-American white

culture, and their individual and social knowledge and experience is seen as "non-mainstream," ergo, "non-truth," deficient. Thus, their differences in knowledge, behavior, and identity are perceived by educators as requiring change through appropriate education. The public school system has become a strategically important vehicle that promotes the deculturalization of African American children to Euro-American norms and creates confusion in the consciousness of these children (Boateng, 1990).

This ethnocentric deculturalization is exemplified by the textbooks used in urban schools, which tend to "reinforce the dominance of the European American perspective and sustain stereotypes of any group perceived to be outside the mainstream." (Nieto, 1995, p. 74-75) In a study of textbooks used in schools, Sleeter and Grant (1991) found the following:

> Whites consistently dominate textbooks, particularly white males; Whites receive the most attention and dominate the list of accomplishments in textbooks; Women and people of color are shown in a much more limited range of roles with limited accomplishments; Textbooks contain very little about contemporary race relations or issues that most concern people of color; Textbooks convey an image of harmony among groups and contentment with the status quo; Lives and experiences of African Americans, Mexican Americans, Puerto Ricans, Asian, American Indian and other groups are omitted or stereotyped (Sleeter & Grant, 1991; cited in Nieto, 1995, p. 75).

In a survey undertaken by my own students for their student newspaper, they reviewed each textbook used by the 7th and 8th grade classes, some fifteen texts in all. They found that whites were mentioned or shown in pictures over blacks by a 4 to 1 margin, whites to Hispanics by 7 to 1, and Asians went unmentioned except for one California historical reference. They discovered that in all of the textbooks, there were no black scientists or mathematicians depicted or mentioned whatsoever, and only five black historical figures were named or pictured. The English texts had no anthology material by Hispanic or black authors; all prose and poetry selections were from deceased European or American whites. The context of all texts in this particular urban, primarily black school was Euro-ethnocentric, which is all too common within inner-city education in this country (McLaren, 1988b; Nieto, 1995; Kozol, 1991; Giroux, 1992). This

Eurocentrism, at the core of the dialectic of deculturalization and assimilation, provides both a standard for normalcy and for difference.

> Much of Western history conditions us to see human differences in simplistic opposition to each other: dominant/subordinate, good/bad, superior/inferior. In a society where the good is defined in terms of profit rather than in terms of human need, there must always be some group of people who, through systemized oppression, can be made to feel surplus, to occupy the space of the dehumanized inferior. (Lorde, 1990, p. 281)

Lorde argues that this Euro-western conditioning constructs and furthers a hegemony of what she terms as the "mythic norm," where the standard is defined within terms of a white, middle-class, heterosexual and Christian male. McLaren (1988a) speaks of a "transparent norm," which has similar conditions and is akin to an invisible grid overlaid on all social and cultural perceptions but especially educational.

Whether we use the term Eurocentric or ethnocentric, the reference is still to a dominant worldview that exclusively values western European culture and its American simulacrum and denigrates and/or subordinates the cultures that are different from the "mythic norm." In this country, Eurocentrism acts as a selection process used to screen out information and understandings that do not support the superiority of western culture's social, political, economic, and spiritual manifestations (Schwartz, 1992).

As an example, this Eurocentric consciousness depicts a preaching, nonviolent Martin Luther King, Jr. (which is the standard image of Dr. King presented in inner-city schools) rather than the violent conditions about which he preached. He becomes acceptable as a dreamer and preacher of American democratic values, but the unequitable social relations that were his motivation are submerged:

> These separations of "acts" from their causes and effects restrict the development of consciousness about social conditions through absorption of the "act" into an acceptable dominant ideology. (Schwartz, 1992, p. 35)

This Eurocentric norm, particularly with its linearity and polarization, is pervasive; the effect is profound and unconscious. This is vital in coming to an understanding of urban education. This "norm" affects all phases and levels, from texts to teaching to the students' own consciousness of themselves. It pervades and shapes the kind of knowledge teachers transmit and honor in the classroom, the way in which the students perceive themselves and their own cultures and languages, and the manner in which appropriate learning and behavior is rewarded.

It needs to be equally asserted that the imposition of the "norm" is not without resistance or questioning. Students do not always accede: e.g., an example of this occurred during the questioning of students about careers by a speaker (who was a white older male from outside the community):

Speaker: "What kind of career do you want, young man?"

Student #1: "Ah wants to be a doctor!"

Student #2: "Ya can't be no doctor, stupid, niggahs can't be doctors!"

Student #3: "Liar, dey can too, ah knows an African doctor, he's black."

Student #2: "Yo momma! He ain't black, he's African or he's a oreo; niggahs can only be janitors or on the county line [welfare]."

This is an example of both the accommodation/assimilation consciousness (Student #1) and the resistance mode (Student #2), evidencing the "norm" and the contradictions felt by the students. This struggle permeates the everyday lives of the students, balancing the messages and pressures of the institution against their own cultural experience and knowledge (Solomon, 1992; Sleeter & Grant, 1991; Yeo, 1992). Although students and parents may be able to bring the contestation to a stalemate, the power of the institution and the parameters of compensatory programs and mandated evaluations of students' knowledge and behavior tend to result in either the student's eventual acquiescence or dropping out. Of course a significant number of students do attempt some higher level of assimilation in achievement.

Formulated by theories of cultural and other deficiencies, justified under rubrics and rhetoric of compensatory programs, and particularized by "experts" conceiving of specifically designed, often "teacher-proof," curriculum and pedagogical techniques, specific curriculum and pedagogical packages have been assiduously designed and mandated for urban school systems. The curriculum and the requisite pedagogy (enforced through teacher evaluations) are infused with formulations constructed by an amalgam of deficiency theories and Lorde's "mythic norm." Accepted by districts often because of enabling funding, the resultant "Basic Skills" curriculum has come to be the dominant approach to the actualities of classroom education in urban schools (Carlson, 1989). The next section will describe and critique the "Basic Skills" philosophy, content, practices, and the examples of curriculum, pedagogy and classroom interactions framed by this approach and demonstrated in Chapter Three.

II. Curriculum and Pedagogy in Urban Classrooms: The Techniques of "Basic Skills"

Education, as it is ground out daily in shabby inner-city classrooms, constitutes in large part what has become the focus of mainstream educational concerns for education in general: such issues as testing, grades, a presumed linearity between curriculum and jobs, "time on task," regimentation, competition—a "trivialization" where the stress is on the technical and technique rather than social and moral issues (Purpel, 1989; Nieto, 1994). Given the impoverished conditions of schools and communities in urban areas, it seems ironic that urban districts, administrators and teachers have equally reduced the purposes of education to a level of trivialization where success is almost purely measured in numerical productivity, with little concern for the human lives masked by the statistics. At all levels in an urban school, the emphasis is on discipline, grades, diplomas, "succeeding," "making it," adherence to school rules and deculturalizing the marginal.

Sonia Nieto, in her 1994 *Harvard Educational Review* article, cites Martin Haberman's (1992) critique of what he terms the "pedagogy of poverty," which is defined as the basic urban pedagogy used with children who live in poverty and consists primarily of giving instructions, asking questions, giving directions, making assignments, and monitoring seat work—"such pedagogy is based on the assumption that they must first master "the basics'" (Nieto, 1994, p. 405 citing Haberman, 1992). Nieto points out that educational researchers have found that teaching methods in most classrooms vary little from traditional "chalk and talk" methods. Textbooks are the dominant teaching materials used, and rote learning is generally favored over creativity and critical thinking (Nieto, 1994).

The irony in urban pedagogy is the effort expended by the schools and teachers to incorporate dominant values, beliefs and knowledge in marginalized urban children of color for the purpose of achieving "success" in a mainstream society that at best is ambivalent about accepting them in the first place. The contradictions go unchallenged at both the official and classroom levels.

A. *The Regime of the Test: Standardization, Meritocracy & Failure*

Although the emphasis throughout this book is on cultural aspects of urban education, an analysis of curriculum and pedagogy in inner city schools would be incomplete without some discussion of the practices promulgated there by mainstream ideologies, such as positivism and meritocracy. These have resulted, as in many other schools in this country, in an inordinate reliance in teaching on instrumentalist techniques, constant evaluation of student learning, competition, enormous efforts on testing and tracking (Giroux, 1988, McLaren, 1988a):

> Most classrooms reflect the perception that learning can best take place in a competitive atmosphere. Techniques that stress individual achievement and extrinsic motivation are most visible. Ability grouping, testing and rote learning are the result . . . students learn other lessons as well; that learning is memorization, that reciting what teachers want is education and that critical thinking has no place in the classroom. (Nieto, 1995, p. 77)

Even though Nieto's description was about schools in general, it is especially applicable to urban classrooms, where teachers are primarily concerned with the "techniques" of discipline and teaching (in that order) and being evaluated on their respective efficaciousness as, in turn, they evaluate students. The prime motivators used with students are grades and the promise of future jobs, backed up by disciplinary procedures running the gamut from in-classroom "assertive discipline" techniques to district expulsion. The pedagogical emphasis is on "practices," not on the explication of deeper understandings of students' lives or understanding of social beliefs and practices such as racism and poverty.

In fact, the term "practice" in mainstream discourses has come to mean workable programs, which merely allow for the incremental modifications necessary for the maintenance of existing institutional frameworks and power relations (Weis, 1988). Within this definition of practice as an essentially static modality, the "educational process constitutes a political process in which women, minorities, and the socially and economically disadvantaged are disenfranchised," and their interests and cultural values and knowledge are delegitimated (Weis, p. 31).

A great deal of educational literature has been written since Paulo Freire published *Pedagogy of the Oppressed* in 1970, yet much of it has bypassed the urban schools. Freire is worth quoting here at some length even though readers may be familiar with his conceptualization of education and schooling, since what he describes as "banking" education is absolutely applicable to urban education. In fact, if the reader will refer to Nieto's and Haberman's descriptions of urban pedagogy while reading this section on Freire, he or she can quickly begin to understand that the kind of necrotic teaching Paulo dissects is the same that millions of inner-city children are subjected to on a daily basis. Worse, it is the kind of approach to teaching advocated for urban schools by both the State and by mainstream educators (many found in teacher education, unfortunately).

Specifically, Freire attacks education for being consumed by two interlinked concepts: first, it has become dominated by a "narrative" characterization that objectifies knowledge, experience, and students. Second, he decries the paradigmatic understanding that comprehends students as "empty vessels" or "containers" to be passively filled by teachers, which he calls "depositing." Freire labels this kind of education as the "banking" concept of education in which the scope of action allowed to students extends only as far as receiving, filing and storing the knowledge. (Freire, 1970, p. 225)

These two notions are connected in the sense that it is the contents, the minutia of the narrative(s) that are containerized for students, and passive recipiency is rewarded, as are the best narrators (teachers). This would seem to be borne out in the increasing number of states that inflict course-end, year-end, and summary tests on students to gauge the level of deposits, i.e., the "Dow Jones Indices of Education." Not only are students' relative personal and academic worth based on these indices but so are those of teachers, administrators, schools and whole communities who advertise themselves as worthwhile living places based on their respective schools' depository indices.

Freire describes "banking education" as mired in the past, static and fixed, promulgated through particularistic visions of knowledge, values and culture that inordinately value a concretized, essentialist visualization of the past. The curriculum itself, with its totalizing emphasis on western white culture, becomes what Madeline Grumet refers to as "ancestor worship":

> . . . proclaiming the texts of dead men to be our standards for human experience. Drawn to the beginnings, we have denied the capacity of people to be active agents in the development of their own character, reducing them to biologic, genetic or social determinants. (Grumet, 1992, p. 25)

Freire typifies mainstream or "banking" education as alienating, objectifying, and predominantly for the benefit of the particular society's dominant class. Specifically, he constructs a descriptive list of "banking" education, a few points of which should serve to convey the gist of his critique:

(b)   the teacher knows everything and the students know nothing;
(c)   the teacher thinks and the students are thought about;
(g)   the teacher acts and the students have the illusion of acting through the actions of the teacher;
(j)   the teacher is the Subject of the learning process, while the pupils are mere objects. (Freire, 1970, p. 226)

The scenario of banking education is played out daily in inner-city schools; students are taught, generally by use of lecture or worksheets (from pre-packaged materials), isolated "facts" without connection or efforts at relevancy. The teacher is generally authoritarian and distant; materials are the same for all students as is the pace of any lesson. There is a consistent use of "recall" style tests and quizzes, and yet, as evidenced by the low scores, there is little retention of the materials by students. The students' reactions range from acceptance to outright resistance and disruption, with the emphasis on the latter. Rarely are students encouraged to decipher the material or question its relevancy or meaning; they are admonished to simply memorize it, copy it, i.e., deposit it (Carlson, 1992b; Yeo, 1992).

Within my own experience of viewing other teachers in an inner-city school, the style of teaching generally in widespread use is exactly this "basics" pedagogy about which Freire's critique is so apt. What is often not noted by educational researchers is the inordinate amount of discipline and administration power that supports this approach to pedagogy. In any day, in most inner-city schools, there is a steady stream of children being sent to the office for admonishment, detention, or outright suspension for violating the strict classroom order that structures "Basic Skills" education. For example, one of the teachers regarded highly by the administration primarily for his ability to maintain control and keep order had students spend every class period throughout the school year copying out of the history text. Through the course of the academic year, the text was copied verbatim, from cover to cover, into a student notebook which was checked for accuracy to determine the final grade. There was no discussion, no group or cooperative activity, no talking—just laborious, meaningless copying. Any infraction was immediately dealt with by sending the student from the room. Other teachers advised me that this style was both common and touted through the district and that this teacher had been awarded "teacher of the year" on several occasions.

In a similar critique, Kanpol (1992), in a study of a primarily urban Hispanic district, noted that the schools' centering was primarily on facilitating and justifying an inordinate emphasis on

> . . . testing, instruction geared to tests, autocratic rules, rigid assertive discipline measures, a top-down hierarchy, and a strict adherence to an official subject-based curriculum in which the teacher and texts are the main (and often the only) sources of knowledge . . . standardized teacher evaluation, rigid role definitions, unflagging administrative authority . . . with an emphasis on predictability, control and stability. (Kanpol, 1992, p. 227)

This reductiveness, the emphasis on objectivity, testing and above all, control, is endemic in urban schools; almost as if through the distillation of mainstream educational paradigms and practices, the marginalized can attain acceptance.

More specifically, within inner-city schools, these emphases are played out within the confines of a specific, regulated (by district, state, and county educational officials) style of curriculum and pedagogy gener-ally known as the "Basic Skills Program." This program is mandated by State departments of education and acceded to by the urban schools, and represents Freire's "banking" education concept at its height.

B. The "Basic Skills Program": The Heart of Urban Teaching

This program has been designed by the State educational bureaucracy and mandated by regulation with the expressed mission of insuring that urban students attain certain objectively (empirically) defined minimal literacy and computational skills to prepare them to enter the work force (Carlson, 1989). Once again, there is the direct linkage between curriculum and employment as well as the imposition of an explicit scheme of deferred gratification. The question the schools, administrators, and teachers never ask is "what jobs?", thereby underscoring one of the classic paradoxes or tragedies of urban schooling; the disconnection between urban educational schema and students' existential realities. "The absence of employment for youth and adults in inner cities not only makes the young deeply pessimistic about their futures and the value of school, but also means they have no opportunity to learn how to work" (Heath & McLaughlin, 1993, p. 40).

The Basic Skills Program has been initiated and imposed on urban institutions as a "reform" by state governments, grounded in the notions of a "functional" curriculum, "out-comes based" evaluation based on instructional objectives, and "minimum" competency testing. Carlson (1992) argues that these programs were instituted in response to economic changes in urban employment (Carlson, 1992). The major components of the "Basic Skills Program" agenda are:
1. Performance-based evaluation guidelines that require quanti-tative data on student and school achievement.
2. Performance based "skill" kits; workbooks, drillsheets and texts.
3. Criterion referenced pre- and post-tests for use with specific curricular materials for specific subjects.
4. Teacher evaluation procedures which emphasize a "teach to the test" and "time on task" perspective. (Carlson, 1989, p. 89)

The focus of the Basic Skills Program is on functional literacy and job skills (Carlson, 1989) and is resourced on the basis of specific texts, workbooks, drills, and packaged texts. Equally important from the school's point of view, it is also designed to depersonalize authority relations and routinize classroom work so as to lessen teacher-student conflict (i.e., reduce student resistance). The use of packaged materials allows the districts to hire non-credentialed people, maintain high student-teacher ratios and horrendous class sizes (although as noted in Chapter Three, much of this is disguised by fallacious statistics generated by school and district offices) as well as compensate for high teacher turnover.

In general, the program's control function works through a lessening of discipline problems as students are "kept busy" (in conformance with the constant rhetoric of "time on task"). Teachers rationalize the authoritarian classes through a constant harangue about tests, CAT tests and threats of future joblessness unless the material is managed. This is reinforced through a constant stream of students being sent to the office for often minor infractions.

The emphasis on the job connection, passing standardized tests (e.g., CAT, CAT/E), and discipline has resulted in a stylized pedagogy common to urban classrooms of routinized, repetitive work, a high rate of in- and out-of-school suspensions, and mundane, boring classes constantly punctuated with student attempts to relieve ennui and irrelevancy.[4]

The "Basic Skills Program," in addition to setting the tone and context of education in these schools, is replete with contradictions that undercuts its own mission. Teachers and students quickly fall into a pattern of going through the motions, of completing learning activities without much awareness of, or concern for, the topic being studied (Carlson, 1989).

As Carlson (1989) noted in his study of urban schools and as borne out in my own experience, given the increasing fiscal losses to these districts and the increased costs of monitoring the "Basic Skills Program," many of the schools have increasingly deleted elective courses, so that students often find themselves repeating the same basic classes during the course of the school day. Ironically, this does not result in increased subject learning; witness my own experience (see Chapter Three) of students who attended two math classes per day (all operated per the Basic Skills format), yet who were incapable of telling time, performing basic math functions, or even making change.

Math, social studies, English, and science courses are taught in such a way as to denigrate student experience or their cultural knowledge and inculcate mainstream understandings of these subjects. For example, in terms of social studies, history content is restricted to only that which will be tested, generally white, Euro-American memorizable material—names, dates and events. Black, Hispanic, or Asian names or events rarely appear. Geography is memorizable data such as states, capitals; all American and/or European. It seems ironic that schools have failed African American students to the point where many cannot identify Africa or its salient features or history.

Another contradiction comes in the form of the students' own experience. Balanced against the drum-beat of the rhetoric and practices of the Program, and particularly its espousal of a correlation between success in the form of grades and future jobs, is the students' own awareness of the lack of legitimate employment opportunities in the community. An example of this, at my school, was the principal's insistence that scoring well on the 8th grade CAT Test would help students get into college and/or obtain a job *after* high school (4 or 5 years later!). The students were equally aware that the scores were never released to colleges or employers, so why bother? And they were equally aware of the high unemployment rates in the community through relatives with high school diplomas who could not find legitimate work.

Overall, the program has reduced "learning" to a rote emphasis on specific tests and has fostered a mentality of doing anything necessary (including assisting students) to raise student test scores in order to demonstrate increased "competency" for state and local officials. It promotes a style of control calculated to support teacher and administrator authority yet undermines it at the same time with its irrelevant, boring, repetitive work, which fosters student resistance (Carlson, 1989).

A last irony is that the "Basic Skills Program" is materials-intensive (texts, booklets, worksheets, tests, etc.), and many fiscally poor inner-city districts cannot afford annual replacement of the materials (Carlson, 1989). Thus a program that touts its individual emphasis is reduced to numbers of students sharing the same worksheets, tests, and the requisite texts (of which there are never enough).

The "Basic Skills Program," as instituted by states and local governments, has been successfully implemented or imposed on urban schools; however, it is an abysmal failure. Its determinate, test scores, are unreliable; its methodology is alienating to all involved, and certainly it would be hard to claim that urban education is improved by its incorporation. Additionally, the emphasis in the "Basic Skills Program" is on competition, individualism, and meritocracy which runs contra to the value system of the black community, which emphasizes holism, group orientation, and self-effacement (Fordham, 1988; Fordham & Ogbu, 1986; Ogbu, 1988; McLaren, 1992) and therefore is profoundly resisted by the students. The results are massive dropouts, illiteracy and school rhetoric to justify the failure of a white, Euro-western education for Hispanics, Asians and African Americans by blaming its clientele.

If there can be posited a chief problematic for the "Basic Skills Program," it is within the alternative cultural ways, knowledge, and values that urban students bring to the classroom. Inner-city students enter urban classrooms with intact, experientialized worldviews that conflict with the mainstream belief systems that undergird urban education (Ogbu, 1988; Solomon, 1992). Neither the value systems underlying the "Basic Skills Program" or its practices give credence to this dichotomy. As will be seen in the next section, urban students enter the school perceiving school practices and knowledge from within their own personal experiences but also from within culturally mediated consciousnesses formed through the black experience in this country or the Hispanic, Asian, Native American, etc.

> The means appropriate for teaching poor, urban black students differ from those appropriate for teaching other students because teaching and learning are sociocultural processes that take place within given social systems. Many of the instructional procedures used by schools stem from a set of cultural values, orientations, and perceptions that differ radically from those of poor black students (Pang & Barba, 1995, p. 342, citing Gilbert & Gay, 1994).

The first section in this chapter attempted to describe the primary cultural ideologies and mores constructing the urban educational scene, while the second section discussed the more specific curricular and pedagogical theories and practices found in urban teaching. This third, and last, section, will discuss the nuances and interactions, personal and collective, of urban education from the standpoint of the school clientele, the students themselves and their parents and guardians as representative of the community, its historical values and beliefs and inevitably, its culture.

III. Cultural History and Experience: Roots of Educational Conflict

In a 1986 study of an urban school, Sleeter and Carl Grant (1991) noted many of the same characteristics of urban curriculum and teaching as I experienced (see Chapter Three). In their interviews with teachers and administrators, educational content was described by the study participants as teaching basic skills and academic (reified) knowledge and "preparing students for lives outside of school" (Sleeter & Grant, 1991, p. 53). The interesting contradiction is that many of the teachers did not comprehend or value the students' lives outside of school. A standard rationale for student "failure" was perceived or assumed deficiencies in the students' home backgrounds that culturally limited learning aptitude (Sleeter & Grant, p. 54). Often there is no evidence for the beliefs as to students' home lives, but they form part of urban teachers "common sense." Their description of the pedagogy used by the participants corresponds to the "basic skills" motif: passive students, teachers' lecturing, worksheets to take up class time, tests emphasizing recall and rote memorization, individualized classwork, and a heavy emphasis on grades and future connection to employment (Sleeter & Grant, 1991).

One constant of school knowledge for most students is its profound irrelevancy. It is not necessarily meaningless; students simply use it for accomplishing tasks imposed on them by adults within a narrow, relatively unimportant niche in their lives. Listening to students in classrooms, hallways, or on the grounds tends to confirm this. Students rarely talk about classes in the first place and even less about any content. Most of their talk is about moments of their own lives, in terms of relationships, of their experiences and meanings outside of school and/or the classrooms. They also found that rarely is student experience, cultural knowledge or history a subject of the curriculum. As Sleeter & Grant (1991) noted:

> Their [students'] cultural knowledge did not simply compete with school knowledge—school knowledge was subsumed within it, and understood as a set of tasks to do. School knowledge was

> compartmentalized within their own conceptual system and
> thought of as sets of activities done for someone else in a social
> context. (Sleeter & Grant, 1991, p. 63)

Thus, while the school discounts and/or repudiates most of the
worth and/or value of ethnic, racial minority student cultural heritage
and experience in favor of its programs and paradigms, students,
parents, and many community people have come to distrust the
schools' practices because of this educational devaluation as well as
historically constructed memories.

This "contestation" derives from a number of sociological,
linguistic, and cultural factors, including that of racial history as
experienced by many subordinate groups in this country and which few
educators take into account. Yet the conflict of values, beliefs and
preferred knowledge is also multifaceted. While the students may indeed
be contesting for legitimacy with a school curriculum and pedagogy
that derogates their own, there are also moments and forces of
acquiescence when students, due to culturally based historical
understandings, attempt to accept and assimilate into the school's
mainstream values, beliefs, and cultural standards. This often places the
students in opposition to their own peers, certain strands of their
community and ethnic history and perceptions, and their own
internalized understandings as members of an oppressed racial minority.

A number of ethnographers (Ogbu, Weis, Solomon, Grant,
Fordham, et al.) support the contention that this represents a
paradoxical and conflicting lived-situation for racial minority students:

> Black youths do not consciously reject school meanings and
> knowledge. In fact Black youths state emphatically that schooling
> is important to them and that they want to get an education in
> order to escape from poverty and other problems of the ghetto
> community. (Ogbu, 1988, p. 170)

Black students will affirm a strong desire to attain educational
success in the mainstream sense yet will then act in ways to undermine
that very achievement. Lois Weis notes that blacks as a subordinate
cultural group evolved socially high aspirations for education as a way
out of the subordinate status; i.e., "education became a form of
opposition against whites who denied them educational access" (Weis,
1988). As Darder (1991) notes, public education has historically been
the only legitimate hope for escape from poverty for the majority of

people of color in this country. Parents, contrary to the stereotype, are often actively involved in supporting the education of their children.

For minorities, a conflict often arises within the communal knowledge and history; education, however assiduously striven for, still did and does not work for them the way it did and does for whites (Ogbu, 1988), thus it was to be opposed and resisted. This ambivalence about education in the black community evidences itself in two contraposited sets of beliefs, rhetorics, and behaviors. The first is that of the distrust of and opposition to the schools and teacher practices and rhetoric, which are seen as "white" (even in the urban schools where faculty and administration are predominantly black) (Erickson, 1993; Ogbu, 1990). Second, there is a parallel dimension wherein students and parents ascribe to the mainstream notions of school, achievement, etc.

This oppositional cultural frame, as Ogbu (1988, 1990) references, is what we and/or the media ascribe to urban schools—the destruction, the behavior and discipline problems, the refusal to learn "basic" skills, etc. Yet these incidents and the understandings of the children who engage in such overt opposition are not derived particularly as part of the school experience itself, since black Americans generally equate school learning with the learning of the dominant group, or white culture. Within the historical sense of the black community, it is often believed that schooling can only result in giving up black culture [and identity]. "He or she must learn to think and act white . . . a minority person must give up his own group attitudes, ways of thinking and behaving, and, of course, identity . . . a subtractive process." (Ogbu, 1988, p. 177)

To do so, to become "white," is fraught with anxiety, because a white society replete with racism may not accept the "whitened" minority person in the first place, and there is the problem of abandoning black culture, causes, and community (Ogbu, 1988). The result is that these students, in many cases, act in opposition to school practices, rules, etc. to avoid disconnection from their community. This duality is rarely acknowledged or understood by the teachers, even though many have lived through it themselves.

The "oppositional" frame delineates not only how students but also parents and the inner-city community act and react to school culture and knowledge. The schools, which are perceived as "white," or at the very least as culturally oppressive to the students and parents who have contact with them, are understood to be repressive in their overuse of rigid tracking schemes, derogation of community mores, high rate of condoning and/or facilitating school failure, and virtual isolation from the community. African Americans often perceive an inferior education being perpetuated on their children (having experienced it themselves) through devices they suspect are white originated (e.g., biased tests, tracking, texts, counseling, etc.) and they doubt that these schools understand black children and their needs (Ogbu, 1990). The irony is that most of the teachers and administrators are African American but viewed as "white" by inner-city students and parents.

Parents and students distrust and resent the use of "discipline" derived from schools' view that "ghetto kids" are unable to handle freedom or innovative classroom experiences. This is exacerbated by the feeling of being betrayed by black teachers whose structure and control emphasis is felt as a non-black distancing (Glasgow, 1980). The schools' promulgated cultural skills, knowledge and values are perceived by many parents and community people as being profoundly racist, of being "abductive," a process in which teachers participate, often unknowingly, as a result of their own miseducation. This "abduction" includes:

> Biased school knowledge, illusions of social normality as espoused by the educational establishment, the miseducation of teachers of a dominant but decaying vision of social equality, and barriers in ways of knowing and perceiving presumed truths. These biases help to maintain hierarchies of human worth; they are elements of racist epistemic authority that construes difference as illegitimate . . . and subscribes to concepts of Blackness as non-good "Otherness." (King & Wilson, 1990, p. 11)

These minority oppositional cultural references and behaviors are deeply rooted in the conflicting impulses by which ghetto residents perceive educational practices. Within the black culture there is a paradoxical conflict; historically blacks fought for education and literacy as oppositional to slavery and "Jim Crow" and still see education as a way out of the ghetto, yet their encounters with school have resulted too often in destroyed aspirations and failure (Glasgow, 1980; Weis, 1988; Ogbu, 1993). The lives of parents, adult relatives, older siblings, and neighbors demonstrate the utter failure of education to bring good jobs or end black joblessness and poverty (Berry & Asamen, 1989). "These adolescents live in communities in which the rhetoric that stresses education as the route to mobility is subverted by daily evidence to the contrary." (Fine, 1991, p. 106)

This paradox described by Michelle Fine (1991) typifies inner-city classrooms, where students will simultaneously argue that they "want" an education but act to disrupt the schooling that they see as irrelevant personally and oppressive culturally.

> These ambivalent attitudes toward education have made it difficult for Black students to adapt and succeed in educational settings. Many of us have found that to succeed at the very education we have been encouraged historically to seek . . . we have to separate ourselves from the experience of Black folk, the underprivileged experience of the Black underclass that was our grounding reality. (hooks, 1989, p. 99)

Additionally, there is a tension between middle-class teachers and administrators who do not live in the community and underclass parents and students, the first preferring disconnection from the latter. It is not uncommon, possibly even the norm, for teachers to live in suburban areas and teach in inner-city schools many miles from home. Another explanation has to do with the practices themselves. Mainstream pedagogy emphasizes practices that are at variance to black cultural experiences and knowledge (Ogbu, 1990). For example, mainstream education stresses individual access to knowledge and teacher attention. However, within various minority cultures, there is a more group-oriented, holistic approach to acting, epistemic understandings, and activities (Fordham, 1991).

Conversely, to suggest that student behavior is entirely oppositional is simplistic. As discussed above, students generally come to the schools within an historical consciousness that places significant value on education as a means to escape oppressive lives and conditions. Although this dissolves relatively quickly due to the perception that urban schools are maintaining the oppression instead of providing the wherewithal to combat or end it, there is still a consistent attempt to acquiesce with school routines, culture and knowledge. However, these attempts are conflicted. Students who attempt to achieve within the school's definition of achievement are not just perceived as "nerds" or other similar epithets as they would be in suburban schools but are often cast in the role of trying to be "white," of attempting to cast off their black heritage (Fordham, 1991). There is a constant pressure from peers within an urban school to avoid acceptance of achievement, although this oscillates as peers move through the same conflict.

> The influence of this black peer cultural orientation on students' orientation toward academic achievement was profound. Black students who acted "white" in school risked being ostracized by their peers, and few of the activities associated with school success were deemed appropriate. . . . In other words, school achievement came with a high price; give it up and fit in or pursue it and risk losing one's peers. (Eisenhart & Graue, 1993, p. 172)

Again, teachers and administrators seem oblivious to this ambivalence that marks much of students' attempts to succeed academically, even though many may have experienced it themselves. If aware, they rarely seem to take it into account in dealing with youngsters struggling to do well in the face of peer pressure.

Thus, there is a constant intermix or movement within the school so far as students are concerned; they are neither passive recipients of cultural transmission and knowledge from the school nor the standard-bearers of racial ideology.

The amalgam of student perceptually generated behavior, although seen (particularly by school staff) as directly oppositional to school authority or its knowledge, is instead a complex mix of direct resistance, historical understandings of education, perceptions of current educational betrayal of that history, and a constant flux of wanting to achieve but not at the expense of group identity. Added to the effects of the cultural paradigms of the school and the mainstream practices of curriculum and pedagogy, this complex array of beliefs, values, and behaviors constructs both the multiplicitous experiences and the normative understanding of urban education.

Societal and Governmental Responsibility

Any description of urban education must include an indictment of the socially and politically promulgated injustices inflicted on these schools—the governmental policies that through a negligence bordering on malfeasance or malevolent intentionality maintain the conditions, educational policies, funding, and practices endemic to urban schools. To place culpability within the boundaries of the inner-city community is both fatuous and inane. It is inconceivable that a community would opt for schools where class sizes regularly exceed forty or fifty students, where there are virtually no educational resources, where the few textbooks available are in excess of 20 and 30 years old, where expulsion and dropout rates exceed 50 percent, where violence is endemic, and where the public at large seems indifferent. It is beyond the realm of common sense to suppose that anyone would voluntarily choose such schools for their children, compensatory theories notwithstanding, and therefore, the ultimate responsibility for perpetuating these institutional purveyors of trauma and failure must lie elsewhere.

These schools in 1996 represent institutionalized racial and ethnic segregation to a degree not seen in this country since before the civil rights movements of the 1960s.

> Some forty years after the highest court struck down racial segregation in our nation's schools on the grounds that a separate school system denied black children their right to equal educational opportunity, racial discrimination in our public schools is alive and well and the outlawed dual school system is still with us. (Carter, 1995, p. 619)

The striking thing noted by many educational sociologists is the degree to which state agencies and influential groups such as business or the media show little inclination to question the matter. While the violence and human tragedy are documented, the underlying governmental policies and social values of a society that would tolerate such human degradation, especially as to children, go virtually unexplored and unquestioned. Again, as Kozol writes:

> One searches for some way to understand why a society as rich and frequently as generous as ours would leave these children in their penury and squalor for so long and with so little public indignation. Is this just a strange mistake of history? Is it unusual? Is it an American anomaly? (Kozol, 1991, p. 40)

Overlooked and/or intentionally neglected is the degree to which governmental agencies have acceded to and/or cooperated in the establishment of these schools *and* their conditions. Public support for these districts and their young clientele is notoriously disparate (Kozol, 1991; Hacker, 1992); the spending gulf between minority districts' funding and that of suburban (predominantly white) districts is blatantly inequitable (Kozol, 1991; Hacker, 1992). From wherever the source of public funds for education, it is generally distributed on the basis of district derivation (Kozol, 1991); hence a wealthy district receives significantly more state funds than an impoverished district. Thus, the impoverished conditions of urban districts are maintained through the taxing and spending powers of the state governments. The inherent inequity is that states require public school attendance supported by county and other local governments enforcing public school attendance in the district of residence yet fail to ensure resource equity, thereby effectively condemning urban children to an unequal and inequitable education.

This institutional bias is rationalized within the same belief constructs as discussed earlier. In a blame-the-victim self-fulfilling moment, community leaders question "throwing good money after bad" when asked about redistribution of public school funding (Kozol, p. 79). Kozol (1991) notes specifically how Chicago city and state agencies have argued against additional urban school funding on the spurious basis "that you don't rearrange the chairs on the *Titanic*" (Kozol, p. 80). In other cities across the country:

> Investment strategies in education are often framed in the same terms: "How much is it worth investing in this child as opposed to that one? Where will we see the best return?" . . . it is clear that certain choices have been made: who shall be educated? Who shall live? Who is most likely to return the most to society? (Kozol, 1991, p. 117)

Thus, the urban school, in addition to its deleterious educational practices, has been subjected to institutional and government discrimination that furthers and/or maintains its abominable conditions, resources, and funding. Given our society's reliance on Horatio Algerism, competition, and a sickening justification of "who deserves," urban educational hopes for ameliorating change seem farcical.

Requiem

All too often, sociologists, politicians, educators and civic leaders diagnose the lives of inner-city school children through the lens of white, middle-class frames of reference. They, and this includes all too frequently the school administrators and teachers who spend their days with these children, condemn the dropouts, the teen pregnancies, the deaths, the gangs, and the street behavior in terms of perceived deficiencies in the families and attitudes of the community (Heath & McLaughlin, 1993). These folks, so invested in the commodities and values of middle-class America, believe that these children live the lives they do almost by choice because of perceived low motivation toward schooling as offered in urban schools, low self-esteem, and perceived parental indifference. They do not hold society and/or its institutions accountable; instead they persist in "blaming the victim" and continually seek solutions that are meant to fix deficiencies but not problems.

Before we move on to a narrative analysis of teaching in an urban school, the worldview, the subjective self-identificatory subjectivity of inner-city students needs to be put into perspective. Again, I will draw on anthropological descriptions of life in the "hood" that becomes lives in the classroom. In order to come to terms, to accept who these teens are, where they come from, in order to teach them,

> there is the need to recognize that the public ideal of leisured and paced mainstream middle-class childhood, adolescence, young adulthood and adulthood, often portrayed in the media, lies outside the realm of possibility of those who grow up in inner cities at the end of the 20th century. (Heath & McLaughlin, 1993, p. 215)

Please keep this in mind as we proceed through Chapter Three: underneath the numbers, the theories, and the stories are young children whose only crime is that they happen to struggle for identification of self and community in a place Derrick Bell (1992) has aptly called "the bottom of the well."

Notes

1.   A street rap from Watts (circa 1970) quoted in Douglas Glasgow, *The Black Underclass*, San Francisco: Jossey-Bass Publishers, 1980.

2.   Most state education departments produce and publish a series of subject-matter content guides entitled "Frameworks" or "Curriculum Guides" or "Basic Curriculum," etc. These more or less mandate curriculum sequence, content, evaluative stages and instruments, goals, objectives and overall purposes of the State's vision of curriculum for

the public schools.

3.   Examples of this siphoning of entitlement funds are endemic in urban districts (Kozol, 1991; Yeo, 1992). Unfortunately, federal and/or state oversight has been cut back due to reduction of educational budgets, so little action is taken to correct the problem.

4.   A similar description in more detail occurs in Jean Anyon's description of a working-class school. See J. Anyon, "Social Class and the Hidden Curriculum of Work," *Journal of Education*, 162, 1980, 66-92.

Teaching in an Urban School: A Personal Narrative

As indicated previously, Chapter Three embodies the theories and educational practices categorized as urban education. Although framed within the broad category of ethnography, this chapter constitutes, more specifically, a narrative, the story of a white, forty-year-old, middle-class male who happened to enter someone else's world. Much as Peter McLaren noted in the foreword to his book, *Life in Schools* (1989), about teaching in inner-city Toronto, I entered as:

> a young, liberal teacher both fascinated by and fearful of the marginalized, the disaffected, the disenfranchised and the indigent—fascinated because their poverty and behavior seemed to be born of defiance rather than despair; and fearful because their anger, pain and hate had clearly been constructed out of the neglect and greed of a democratic society. (McLaren, 1989, p. ix)

Defining the Approach

The framework of this chapter is eidetic or phenomenological, set within the notion that knowledge of people and events is not objective but is exquisitely situational. Specifically, the frame is the phenomenological concept that the structure of the meaning of events and human interactions is that which the actors give to the events, often through their language.

The concept of eidetics derives from Husserl's development of phenomenology and Heidegger's insistence that any claims to truth or knowledge can never be more than partial, incomplete. Thus, there cannot be transcendent, absolute truth about experience, and what we see and experience are mere appearances or phenomena—they indicate something else behind.

> What is being proposed here is a way of describing everyday school situations in a manner that takes seriously the basic insight of phenomenology. If we want to know what is going on in classrooms, we can have direct access through our empirical senses, through our experience. But also, what we see and experience has an eidetic quality—it speaks of something else. (Pinar, 1988, p. 422)

Thus, an inner-city student's school failures, language, or behavior must be understood as phenomena—they speak of something else. The purpose of this book is to try to locate the "something else" in that milieu. This approach has spawned a number of research efforts referenced as ethnography ("critical inquiry," "qualitative research," "interpretive inquiry," etc.). In the main, ethnographic or interpretive research generalizes from observation; attempting to derive the meaning of events and human interactions from a variety of languaged symbolic patterns versus Positivism's search (or re-search) for objectified knowledge. Ethnography accepts the partiality of knowledge within the totality of experiential expression (Pinar, 1988; Lather, 1991; Nieto, 1995). Grounded in this notion that observations and occurrences do not speak for themselves (McLaren, 1989), phenomenological research asks, What is the participant's experience like and what does it mean? (Barritt et al., 1983).

The definition of ethnographic methodology has periodically raised the question of its validity, although recently this debate has subsided (Eisner & Peshkin, 1990); (Lather, 1991, 1989; Pinar, 1988) as broad use of qualitative research has created an intrinsic legitimacy. Lather (1991) suggests that even posing such an issue, however, reduces ethnography to a positivistic schema which expunges its inherent experiential validity. At the other end of the spectrum, researchers such as Miles & Huberman (1984), Bullough (1989) and others posit that ethnography must address the validity issue by "evolving a set of valid and verifiable methods" (Miles & Huberman, p. 23). Such a stance seems antagonistic to the phenomenological emphasis on experience and interpretation whose antithesis would be a reductiveness to typologies of method.

Eisner (1981, 1990) argues that interpretive research is inherently artistic and that the canons of reliability and replicability are inapplicable:

> Its [research] validity is to be determined by our view of its credibility, and not by reduction to some average by using only that portion that it shares with others. Validity is the product of the persuasiveness of a personal vision; its utility by the extent to which it informs. There is no test of statistical significance, no measure of construct validity; what one seeks is illumination and penetration. (Eisner, 1981, p. 6)

The resultant qualitative "data" are thus constructions of other people's constructions of what they and others are up to. "Analysis is sorting out the structures of significance . . . and determining their social ground and import." (Geertz, 1983, p. 15). Within interpretive research, the use of the narrative has come to be increasingly utilized and validated (Wexler, 1987; Eisner & Peshkin, 1990; Quantz & O'Connor, 1988). The value of this particular approach is its emphasis on the meaning-making of the narrator:

> One of the significant ways through which individuals make sense of and give meaning to their experiences is to organize them in a narrative form . . . to find and speak in their own *voices*. (Lather, 1991, p. 118)

The use of the narrative and voice makes particular sense when attempting to interpret experiences on the margins (hooks, 1990), and especially within the borders of a school where multiple voices are in constant struggle for legitimacy (Nieto, 1995). Although significant research (in both the positivistic and qualitative formats) on urban schools, students, and cultures has been performed, little has been attempted within an interpretive framework of a participant teacher. One exception is McLaren's *Life in Schools* (1989), which was constructed as a specific juxtaposition of his daily journal and certain notions of critical pedagogy (McLaren, 1989). The voices of the students serve as exemplars, often without specific connection to the theoretical concepts discussed. The experiences and voices that follow constitute an interpreted reality set within everyday encounters; I have attempted not to discount the voices and experiences from their understandings. I have tried to "allow the data to generate the propositions in a dialectical manner that permits use of a priori theoretical frameworks, but which keeps a particular framework from becoming the container into which the data must be poured." (Lather, 1986, p. 267).

Sources and Selections of Materials

All of the narratives and experiential material used in this chapter (and referenced in others) was derived from everyday occurrences within my classroom, on the basketball courts, in the teachers' lounge, or elsewhere around the school. Unless otherwise noted, it was taken down at the time, on breaks, between classes, or from collected student writings and/or official memos and notices. The material was collected over the three and a half years I taught at a south Los Angeles (Watts) middle school. In cases where I was unsure either of my hearing or my understanding, I asked the speaker(s) for repetition or interpretation so as to improve my own teaching.

I began to keep, with their permission, copies of student writings (essays, poems, biographies, etc.), and where possible, gained access to personal meaning and/or experiences that underlay their written efforts. As advisor to the school newspaper, I had access to contributed writings from all over the school, and I continually solicited interpretive input from the students in an attempt to see their world through their eyes.

I have not selected the material on the basis of a particular typology of student ("successful"—Nieto, 1995; "dropouts"—Fine, 1991; "gang members"—Glasgow, 1980; "female"—Weis, 1988, etc.), but because the statements were representative of themes, contradictions, resistance, and accommodation to school practices and their personal clarity of insight into their own lives and circumstances.

The choice of descriptive language is intentional on my part. Emotions are often the internal framework on which we phenomenologically structure our interpretations of the world and others. The struggle here is to try to understand these people on their own terms; what they express is in the context of the experiences and communities from which they came.

Their words are their own, the language used, the phrases, the slang, the choice of vocabulary are wholly theirs. Unfortunately, the use of participants' language can be and has been taken as implicit disparagement, as stereotyping, with the connotation being that their voices should be heard in other, more "acceptable," ways. I have rejected this as additional deculturalization and silencing, from which they already suffer too much. If the reader is uncomfortable with the use of students' vocabulary, that is the reader's problem, not my students'. To understand their realities, we must meet them as they live.

> We encounter each other in everyday life by means of roles and patterns that are habitualized, consciously or unconsciously learned. But what is everyday life? It is important to recall that it constitutes an *interpreted* reality—interpreted by men and subjectively meaningful to them in a coherent world. (Greene, 1978, p. 213)

Setting and Parameters of Their World

It must be emphasized that this chapter represents a teacher's narrative from a corner of the inside, not a stranger's outside research peering in to catch a glimpse. This interpretive narrative is about an institution and individuals whose lived experiences, systems of practices, and ways of life differ from the dominant American culture. As was true of Solomon's study of West Indian students in Canada, conflict and tension characterize students' relation to school authority as they break rules, disregard expressed and unwritten codes of conduct, and struggle to impose their own values and language on the school culture (Solomon, 1992).

The school, Washington Middle School,[1] is an inner-city school with a population of about 800 students and 28 teachers (both very transitory) and 6 administrators (3 were counted as teachers for class size calculations, even though they never actually taught). The students were predominantly (90%) African American with the balance being recent immigrant Hispanics, divided into 6th through 8th grades. The teachers were mostly African American, self-identified as being middle class, and predominantly female (4 male teachers, including myself). The administrators were all African American and female. Four of the teachers and all of the administrators had taught in the district in excess of 20 years; the other 24 teachers had taught from one day to a few months; turnover was unofficially calculated at 250% each year. At any given time, most of the teachers were (and still are) on emergency contracts (without credentials) or were long-term substitutes. Numerous others are teaching out of their credentialed subjects, and the few teachers who were not African American (although black) were foreign (e.g., Filipino, Sierra Leone, Nigerian, Zairian, etc.) with limited standard English abilities and no experience with American black or Hispanic inner-city children.

School attendance was high and class sizes ranged from 25 in one teacher's classes (she refused to take any more, daily sending the excess to the office) to the more usual 40 to 50 students each period.

The school is located in Watts, a predominantly black underclass community haunted by gangs, drugs, street violence, and crime. There are numerous small businesses, most with boarded windows. Alcohol and drug abuse is pandemic. From the students' standpoint, the school's culture is strongly influenced by gang identity, violence (of several types, including epidemic levels of sexual and physical abuse), and poverty. The students are representative of lower-class black America [Ogbu, 1988]; they come from primarily single-female-parent homes, have multiple stepsiblings, low socioeconomic status, and are, in part, typified by their music, language, and dress. The area still shows the scars of the "Watts Riot" of 1965 along with the more recent signs of conflict in April 1992.

I came to teach here in 1988 and stayed for several years. The interpretive narrative you are about to read is mine, but it is not unique: it is mirrored thousands of times a day in inner-city schools across America. As you read, keep in mind the ideologies, practices, and foundational values described and analyzed in Chapter Two, particularly those dealing with "blaming the victim," because it is hard to tell who the victim is. Perhaps, teacher and student, we're all victims of the social construction that configures, condones and sustains what is at "the bottom of the well" (Bell, 1992).

Teaching the "Faces at the Bottom of the Well"

> In these bloody days and frightful nights when an urban warrior can find no face more despicable than his own, no ammunition more deadly than self-hate and no target more deserving of his true aim than his brother, we must wonder how we came so late and lonely to this place. (Angelou [2])

Driving to my teaching job each morning, I pass from a world of clean, quiet residential streets and corner shops to one of graffiti, police and ambulance sirens, the ever-present whop-whop of the police helicopter, and brooding faces. Walking onto the school grounds is to be immersed in a sea of black faces, of shouts and thrown epithets and obscenities, of a sweaty Brownian motion of bodies dressed in L.A. Laker jackets and red bandannas. To walk down the hallways is to be jostled and heckled amidst broken lockers, a litter of paper and pieces of refuse. The windows in Room 24 are broken; the door needs to have the gang signs and references to sex and drugs painted over; the room itself is as I left it yesterday; broken light fixtures, desks with taped-up legs (two balanced on a stack of books), stucco walls with faded charts (falling off as the tape wears out), and the voices:

> Hey, Mr. Yee-ho, didcha hear, man, Shamika's Mama gots busted?

> Good morning, Mr. Yo, my Mama needs to talk wid you about dat boy, he been botherin me agin.

> Man, keeps yo hands to yo sef, hey, Mr. Yo, hey, Fred, whats happenin, ya hear about Jemal, his bro gots shot by Crips, man he be deaded.

> Hey, Mr. Yeo, can yo talk to Mrs. Smith fo me, dat ole bitch won't let me take a test cause I cussed her ole bootie out?

It's 8:15 a.m., 1st period, Monday, at Washington Middle School, in the ghetto that is the site of the movie *Boyz in the Hood*. Located in south central Los Angeles, the area known as Watts; we just call it the "Hood." Bounded by freeways dividing the area from more prosperous neighborhoods, it is separated from the beautiful large shopping malls, movie theaters, office buildings, and quiet residential areas. This—this be the ghet-to, here there be the Crips, the Bloods and the Pirus; boarded buildings, run-down stores, abandoned vehicles in the streets (folks live in them), graffiti, burned-out hulks of long-gone enterprises and everywhere there are the liquor stores and the quiet but tense clots of men (young and old, standing in separate groups) sipping from bottles of cheap wine or Colt-45, watching, staring, waiting. . . .

At the school, I teach 8th grade science and math and coach the girls' sports. I came here because I needed a job; I stayed because I needed the kids. I was forty years old, fresh out of a private college's teacher education program. I had taken courses in methodology, teaching strategies, evaluation models, and curriculum. I had learned how to construct lesson plans, assertive discipline schedules, different learning styles, and the taxonomy of cognition. I knew how to construct tests, quizzes, and reading assignments. I knew about different world cultures and had passed the California Teacher's Exam. I was prepared for the interview questions we had been told would be asked on Bloom's Taxonomy, lesson planning and teaching strategies. I had recently closed down a law practice and wanted to teach because I thought I knew a lot about science and kids.

It was mid-October. School had already started when I applied for an opening to teach biology at a district high school but was told in the interview that the notice had been an error; however, would I be willing to teach science at the best middle school in the district? The teacher in the position had recently left for "personal" reasons.

Sure, why not, I can handle 8th graders, I had been a Scoutmaster.

Hey, Flo [the principal at Washington, who was passing by], this here white boy Eagle Scout wants to teach at Washington! Dontcha need a science man?

I was hired on the spot—no questions, except if I knew anything about computers and science equipment. I was told to report to Washington Middle School on Monday at 8:00 a.m. (classes start at 8:15 a.m.) and given directions. I wasn't even asked about Bloom's Taxonomy or for samples of lesson plans, although I recall wondering why the Assistant Superintendent kept emphasizing that I was to come see him when (note: not "if" but "when") I wanted to leave—leave, I just got here!

Although I was aware that the surrounding area was known as the site of the 1965 "Watts Riot," somehow the ethnic connotations went unnoticed. Ignorant of both inner-city schools and the ways of students and teachers, armed with the techniques of teacher education and the excitement of embarking on the experience of teaching science, I approached my assignment at Washington Middle School with what I think was probably only the normal trepidation of any new teacher.

The First Day

I arrived at the school at 7:45 a.m., parked my car and strolled to the office as nonchalantly as I could through a milling crowd of black students, all yelling at each other, slapping palms and jostling. I waited for the secretary to notice me and watched the teachers come in, silent, a few smiles, grabbing papers out of boxes and slipping long cards into a time clock. Finally at 8:20, the secretary finally asked if she could help me. When I told her why I was there, she hollered for the janitor to take me to the room and went back to the phone—nothing more was said.

Escorted by the janitor, without a gradebook or class roll (or a welcome by the principal or anyone else), openly gaping at the broken windows, trash, and graffiti, I clutched my carefully crafted lesson plans and entered the room. It was filled with 44 students, all yelling, arguing and pushing, the cacophony exacerbated by the sheer din. What I had not registered earlier came into my consciousness—"They're *all* black!" I was immediately and vividly conscious of my whiteness—and their blackness—that this was their school. I was a stranger—an alien!

In a sudden hush, I walked to the big lab table, placed my plans down, and turned to an unnerving sea of dark eyes.

Good morning, I'm Mr. Yeo, and I'm your new science teacher. . .

Hey, white man, can you blow things up?

Jemal, shut up man, the dude's talking, yo dumb nigger!

Who you callin a nigger?

OK, quiet down [what do I do about the "N" word?] I don't have a roll sheet yet, so why don't you tell me your names?

Her name's ho, she's a ugly bitch . . .

Who you callin a ho, blood—yo momma's a ho!

. . . and the two girls flew across three aisles of desks to claw and flail at each other—welcome to Washington Middle School. . . !

Within the first 15 minutes, my lesson plans became spurious, and techniques of classroom management were drowned in the sheer volume of fights, obscene language, and talk. When I asked where they were in the text, there were catcalls and obscenities. Becoming angry and frustrated, I was admonished to "chill out, bro!" The "broken record" approach splintered in the face of derisive laughter, denial, and teasing. I was embarrassed when asked, "Hey man, how come they send us a white boy like you?" I tried assertive discipline methods I had memorized; there was a great deal of laughter as I wrote names on the board (mostly they were the wrong names) and misspelled "Jakiesha," "Tazshamesha," and "Chantyeneka." They said they had no textbooks and the previous five (five??) teachers (this was only mid-October) had left them alone. This between a few other fights, screamed epithets, and the beginnings of an Excedrin headache.

The room was concrete blocks, only partially painted; the chalkboard was cracked; map hangers had no maps; two of three windows were broken by what appeared to be small round holes; there was a large American flag (with 48 stars!); a scarred metal door led to the outside corridor, and there was an inner door, which I discovered led to a "stockroom." When I pushed open that door, I discovered a room full of shelving (mostly bare), a floor 12 to 15 inches deep in paper, broken glass, half-open chemical bottles, and the smell of stale beer and sulfuric acid hung in the air. A few microscopes drooped on one shelf, and there were some unbroken bottles of chemicals and some beakers on another. There were piles of booklets from power companies advocating energy saving and professional careers; along with a large pile of U.S. Army recruiting materials. It became a place of refuge for myself and the other science teacher to talk quietly, drink a little coffee, and laugh about the latest antics of either the students or the principal.

The students (all 44 of them) were black, ranging in complexion from dark to light and from petite to one girl who must have weighed in at 300 lbs. and was about 6' 3" (she turned out to be sixteen and was visiting someone's cousin). Their dress went from what appeared to be discards from the Goodwill Store to what the kids called "church rags." When they weren't insulting each other in language I had not heard since boot camp, they were loud, laughing, and highly energetic. Their bodies were constantly in motion, touching or hitting each other, and the voices were shrill and constant, speaking what sounded like a southern dialect, with vowels dropped, esses added, and misplaced verbs. Their hair styles ranged from long straight tresses to wild Afros, and many of the boys had initials and words shaved in the back. Their favorite words were "mo-fo," "bitch," "posse," and the ever-present "nigga." And the names; Sutoya, Travahar, Kenya, Sharnell, Devenniyon, Roosevelt, and Ka-Ssandra.

Completely nonplussed, I calmed down the two girls, got the class to stop shouting "whoo, whoo, whoo," and started teaching my first science lesson. What I had anticipated would take 15 minutes took the rest of the period between a few more fights, requests for passes, questions to deflect the topic, throwing of miscellaneous materials, and the never-ending "bagging" (the practice of hurling insults: the trick is to get a good one back before the teacher stops you both).

At 8:45 a.m., the PA speaker high on the wall coughed on, and a voice who identified herself as "Dr. Johnson" came into the room. She talked about people whose names and faces I didn't know and school events about which I knew even less (nor did it seem did many of my students, who were paying little attention). At the close, she called for all students to repeat with her the school motto:

We are Washington High
When we draw nigh. . . . . . [nigh?]
To April's summer day
And take the CAT and CATE tests
We'll be the best in the USA

When I asked, the students had no idea what she was talking about nor did they appear to care. At the end of her spiel, Dr. Johnson reminded all the students that they should obey the school rules, follow their teacher's directions, and study hard so they could get good jobs when they grew up. Catcalls and obscenities erupted! I wondered why—she had made sense to me.

The rest of the morning periods passed in much the same manner except that my headache from the confusion and noise continued to mount. More names I couldn't spell or pronounce, half-understood language swirling around me, and desperate attempts on my part to talk about geology, mountains, and deserts. By lunch, I was already hoarse, but I felt comforted that I had gotten through five periods. Lunch was to be followed by a computer class, which had to be better. I closed the door and walked to the cafeteria, anxious to meet my colleagues and, perhaps, Dr. Johnson.

As I entered the large student cafeteria, the volume of voices was truly astounding as was the splattering of food on floor, tables, and walls. There were three big trash barrels in the center of the room, filled to overflowing with paper plates, half-eaten food, and empty milk cartons. Students would walk by and make a tentative toss at the barrel, while yelling at their "homies." I reached the inner door that said "Teachers Only" and gingerly pushed my way in. Seated at two tables were about 15 black women. Most looked up, glanced my way, and went back to eating and talking. No one said a word to me, not a "hello," "welcome," or a name.[3] I was excruciatingly conscious of being new, white, not belonging—the Other. I sat on a chair alone, listening to a cacophony of complaints about the school, the principal, other teachers, and, of course, the students—who they usually referred to as "fools." All of this interspersed with laughter, jokes about whites, and all conducted in what sounded like a southern dialect.

Escorted again by the janitor to the "computer" room since I didn't have a key, I was looking forward to teaching a computer class. I was assuming it would be a quiet room, filled with computers and industrious students. Outside the door, milling around and poking each other, were about 35 students; they looked like the same ones from this morning! When the janitor and I entered the room, they all crowded through the door pushing and yelling. The room was the same concrete block style, with bare walls, lined with long tables. Scattered on the tables were monitors, a couple of old Apple II CPU's, and wires running all over the floor. There was not a single assembled computer in the room, just pieces and parts of systems. Some of the students sat on the tables, on the few chairs, but most sat on the floor, still jostling and talking.

After getting their tentative attention, I asked the students what had they been doing in this class. Some responded that the previous teachers had been taking them out to the PE area and letting them mix with the PE classes to play basketball. I asked a few why they had opted to take the class and was told that it was the school's only elective, that they were all in a GATE (??) (which I found out later meant Gifted and Talented) class, and Mr. F., the guidance counselor, had placed them all in it to learn job skills. None had ever worked on a computer; they had no idea how computers worked, and to their knowledge, in the three years they had been at the school, no one had ever worked on a computer in the class . . . we went to play basketball, which I discovered meant 55 minutes of standing along the walls of the PE building talking to friends. In their favor, of course was the lack of any whole computers to even attempt any learning on, just pieces and parts and frayed wires.

When I left at 3:00 p.m., I still had not met another teacher or seen any of the administrators. I had no idea what I was doing, who these kids were, or if I could or should continue.

Survival and Growth: The Changes in the Story

As that first week went by, carefully prepared handouts littered the floor; assigned homework was never done; test taking was a farce in the presence of the shouting of answers (usually wrong); essay responses were generally unreadable, nonsensical, and obscene, and my attempts at reflective dialogue floundered in the face of street language in which I was the illiterate. The office informed me that I couldn't use the xerox machine "cause you teachers always fuck it up" [secretary]. The "bad" students (it seemed that most fit that category) taken to the office for discipline beat me back to the classroom and celebrated my chagrin with victory swaggers and a great deal of hand slapping with the others. What was I supposed to do when even the smallest kids wanted to physically intimidate me—"whatsa matter, white man, scared?"

Pleas for administration help were met with closed doors or references to the school handbook, the other teachers were often aloof, angry, and hidden behind closed classroom doors. The gradebook was a litter of forms I had never seen. Where was my "teaching practice" in the welter of memos, P.A. announcements, half-destroyed texts, disappearing principals, and no supplies?

I discovered that the science text was over 30 years old and we only had enough for a classroom supply, yet the principal demanded daily that we assign homework in the textbook. There was little science equipment, and what did exist was often unserviceable. The stockroom had been a place for teachers to meet and drink during the day, or so the kids and the bottles littering the room suggested. Mrs. Netty, the 7th-grade science teacher, said that there hadn't been any monies to spend on science in her three years, and there were none this year. There were no field trips, no overhead projectors, no film projectors, no audio-visual equipment.

> Mrs. Netty: We did get donated some TVs and VCRs last year, but
> the principal and the counselor took them home; we ain't seen

them since.

I was one of four males and the only white person on the campus!
Silence or snickers followed as I walked the corridors, obscene and
violent language assaulted my senses, and classes and instruction
continued to be an unmitigated disaster. Nothing in my experience,
certainly not teacher education, had prepared me for the crushing
humiliation and frustration as the "white boy."

As time progressed, although I didn't know the term, I became
inundated with the paperwork indigenous to the "Basic Skills Program."
I struggled with pre- and post-tests, futilely demanding attention to stop
cheating and "please stop talking!" I wondered how the other teachers
survived—was it a "black thang"? I found other classrooms were
structured with rows of desks, worksheets, and a plethora of packaged
tests. I listened while teachers routinely yelled at students to "shut up"
and pushed them from the room for trivial excuses (anything, they
would say, to lighten the load!). I listened to the PA announcements to
work hard, follow directions, be on time, stay on task, in order to
graduate and get a job. I learned from students that there weren't any
jobs except on the street selling "crack" and "snow."

As I talked more and more with students, I discovered that for
them, school literally had little meaning in their lives. I heard staff rail
against the gangs, and the students describe how joining meant survival
in the "hood."

Yeo: So why the red shoelaces, Jemal?

Jemal: Man, Mr. Fred, if'n you don't gots red, de Bloods be
fuckin you up on de way home, but ah gots some blue ones
too for de Crips.

Yeo: Does everyone belong to a gang?

Jemal: Man, ah ain't no banger, ah hates dem, all that
shootin and shit, but ya gots to belong, they gives you a job,
protects ya, ah even gots me a cah so ah can drive mah bitch
around. The teachers always be baggin on it, but we gots no
choices, man.

Many of the students had two sets of clothes, one blue and one red—they would change as they walked home and crossed gang boundaries. Gang membership provided protection, identity, and jobs (usually involving drug sales). On the other hand the students universally would denounce what they called "banging" or "gang-banging" to a teacher and walk away slapping palms with each other as if they had put one over. There was a bitter rivalry between gangs, even at the school, which was generally regarded as a "safe zone." This prompted numerous fights, "baggin," and disruptions. Simultaneously, however, there was continuous angst about gang activities, especially the omnipresence of "drive-bys," where a car of gang members (often in their early teens) would drive by a rival house and spray it with unaimed gun fire. It was a regular occurrence for students to come to school mourning friends and/or relatives killed in this insanity. [4]

I talked at first about oceans, geology and space and then began to listen about lives of abuse, hunger, and only knowing a few square blocks of squalid streets. Kids who lived three miles from the beach and surrounded by mountains had never been to either. I discovered we couldn't even explore such places vicariously, since both film projectors were broken (not to mention that the librarian was reluctant to loan any films to a new teacher). I wondered why they refused to stop talking to each other during tests, until I realized they walked, talked, and lived in a group-cooperative world. I learned gang signs and how to speak "street"; they learned about whites. I wondered how they could have so many brothers, sisters, and cousins. I found out that many could only read at about a 2nd grade level; math skills were four or five years behind or in some cases nonexistent. I discovered it was "no big thang" to be pregnant, that in fact it was kind of looked up to, although they used terminology like "being in trouble," "loaf in de oven," etc. I found out that most didn't live with their biological parents, and those who did lived with their mother—fathers were gone, in jail, or deceased. One incidental conversation with a group of four female students who spent the entirety of each period doing each other's hair in the back of the room stands out to illustrate something of the conditions these children dealt with. For a week or two, I had demanded their attention and participation (although I'll be the first to admit that in a class of 52, they did sort of blend into the back of the room), and, when it was not given, I sent them to the office (discovering later that they never arrived—they just "floated" until the next class period). After several weeks of this, I decided to be dialogic about the whole thing and confront them:

Yeo: Aren't you tired of me sending y'all to the office; I mean it happens every day. How are you going to learn anything?

Shakeesha: What's to learn, we all is goin to be hair designers.

Yeo: Maybe, but in the meantime how do you expect to get out of the 8th grade and graduate from high school without science?

Jamika: We don't care, won't grageate anyway—most don't.

Yeo: What do your parents think about this?

Shakeesha: What parents, we none of us gots no parents!

Jamika: Hey, I have a brother, but he's in jail.

Yeo: So where do you live then, who takes care of you?

Shakeesha: We lives over there (pointing out the door toward a vacant lot with some old cars)—we looks after ourselves, don't need much, sides parents just do shit to ya and other stuff.

Jamika: Shit, I had a step Dad, and he always wanted to do it with me, my momma weren't around much, but she's gone.

Yeo: How do you eat, and do things like buy clothes?

Jamika: Hey man, we has friends and we earn money doing stuff fo guys, ya know what ah means?

I wrote most of this down that day, because somehow it struck me then as a microcosm of my students' lives. These girls lived in two abandoned cars on a vacant lot, unbothered by police or social workers. Their parents had disappeared (or perhaps threw them out) and they obviously were making money through prostitution—and these girls were just 13 years old! It was hard to insist after this that they focus on science. I kept track of two of them—they were right—none graduated; one ended up in jail and one disappeared. Two did get jobs in local businesses as hair stylists. Although perhaps most of the students in the 8th grade were not in such extreme circumstances, many were in similar ones. Other teachers and the one counselor did confirm that many did not graduate from high school; over half of the girls were involved with parental sexual abuse, and many of the boys were actively involved in illegitimate enterprises.

After two weeks, I realized that it was quit or survive. To do the latter, it was clear that the paraphernalia of teacher education needed to be jettisoned. Instead I used humor, self-deprecation, and listening and began to identify students (they didn't all look alike) and their personal histories, voices, and the nuances of their culture. Since this took a great deal of class time, I discarded "sponges," structured lesson plans, *and* assertive discipline. I questioned students about their language, the streets, and their sexual attitudes. I learned about red shoelaces and scarves, dread-locks, the "hood" and mastered the art of "baggin." I asked them to define and interrogate their favorite insults—"nigger," "mo-fo," and "yo momma." I answered questions about what it was like to be white and old (40!). We talked about pollution and population and whether it applied to blacks or were these inventions of the "Man" (whites). We argued over whether AIDS came from monkeys or if it was a white plot to kill blacks. We discussed jobs, religion, racism, music, and what school was really about. We formed groups to go outside and see who or what lived on the school grounds, bet on which type of clouds and weather would occur tomorrow, and "rapped" about stars and planets. I asked them what they wanted to know about a science topic and went from their questions (no lesson plans, besides the principal never looked at them, much less visited the classroom).

The lesson plans became a focal point for teacher resistance when the new vice principal announced we all needed to turn in a week's worth of lesson plans for his review each Monday. I dutifully started a 3-ring binder, typed up five days of lesson plans, and turned in the binder. After several weeks of this and receiving them back without any comments, I became suspicious that they were in fact never read. So I duplicated the prior week's plans (including the old dates) and placed them in the folder. When nothing was said, I duplicated one day's lesson plans, including the same date, five times and stuck them in the binder and turned it in. For the rest of the year I used the same exact lesson plan to fill out the binder. When I told several of the other teachers what I was doing, they agreed it was more "head office boo-shit," borrowed the plan, duplicated it, and we all turned in my same lesson plan week after week (duplicated five times per week in each binder). For several years, a growing number of the teachers (in a number of subjects) turned in that plan to the vice principal. Perhaps they still do!!

In talking to the other teachers (who goodnaturedly had thought I was funny because I was so white and scared), I discovered they faced similar conflicts between what we had been taught and what we experienced. They, too, struggled with the street language and urban culture, slipping in and out of the black English verbalisms. They believed fervently that "white" education had trashed and forgotten the black schools. As the only white person there for several years, I was often asked to justify the discrimination they all had felt and lived; I couldn't. Usually, I found myself in agreement and angry at white friends who failed to understand.

Over the several years, as I struggled with yearbooks, the school paper, student councils and coaching, gang signs, the boundaries of the "hood," and other tools of my trade, I was often asked to counsel new teachers—"cause you know how it is here." They uniformly expressed their non-preparation for an urban classroom. They were frustrated by the students, the lack of materials, and the inability to solve their quandaries with formalized lesson plans, assertive discipline, rigid learning techniques, and whatever else they took from teacher education. They came and went in droves. Often new teachers would comment in frustration or anger on their experiences:

> They don't want to learn! Nothing I do works! They have no respect for me or themselves.

> Where is the principal, why doesn't he come to my class to help?

> Why won't they stop talking, pay attention to me—don't they want to learn so they can go to college?

This last teacher was typical of many of the new teachers who had little understanding of the world in which these children lived; that college was a dream for a few and even fewer would make it. No one had prepared them for teaching children who walk daily the edge of survival. It was not that they didn't care—many did deeply—but "culture shock" was real and desperate.

The first year passed in a haze of faces, Africanized names, and a variety of experiments in teaching. I discovered that gopher holes (of which there were many on the grounds) had a multitude of pedagogical uses, such as finding bugs and worms, illustrating ground layers, or, my favorite, trying to talk through one to the Chinese (the kids were fascinated when I brought in a globe of the world and they realized that China was opposite Watts!). The 8th graders loved to convince the 6th graders that this was possible, and for a while lunch-time inevitably included numbers of 6th graders yelling into holes in the ground! Plastic bags and Mr. Thompson's old car could teach about pollution. Potato chip cans made fine telescopes with a little imagination. Chemistry could be taught with pool acid and pieces of iron, although the resulting fumes cleared mine and several other rooms. Biology and health topics were easy to teach if you didn't mind answering questions about sex and whites.

Often it was within these discussions that students would disclose the limitations of life in an urban ghetto. For example, during a lecture on the reproductive system, the following discussion occurred.

Student: Mr. Yee-Ho, how come white folks always gotta buy their babies, cain't they do the wild thang?

Yeo: What do you mean, as far as I know, we do it too!

Student: Yeah, but y'all don't gets no babies, y'all gots to buy em fo yoselves, how come?

Yeo: Where did you get that idea?

Student: Ah saw on the tv the other night that white folks gotta buy their babies. There was this man and his woman and they bof went to a lawyer to buy a baby. The man on the tv said that they couldn't have no babies, so he was sellin them one. Black folks ain't gots no problem havin babies, how come y'all do?

Student: Yeah man, I heerd that y'all steals black babies and then dey turn white fo y'all. Is that the truff?

After some more questions, it dawned on me that these students had seen one of the anti-abortion adoption television advertisements and had assumed that since all the actors were white that whites had to buy babies. Few of the students had known a white person other than myself or another teacher, and whites were a mysterious other from outside their experience. As the discussion moved to the nature of whites in their world, it became clear that since most had only seen whites on television, they were somewhat fictional to them. It explained why so many of them were fascinated by my clothes, my own children, constantly wanted to touch my hair, and wanted to know about my history.

Often these kinds of discussions were part of the contract between us. I would buy fifteen or so minutes of attention to the material with ten minutes of what often was a tangent to me but clearly not to them. Their world was often sadly limited to a few square city blocks, which equally limited how relevant the material was to them. As I came increasingly to realize this, many days the class consisted of all tangents as we each attempted to explore the other's world.

I can remember vividly wondering at the end of the first year whether I would come back to this hell-hole. On graduation day, as we went through the principal's well-ordered drill, in which I handed them their 8th grade diploma as they walked by, I was embarrassed by the number of tears and hugs I received. When the principal gave his (Mrs. Johnson had left mid-year) speech about the year, he mentioned each teacher's name, and, of course, mine was last. I was thunderstruck when over 400 students leaped on their chairs and started calling my name, yelling "whoo, whoo, whoo"! As I tried to smile and keep from crying, I saw tears flowing down faces and I started to break. I turned away inadvertently toward the audience of parents, grandparents, siblings, and community people and through my tears saw the entire audience on their feet waving at me and yelling the same chant. All this for "the white boy"! I have never been so hugged, cried over and unconditionally loved and accepted in my entire life! I returned the next year—and the next—and each graduation was wonderfully the same.

I found myself wondering through the summer, what did the year mean? Why are my school, my kids, so different? What causes their deprivation, poverty, low school achievement, dropping out? Why the high teacher turn-over? Does any of what is taught in the classrooms make sense? Why are the resources so limited? Why are the new teachers so poorly prepared? Is there some way to make sense of the experiences of the year? Do I even want to return?

Making Sense—Or Can It?

As I increasingly realized that I simply had not comprehended much of what was happening around me, in the classroom, teachers' lounge, cafeteria, etc., I attempted to make sense of the tumult, the anger, and the alienation of the teachers and students, which affected significantly what went on in my classroom. I struggled to understand the contradictions between the administration's rhetoric and the students' reactions, and those that were painfully obvious between the curriculum and instructional practices demanded by the administration versus the experiences and attitudes related to me by students and parents.

I wanted to understand why there were so few school supplies, why there were so few job prospects but the administration continued to hammer out the equation of obeying the rules plus studying earns a diploma which would supposedly equal a job. Why did so many students come to school hungry? Why were their test scores so uniformly low—and were the tests relevant? Why did 6th graders get pregnant and 7th graders act jealous of it? Why was there so much anger exploding in constant fights? These and a myriad of other questions framed my daily interactions at the school.

While I often did not understand theoretically the import of what occurred, I began to construct an understanding of how these students' lives were impacted by the economic and educational poverty in which they moved daily. Without a definition, I began to comprehend some of the nuances and framing of their urban culture, which was and is delineated by race, class, gender, and individual and collective responses to social oppression and violence.

I began to read books on black history recommended to me by teachers. I posed questions to students and parents about their lives, their language and their perceptions. I visited other schools and talked to the teachers and got to know students on opposing teams as I coached "my" girls. I asked questions of visiting community service folks (many were young men who had been where these kids were), and stayed overnight at students' homes. I began to understand slowly that there are different realities, ways of making sense of the world, and that the school's knowledge and practices offered little to help these kids.

One might argue that point, arguing that reading and math literacy ought to be important to everyone; however, this school did not or could not teach those skills. If students were poor readers (many were 4-

6 grade levels behind), they were behaviorally managed in the classroom or ordered to show up for detention, where, supposedly, they would be tutored. There were no literacy programs at the school and no tutors in reading or math, and those few teachers who did attempt to work with students were inundated with the problem.

It became painfully clear that equal opportunity was not synonymous with a fair and just opportunity. Not only was I personally conscious of my own race and ethnic presumptions, but I came increasingly to understand that these children and the school, and the district as a whole, were subject to economic and social stigmatization that could only be racially construed.

Comparing other fairly close districts and communities that had more funds, better schools, more teachers, higher levels of equipment and materials, one had to question why this district and its schools were underfunded, dilapidated, and yet filled to overflowing with underprivileged youth. I suppose it could be argued that it was cultural or individual, that somehow, just being a predominantly white, middle-class district in a similar community would make the difference, that poor black and/or Hispanic districts were victims of their own self-abuse. Yet, as I discovered, the state and counties allocate the funding in an inverse proportion to need, and it is the white districts that were allowed innovative programs. I was advised on several occasions by district supervisors that programs had been proposed to state education offices to alleviate reading or math deficiencies only to be rejected on the basis of their experimentality or lack of available funding or that they would not fit into the "Basic Skills Program" approach.

It is in fact the state education department which prescribes the curriculum, the instructional methodologies, the texts, the testing and evaluation, and in some cases, the background and qualifications of the teachers whom the district is required to hire. Funding, texts, allocation schemes, definitions of students (e.g., "at risk," ESL, etc.), cafeteria menus, and virtually every facet of a teacher's life at the school is mandated by state or local educational bureaucracies. Many problems that at first glance appear to be indigenous to the community and/or the school originate at other public levels. I found myself connecting not only to a different consciousness for myself and to my students but to a style or process of both being immersed in the experience and attempting to make sense and meaning out of it.

One construction or meaning-making of the relations and events that occurred daily at the school is that of systemic conflict and profound contradictions that represent many of the "truths," rhetoric, and practices of teachers and administrators. By conflict, I mean the multitudinous levels of oppositional behavior and vocality that occurred between individuals and groups on a constant basis, modulated and, in some cases, exacerbated by varying attempts at accommodation. These complex, oscillating dialectics (both in terms of behavior, educational practices, and voiced constructs) frame the lives and education at the school, and it is from within an analysis of these contradictions that I will frame the balance of this chapter.

Conflict & Contradiction: Understanding the Narratives

There can be numerous rationales posited for the conflict levels that framed the lives of people at this school; however, underneath, it was a cultural conflict—a complicated dance of what Anyon has called "a simultaneous process of accommodation and resistance" (Anyon, 1984, p. 25). This cultural conflict played itself out in a myriad of ways, through sometimes confusing mixtures of resistance or outright opposition, contradictions of motives and meaning, and varying degrees of accommodation (which were often complicated by simultaneous resistance to the accommodation) and always complicated by the effects on all involved of the impact of having to live daily within the effects of segregation and racism.

One example was the GATE (Gifted and Talented Education) program, to which approximately 40 students were assigned. These students were perceived by teachers and administration as the "achievers," the good students, and were jealously fought over. All of the teachers vociferously argued for the right to have as many classes as possible of GATE students, and there was an understanding that only the "better" teachers would have GATE classes. These students moved through the school day as a group, going from class to class with little change in their membership. They had been designated GATE students upon their entry into the school in 6th grade and remained together as a group until graduation. The group was often seen as privileged by teachers, administrators, and other students; they attended classes for special minority students at the local state college, went on field trips sponsored by community groups, and were treated preferentially by school staff (rarely was a GATE student assigned to detention or suspended).

They themselves acted out an ambivalence about this privileged status. On the one hand, they were resentful if a student who was not a GATE student was assigned to their classes; on the other, they assiduously maintained close relationships to students who were not GATE. In fact, many of the romantic liaisons of these students were with students whom teachers labelled as "bad kids," "gang-bangers," etc. They were proud of their academic prowess, but periodically would act out an often bewildering resistance to it, ditching classes, getting drunk at school with the "bad" kids, "going with" another kid who was non-GATE, being a super student one semester and defiantly non-academic the next. [5]

The entire GATE program was replete with contradictions. The administration used the class as a reward/punishment for teachers. Who was assigned a GATE class and who wasn't hinged on how you were perceived by the principal as being aligned with him or her or not. The teachers, even within attempts to show unity against the principal, squabbled acrimoniously over being assigned GATE classes, and it often appeared that the assignments were meant to maintain teacher separation and divisiveness.

One of the most profound contradictions was the dichotomy between the experiential verities of students' lives and the rhetoric of teachers and administrators that schooling and education would equal careers and jobs even in the face of the local community's 65 to 75 percent unemployment. The staff (recall that none lived in the community, but mostly in predominantly white suburbs) seemed to ignore the economic and racially skewed realities that these kids faced every day. In spite of being black themselves, and privately talking about the oppression and racism that they personally had suffered, they publicly spoke to the students as if societal racism did not exist. Contradictorily in the teachers' lounge or in private moments in the hallway, they would use language and dialect similar to that of the students and speak of their powerlessness relative to the principal, of racist incidents they had suffered in their suburban communities, of the "white man," of how difficult their lives had been made by institutional racism in this country. It was almost as if they blamed themselves for what they suffered and believed the children could do better with enough exhortation on their part.

Rist (1970) suggests that minority teachers who have taken on the values and worldview of the white middle class have a detrimental effect on lower-income, minority students, often participating in relegating them to the lowest groups with least instruction (Ladson-Billings, 1990, cited in Grant/Millar, 1992). However, I would suggest instead that this situation represents that ambivalence of which Ogbu writes (Chapter 2) that black Americans bring to education, and that these teachers brought a kind of "tough love" to their classrooms leavened with hope for these children even in the face of the school's conditions.

In reaction to these contradictions, the students generally rejected the staff messages that society and education were neutral and equal opportunity was theirs for the price of studying and following teacher directions. An example of this rejection of rhetoric contradiction often occurred in assemblies where the principal brought in paid speakers (usually from the already slim budget of some other category, such as PE equipment, supplies, or textbook funds) to tell students to study hard, follow the rules, be quiet, and obey teachers to get A's and a "Cadillac job"; students could vociferously be heard:

> That man's fulla boosheet, dere ain't no fuckin jobs fo niggers in Dodge, man!

> Shit man, my homie's gettin me a Cad for heppin ta move da blow [crack selling on the street]!

> My brother grageated from the "Two" (a local high school) wid a four-o and he cain't get no job!

Sometimes the administration's rhetorical contradictions were even more marked. One afternoon after a day of fights, misbehavior and three teachers fleeing (quitting due to classroom conditions), the principal came on the P.A. and announced to the school that students should be good and obey the school codes:

> Principal: If you want to be free, you have to obey and follow our rules!

The students responded with laughter, disdain, and rude comments, clearly aware of and rejecting the contradictions and the message:

> Man, Mr. Yeo, that ole bitch, she be all fucked up—she don't know what she say, do she!

I could only agree and we spent the rest of the science class period talking about rules, who makes them and why. This was often the kind of moment when the students would ask me about whites, racism and why their schools were so poor as compared with suburban schools they had visited for sports.

One of the major contradictions and sources of conflict arose out of the content, style, and structure of the curriculum. The course schedule had been in place for many years without change, with only two electives, computers and home economics. The latter class was held by the teacher to only 20 preselected students, so the rest during this period went to my "computer" class (about 45-55 students), which the guidance counselor admitted privately was seen as a dumping place, much to my frustration. The balance of the schedule was labelled as "Core" and consisted of math, English, social studies and science. Since not all students could take the electives, the counselor scheduled most of each grade level to repeat at least one class (usually math) each day.

Within any given Core class, the curriculum was derived from a subject-specific package, called a "Basic Skills Plan" for that subject (I had one for science, but "lost" it). The package was linked to a text and consisted of sequential chapter plans. Each plan had a number of preunit tests, sets of specific daily lesson plans, and postchapter tests for evaluation. The school year was linked to the plan by date and chapter, and Resource Teachers would collect an evaluation form for each chapter from the teacher showing the tabulated results of student evaluations, which would be collated and passed to the principal and then the district.

The teachers generally adhered to the packaged lesson plans, taught to the postunit tests, and used the chapter worksheets for daily lessons. The students filled in the worksheets, did little homework, and rarely used a text or other activity. The only exception were the English classes, which had ancillary reading books, generally only 1 or 2 copies, which the teacher read to the class before having the students do a worksheet or take a package-generated quiz.

All of the packages were state and district mandated and stressed in their "Purpose Statements" that these packages were for low-achievement schools for the teaching of basic skills to students that would be translatable to post-high-school jobs. This in the face of 70 percent dropout rates, jobs that had long since left the community, and enormous unemployment rates. The test evaluative results were generally fallacious at one level or another, since teachers customarily gave out answers or assisted students during tests. However, the tests were used to compile a state-required public report card on the school indicative of how well the school was teaching. With the exception of statistical materials, most of the report card was fallacious [see Appendix for samples].

In the face of supposed increasing learning levels, particularly in math, substitutes (who did not know the system) complained that students couldn't tell time, measure, multiply using two digits, divide using 1 or 2 digits, etc. When asked to take over a math class for a teacher who left, I discovered that this was absolutely true—none of my students could make change, half couldn't tell time (no wonder they were always late), one-third didn't know the days of the week or months of the year (or the sequence) and these were 8th graders! Multiplying and dividing was a joke, and not one knew how to do ratios or percentages that they had supposedly learned (according to test scores) in 4th and 6th grades. I almost hate to admit to this but I "lost" the basic skills material for 8th grade math and started to teach them about money and counting through card games like Blackjack and Poker. They learned to tell time by timing races and acting as timekeepers at basketball games during P.E. We measured the room, ourselves, other teachers, and around the school. We drew scale pictures of the school and the room and learned how to work ratios and fractions. No tests, no quizzes, and all done in groups. I don't know how they would have performed on the basic skills tests but they knew the math they needed.

The culmination of the ironies (contradictions) was in the annual festival of the CAT tests, state-mandated standardized knowledge tests given to schools all over the state. These tests used a style of English my students had rarely heard and were unfamiliar with and tested reading, writing, and math skills the students were simply not prepared to handle. However, this was the big event for the administration and district. Assemblies were held to exhort students to do their best, follow directions, and "prove to the rest of the country that we're Number One in the USA!" During that week (only) students could get breakfast at school, and the PA announcements were entirely about the tests. Student groups were brought into the office to read their poems about the CAT tests over the PA, and preparatory tests were given by teachers every day in every class for two weeks prior to the tests (as demanded by the administration); all other lessons were placed on hold for the duration. Teachers had to attend faculty preparation meetings three times a week for those two weeks (at 6:00 a.m. or after 3:00 p.m.) during which we were openly encouraged to help students during the test! One year the principal called us individually into her office and told us to give students answers on any questions that they were having trouble on. The resulting test data, although still in the bottom 20th percentile of the state, was heralded by the same principal as showing that the school was improving the students' education!

Teachers' and students' reactions to the test show a clear understanding of these contradictions:

Teachers:
Why does she make us come in so early to learn to cheat, this test don't test nuthin.

This is such bullshit, we get no overtime for it either and it's a waste of time.

Shit, she told us to give them the answers and then tells us these po kids is getting more education—who's she kiddin? I bet white schools don't do this shit!

Hey, YO [Yeo], whys come you white folk always be givin us po black folk these fucked-up tests, they be to test white kids, not black kids; they just use the results to show up how dumb niggers be, so as to not have to give this school mo money.

Students:
Man, this test sucks, I ain't nevah seen most of dem words befo.

Mr. YO, If ah gets an "A" on dis, can I gradgeate now?

How come we nevah finds out how we did? Does dis test mean anything to us? Do it help our grades?

How come dey use all dese white words?

Will it hep me gets a job or inta college?

Hey suckah, what's a yaatcht [yacht]?

The CAT test, and other similar events, were perceived as irrelevant, and even racist, by most of the teachers and students.

However, as perceived by the administrators, they were framed within a complex contradictory scheme of competition, positivistic justification for the curriculum and pedagogic modes of the school, and potential for connection to a white, middle-class-dominated educational state hierarchy.

Another major source of conflict was the often intense, always pervasive, struggle for control of the institutional culture, played out in the arena of the school's language. The administration and faculty in their public language were steeped in the linguistics of official education (rooted in a dominant, white, middle-class context), while the students (and faculty in private) utilized a language expressive of the ghetto and was generally oppositional to the official rhetoric of the school although there were often accommodational or alternative contradictions in both cases.

The conflict arises in part out of administration efforts to control the school's language (and thereby its reality and culture) usually through the P.A. system and a myriad of principal's letters to students or parents (most of which end up in the trash or on the grounds) and the faculty's concomitant effort in the classroom. The students' resistance to the administration's "rhetoric" is both behavioral and cultural [as described by Ogbu (1988), Solomon (1988), Yeo (1992) and others]. McLaren noted that students struggle daily to reconcile the disjunction between the lived meaning of the streets and the subject-centered approach to learning in the classroom (McLaren, 1989).

The rhetoric used by the administration (and faculty) is a mixture of both traditional and progressive themes. Although not well articulated, it is contextually consistent. On the one hand, the administration's language emphasizes traditionalist values of hard work, being on time, being "responsible," "getting an education," etc. The language is usually authoritarian and is often overtly contradictory within the context of its messages; e.g., students are urged to be "creative," but "follow all rules and procedures." The emphasis is on the traditional defining of achievement on the basis of test and grade results. Students are exhorted to achieve "by being good young boys and girls, being hard workers, and making us proud of you" (principal). The language of deferred gratification occurs through frequent reference to "all the jobs you can get if you will just study hard and follow your teachers' directions" (principal).

Alternatively, but often simultaneously in a mixed message, the administration's rhetoric is progressive when telling students that they will have equal opportunity in jobs through schooling. Equal opportunity in employment and higher education is stressed at the same time as students are told that these opportunities are achievable if they will "only work hard at their studies and follow school rules."

The teachers also engaged in furthering the contradictory rhetoric of the school; e.g., Mr. Amandi complains to parents during a Back-to-School night:

> Your children don't respect anything except themselves. They won't follow the rules. [note the contradiction!]

Mrs. Brown tells students that in order to succeed in life, they must learn to obey. Ms. Barundi complains that "only 'A' students should participate in activities, because the rest can't sit still and follow instructions" [this in reference to a dance; she became agitated when a student pointed out that "sitting still" seemed inconsistent with a dance]. The teachers collectively voiced a perceived need for the students to recognize the possibilities of equal opportunity, an unlimited potential for individual success and the "joys" of schooling, if they (students) would only "stay on task" and achieve well on standardized exams.

Much of this exhortative effort on the part of teachers, I believe, had less to do with students' futures and more to do with implementing class management techniques framed by extrinsic motivation, i.e., the threat of tests and grades to enforce student compliance with classroom rules of order. Typically in some classrooms the effort was successful for ten or so minutes, while in others it was an abject failure as students rejected the message and the threat.

It is this mixture of traditional behaviorism and the language of "progressive possibilitarianism" [Apple & Beyer (1988)] that the administration and faculty believe defines the official and cultural rhetoric of the school. It constitutes the overt expression of the dominant (white, middle-class) values and attitudes which the administration hopes to engender in the students and which continually conflict with the students' own language and culture as well as that of the teachers'.

A number of ethnographic studies have documented black students' use of language as resistance to teacher and administration authority. Gilmore's (1985) study describes verbal and body language by black students as a resistance vehicle. Grubb (1986) sees black English as a language form that often hides the real meaning of oral communications in culturally specific semantics. McLaren (1989) and Solomon (1988) both documented and described a pervasive use of language by black students to resist authority and cultural values promulgated by teachers.

The students at Washington were no different in their use of a highly stylized ghetto street patois couched in an ostensibly southern U.S. dialect that is profane, derogatory, and oppositionally coded by their inner-city, historically African American culture. Additionally, they verbalized a scornful rejection of the administration's efforts to inculcate its dominant values and attitudes. In response to administration admonishments about tardiness ("Students should be on task and seated in their classrooms at the bell") and wandering (referred to as "floatin") around the school during classes, they would reply:

> Had ta check up on my bitch; man, don't hassle me!

> Gots ta use the baffoom, man!

Classroom activities were constantly contested by profane catcalls to other students or by posing questions in dialect and about something outside the class material so as to confuse teachers. A few examples are as follows:

> Hey, yo momma, nigga!

> Hey, Mr. Yeo, Royal is baggin on me, he doan stop dissin me, I gonna roll his black ass up!"

> Mr. Yo, is pencils made of wood? If dey is, that makes Kasheema's head a pencil!

These questions and comments were usually accompanied by throwing of paper, making faces, or references to girl or boy friends, sisters or gang affiliations.

In a 7th grade science class:

> Mrs. Nettie, don't Jackson look like he come from apes in de moon?

In a history class explanation of the Declaration of Independence:

> Hey Mr. Thomas, Omar fahted bad! It stink back here, can ah leave? [The whole class did, leaving the teacher standing alone in the room!]

> If we is free, how come niggas doant run things?

or arguing with each other which usually results in a fight, or books being thrown, thereby effectively disrupting the class and deflecting the teacher's rhetoric. There was always a multitude of approaches for "baffoom" passes, to go get water, walking outside ("gotta spit, man!") and a constant shuffling motion of bodies, books and paper. Ultimately, although the administration can enforce a modicum of adherence to the "rules" through punishment and withdrawals of privileges (usually denying access to social events), the students find enough space within the structure of the school to maintain the cohesiveness of their resistance.

The ability of black students to use "their" rhetoric as a form of resistance to resist value indoctrination is regarded by the administration as an unacceptable loss of authority (Solomon, 1988). Even the school's P.A. system represents a place of confrontation between the culture of the administration and that of the students. The black administrator, having been hegemonized into propounding the values and language of an overlaid culture not his or her own (a culture that ironically does not particularly value or esteem a black administrator), is consequently weakened in the ensuing struggle with the lived student culture and language. This weakened position is easily seen in the frustration with which the administration tries to grapple with student values, language, and resistance.

Unfortunately for the administration, the students' linguistic identification has effectively created a collective student sense wedded to a street-based black culture that controls the conflict. In essence, it is the students' culture that dominates the school and their rhetoric which prevails, thereby giving the inner-city school its distinctive nature.

One source of contestation and teacher turnover resulted from the district's policy of hiring many noncertified teachers who were from African nations, e.g., Ghana, Sierra Leone, Nigeria, or the Philippines and other Third World countries under a program entitled "Teach For America." These teachers generally did not last long, usually due to profound cultural differences in spite of a presumed similarity of ethnicity or race. They often complained bitterly that the students did not respect them, had no discipline, and were constantly engaged in verbal exchanges to the distraction of the class.

> Mr. Tahooodie, hey Mr. African Man, watcha gonna teach us today; how come y'all come ovah heah any way?

> Hows come we gets these Africans as teachers alla the time? Don't no one else wanta teach us?

One example of this cultural contestation occurred one morning when the principal requested over the P.A. that I step around the building to see what the commotion was in Room 18 (I was in the middle of class myself). Room 18's teacher was Mr. Gomez who had been teaching 8th grade math for about two weeks. He had come to Watts from the Philippines through the auspices of the "Teach for America" program. The room had doors at both ends, so I could see in without being seen by students or the teacher. Mr. Gomez was facing the board with his back to the class and his arms folded. The students were milling around the room, talking loudly to each other, and generally having a good time! Neither Mr. Gomez nor the students were paying any attention to each other. I recognized the students as my next period GATE class so I knew this was not generally a rowdy group. As I walked in the back door, there was immediate silence, a scramble for seats, and an air of expectancy. Many of the students called greetings as I walked up to the front of the room—"Hey, Mr. Yo, you gonna teach us math?"—"Mr. G just flipped out, man!"—"Mr. Yeo, we couldn't understand him, he speaks foreign." Mr. Gomez had not moved. I told the students to be quiet and open their math books to the page I could see on the board, which most quickly did. I approached Mr. Gomez and asked if I could help in any way. With a tight expression on his face, arms still folded and still facing the board, he replied:

> Mr. Gomez: They are all terrible children. They no listen, I no teach!
>
> Yeo: Is there anything I can do to help, Mr. Gomez?

> Mr. Gomez: They no want to listen, I no teach them.

Yeo: Would you like to take a break and I'll take them. It's OK, I have them next period anyway?

Mr. Gomez: I no teach them, they have no respect!

I told the students to gather up their belongings and to follow me to the science room next to mine. Since the doors between the two rooms could be opened, I could get back to my class and watch this group as well. As we left to walk around the building, Mr. Gomez was still facing the board with his arms folded. I never saw him again, although another teacher said that she had seen him running to the parking lot with his briefcase. The office just marked him absent for several days and brought in a substitute for the rest of that term.

Although perhaps the most dramatic, the incident does demonstrate the problem both students and these teachers faced. The presence of such teachers was usually short-lived. Many complained of the lack of assistance from the office, the poor behavior of the students, and the dilapidated facilities. It was painfully obvious that the causes were often less these reasons (although they didn't help) and more their differences in culture and values and the lack of preparation they received for teaching in an inner-city school. The whole process was relatively common, since we almost always had from four to six of these "foreign" teachers at any one time. I cannot remember a single one who lasted more than a semester and would guess that the average stay was under four weeks.

The third major contradiction and source of contestation within the school was also cultural and seemed to derive from a lack of awareness of their own history and socialization on the part of students and staff and lack of cultural sensitivity to the district's increasing recently immigrated Hispanic population, which constituted from 15 to 20 percent of the student population in the district.

Every year the district allocated one week in February as Black History Week, during which the schools were to emphasize the contributions of black Americans. The principal requested that each teacher turn in lesson plans for the week detailing how he or she was going to conduct a black history curriculum; most failed to do so, giving oppositional reasons:

Its just more booshit she wants us to do—besides she'll never look at my lesson plans, she never has.

> I don't have time for this black history stuff in math, we have the
> CAT coming up.

> I'm going to have them write poems about King, that should get
> me through the week, but I'll make up something else for her.

The same two teachers each year organized an assembly with
songs, speeches by the kids, and a play (usually the same one).
However, in order to practice they had to pull kids out of
classes—which was bitterly resented by the other teachers but condoned
by the principal. The play was usually about Rosa Parks, erroneously
depicting her as a little old lady quietly doing her best to get along, who
just happened to sit in the wrong spot on the bus. Poems about Martin
Luther King, Jr. were read over the PA and stories made up about
Harriet Tubman and Sojourner Truth. The poems and stories were
usually black versions of the Horatio Alger myth, about being
successful in America by being nice and getting along. There was little
mention of civil rights, white oppression, racism, race riots, Selma,
Montgomery, firebombs or the KKK. Slavery was something that
happened a long time ago and was depicted as a mistake. No connection
was made to the social conditions of today or the environment of the
inner city in a wealthy country.

In fact, there was a deliberate squelching of any contested history or
any mention of conflict or racism. One teacher, a young fiery African
American woman, was called into the principal's office after teaching
her music class to sing the civil rights anthem "We Shall Overcome!"
She related to some of us what she had been told:

> She [the principal] told me that the song was inappropriate, cause
> it might irritate some media who might be here on Thursday
> [assembly day]—I told her that was shit, and she said that if I
> kept that up, I'd be fired; she's sold out to the Man!

I asked her to have her students write articles, stories or poems
about Malcolm X and I'd put them in the school newspaper, to which
she agreed. However, the next day I was called into the office and told
that if I printed any of that "inflammatory material," I could be
suspended.

> Yeo: I don't understand, wasn't Malcolm X a great black

leader?

Principal: That's not the point, Mr. Yeo, it would just stir things up and get people mad.

Yeo: I don't see that, and shouldn't people get stirred up over the situation in this community and the school, the lack of funds, the conditions?

Principal: You don't understand, you're white and don't understand our people, you can't understand these kids because you are white, you don't know what its like to be black; we're working very hard to get our kids to fit in and succeed at their education. Our scores are up and I've called Channel 2 about coming to visit and don't want any trouble from you or Miss Hardy; so don't put anything troublesome in the student paper.

I quote the principal at length here because it seems indicative of both the conflicts and contradictions in the school and the black community. There is the acknowledgment of what it "means to be black"; i.e., suffer under racial oppression, which is, in turn, contained by the drive for assimilation and "getting by," typical of what Cornel West (1990) labels as "Black middle-class angst," the notion of having made it in American society and the fear of how fragile a success it is. And note the reliance on the "scores." The CAT scores were being used as the sign of success, which she knew were false anyway, since she advocated our "helping" the students on the test.

During that week, I often asked the kids about Rosa Parks, Malcolm X, etc., and consistently, they wanted to know more and were appallingly ignorant about their own history. I related to them what it was like working for voting rights in the South in 1963 and '64, told them about segregation and Jim Crow laws, and we talked about what Malcolm X had said and Dr. King. They knew next to nothing about Africa (many could not find the continent on a map) and thought slaves got paid or were just the unemployed. They had contradictory notions about today's world, they knew about the "Man," because of white policemen and things their parents had said but thought there was no more racism. They thought that outside of the ghetto whites and blacks were equal because most of the teachers had told them that but admitted that Miss Hardy had confused them some.

I asked them about the use of the term "nigger," why did they use it, what did it mean to them:

Student: Ah don't know, "nigga" is just a insult . . .

Student: Yeah, it just be baggin, don't mean nuttin.

Yeo: then would it be OK for me to use it?

Student: Nah, Mr. Yo, yo is white folk, onliest black folk can call each other nigga!

Yeo: Is it a bad term if white folks say it?

Student: Yeah, real bad, killin bad, but yo be cool.

Yeo: Why can't white folk use it?

Student: Cuz it be our term, mah daddy say we stole it fum de white folk so's they cain't use it no moah, now it be a good word fo us black peoples.

Yeo: So, it be a good word?

Student: Oh sure, like when I say to mah homie; what's happenin nigga, that be OK then, its jest the way we talk.

Student: Yeah, nigga is OK most de time, cause even yo mama cain call y'all a nigga and yo know she loves ya.

I found the term "nigger" to be another example of the resistance/accommodation contradiction buried behind what seemed at first glance to be nonracial connotations, much as Solomon (1992, 1988) and Anyon (1984) described it as:

accommodation *in* acts of resistance and resistance *within* accommodation, which developed as two forms of a single process by which slaves accepted what could not be avoided and simultaneously fought for moral and physical survival. (Anyon, 1984, p. 29)

The term was probably the most common descriptive word used at the school. Students openly referred to themselves, friends, enemies, cousins and strangers with that term. It seemed to have multiple connotations. It might be used in a friendly manner as "hey, what's happenin nigga?" Or as a reference, "who's that new niggah from Texas in first period?" On the other hand, it was a serious insult if used by a white person or if used to refer to a mother, grandmother or someone's child. Teachers used the word in similar fashion, however, only in private conversation and not with students. It was occasionally used by students and teachers in tense situations with administrators but never by the latter.

While the term was symbolic of the resistance at the school to deculturalizing influences, it was the accommodation paradigm that grounded the school's efforts to promote a diluted version of African American history and current social conditions. This follows with the educational system's broader goal of assimilation, job training, and incorporation of a particular set of hegemonic values (Giroux, 1992).

The Ethnic Diversity Problem

A major problematic area and source of another set of significant contradictions were the Hispanic students, who constituted about 10 percent of the school population although there was no Hispanic staff, except the part-time ESL aide. Although their numbers fluctuated constantly, many of these children came from Nicaragua or El Salvador and had recently immigrated to move away from war. Many of these children were suffering from the stress of having lived in a war zone and were poorly educated in their own language as well as in math, etc.

The majority, here black students and teachers, were resentful or condescending to the Hispanic children, teachers often assigning them to the ESL aide or to the back of the room, where they could be ignored. Since many spoke little or no English, they were generally lost in class or assemblies. The teachers viewed them as poor students, troublesome and relatively non-deserving of time and effort. Since they rarely understood or connected to the curriculum or instruction, many of the Hispanic students developed techniques of avoidance, skipping class, disruptions that resulted in being sent from class (to no particular place, just out). In class, the few who spoke English often attempted to translate for the others, but teachers resisted this as disruptive:

> Mrs. Smith: Stop speaking that Spanish shit, I won't have it in my classroom!

> Mr. Black: Why can't these metchicans be put in special ed all day, they're a god damn nuisance?

> Mrs. Green: Do you believe the ESL aide, Mrs. Esparza, wants to put four of those Spanish fools in my 6th period, I won't have it, I'm going to just kick them back out.

More often than not, the kids were just "kicked out" of classes and then "floated" around or just left the campus, at which point the teachers complained that they were "no good" because they ditched class, left school, didn't try, etc.

The district mandated that each middle school have a soccer team. However, the black students refused to play, so the entire team was composed of the Hispanic students. They only played four games (instead of the usual ten played by other teams), the coaches rarely showed during practice or for games, and the school literally paid no attention to the activity (never announced games, no trophies given, no recognition). Usually, one of the two sympathetic teachers were drafted to coach the soccer team, whether or not they knew anything about the game.

The one effort the school made toward the Hispanic students was on one day of the school year, Cinco de Mayo, which is also a State of California official holiday. For that day, the principal allowed the ESL aide to pull Hispanic students from classes which ironically irritated most of the teachers, who claimed that they were missing class. Mind you, these were the same students often kicked out of class anyway! The most vociferous of the critics of Cinco de Mayo were the two teachers who organized the Black History assembly, who stated opinions such as:

Why should beaners get a day, we only get a week?

> Mrs. Esparza is never around anyway to help with these Metchican kids, so why should she get to run Cinco-Me-oh? Besides all they're gonna do is that stupid Metchican Hat

Dance.

They ought to be in class learning something, since they can't speak no English.

The Hispanic kids were allowed two class periods to practice, instead of two weeks, and the assembly was held after school, when most of the staff and students would leave, or late in the school day when many would ditch. Many of the teachers stayed in their rooms.

No teachers included material about Mexico, Central America, or South America in their curriculum, nothing on the extensive Hispanic presence in California, nothing on Hispanic cultures, nor was Spanish taught at the school.

The ESL aide was hired part time, for 20 hours a week, and given about 60 students of all grades to cope with. She was unable to obtain any counseling for the refugee children, who had suffered untold amounts of stress, nor was she able to obtain any assistance from teachers (except two) for mainstreaming her Hispanic students or for trying to incorporate a bilingual program. There were no Spanish texts, worksheets, tests, or materials. These students still took the CAT test each year, and although the State had Spanish versions, they were never available.

New teachers said that they had been given no input in their teacher education or at the district or school level to help them work with these Hispanic students. They could not obtain Spanish texts or materials (the principal said there were no funds, even though the state allocated the district special monies every year for acquisition of Spanish materials), nor did they understand anything about the culture of the Hispanic students (which isn't too surprising since many knew little of the black students' culture either).

Needless to say, the two teachers who did help were overwhelmed by trying to tutor almost 60 extra students. These students were sincere and hardworking for the most part when given the help, although they bitterly resented the way they were treated:

Lupe: Mr. Yeo, why do these Black teachers not want to help us, why they so mean? They're so prejudiced!

Jose: Why do we have sit and hear about Doctor King and no one wants to hear about Benito Juarez? Why do we have to be quiet and they get to talk and laugh in Cinco de Mayo?

Ernesto: I am not a "Metchican," I am from El Salvador; they get mad if we say "nigga" but call us beaners all the time and no one stops it.

Juan: Mrs. Smith, she won't let me help me amigos who no habla engleesh, she's a puta!

At one point, the Hispanic parents became very upset about the overt bias at the school and sent a delegation to speak to the principal. They were made to wait for two hours outside the office and were told (as related to me by one parent) that the principal had said that since they were the minority, they had to learn to cooperate, that the students needed to learn English and we had an ESL person, so there was no need to complain.

The dropout rate for these students just at my school by the 8th grade was 85 percent, which isn't surprising. However, the district claimed only a 10 percent dropout rate for Hispanic students.

Summary

The experiences related here can be interpreted in a myriad of ways; however, it is hard not to acknowledge that the inner-city school is both complex and deleterious. I have attempted to portray the interactions between a predominantly middle-class black staff and urban, underclass students. I also recognize that given my own history and ethnicity, what little I did understand is necessarily only partial:

> Cultural analysis is intrinsically incomplete. And, worse than that, the more deeply it goes, the less complete it is. It is a strange science, in which to get somewhere . . . is to intensify the suspicion, . . . , that you are not quite getting it right. (Geertz, 1983, p. 29; Wolcott, 1990, p. 127)

Although it might be presumed that because these teachers were African American themselves they understood the lives, experiences and perceptions of these children, such a presumption is highly erroneous as

I've attempted to indicate. Students and staff spoke different languages within different symbolic systems, which framed much of the school conflict and contradictions. As I have noted however, this generalization is complex because depending on the circumstances, staff (except the administrators) would also use language similar to the students to describe or act out similar feelings of alienation and oppression.

The students themselves perceived little at school, except their "homies," as relevant to their lives, although they were vociferous about getting what they called an "edjumication." This dialectic of desire and resistance formed a constant in their lives as discussed in Chapter Two.

Neither the teachers or the administrators were prepared to teach in this environment to these children, black or Hispanic. The techniques and procedures of teacher education were in every case abysmal failures, and those teachers who did do well (in terms of teaching and relating) did so by, in their words, "trashing educational techniques," "teaching what the kids wanted to learn," "teaching the kids about themselves," "paying little attention to the office," etc.

I have been away for a few years from the school and, through calls and correspondence with teachers and students, have been told that nothing has changed, except the turnover is greater (for both students and teachers).

The profound tragedy is that most of these kids are bright, loving, compassionate preteens (who happen to live in the inner city and be black or Hispanic), eager to learn and fun to be with. And yet, through stultified, irrelevant teaching practices compounded by an uncaring state and local bureaucracy, they are being "trashed," relegated to a cycle of violence, failure, poverty, and alienation.

Connections

This chapter represents neither pure research nor analysis but a narrative interpretation of the everyday realities of teaching, associating, and relating in an inner-city middle school from the perspective of a teacher who found it impossible to remain the Other. It is an attempt at a transfiguration of image, however partial, by placing the children of the ghettos and barrios into the picture of theory. The chapter is ostensibly a story whose validity is grounded in the verities of experience and the nuances of interpretation in an attempt to make fully present the situated, embodied character of who goes before and after the theories configure the practices of urban education.

In this narrative analysis, I want the reader to feel the pervasive, soul-searing contradictions of living every day in a society that, founded on the aspirations of freedom and democracy, continues to maintain the injustice of relegating human beings, children, to dehumanized status. To quote Roger Simon, I write this such that in no way does it represent

> . . . a seamless web, these experiences rub against the grain of my participation in existing relations of domination. Such rubbing, of course, cannot eliminate this participation, but it can highlight the rough spots, the points of contradiction. (Simon, 1992, p. 6)

Inner-city education does not exist in a vacuum, separated from other social and/or educational endeavors. Certainly affected by efforts generated by a mix of reform adherents (coming from a multitude of rationales and purposes) promoting programs to cope, solve, and ameliorate the perceived "problems" of diversity, urban schools have been forced to adopt both curricular and pedagogical reforms as to multicultural education. In fact, multicultural education has at the same time been touted as the panacea for urban schooling problems, as the programmatic fount of increased achievement for urban students, and as the newest imposition on teachers in urban schools. In the next chapter, I will address the issue of multicultural education from several stances but primarily to discuss and critique its approaches, uses and effectiveness within inner city classrooms. Obviously, given its current popularity as a topic of public and educational debate, the question arises as to whether multicultural education offers potential for real change in these schools or is merely another placebo intended to deflect critique and maintain the status quo. For an answer or at least an analysis of that question, we turn to Chapter Four.

Notes

1. Not the real name of the school, nor do I use the actual name of the district. Student and teacher names do not represent actual names of conversants.

2. From Maya Angelou, "I Dare to Hope," *New York Times*, 25 August 1991, 15; quoted in Bell (1992), p. 1.

3. I was told months later that there was usually a pool on new teachers to see when they would "run" away; mine got up to $50. Few pools lasted longer than two weeks.

4. Violent and senseless death provided a pervasive background to the students' lives. Drive-bys or drug-related homicides were common enough to be a constant undertone in student talk. No student that I knew had not experienced the death of a relative or friend, usually another adolescent. For additional reading, I would recommend J. Alleyne Johnson's "Life after Death: Critical Pedagogy in an Urban Classroom" published in *Harvard Educational Review*, 65:2, Summer 1995, pp.213-230. This article is a superb ethnography of both this topic and how a teacher dealt with it in an inner-city classroom.

5. Signithia Fordham has written a number of articles detailing this ambivalence of students to academic achievement, the peer pressure and the fear of "becoming white." See Fordham, Signithia, "Peer-Proofing Academic Competition Among Black Adolescents: 'Acting White' Black American Style," in *Empowerment Through Multicultural Education* (Sleeter, C., Ed.), New York: SUNY Press, 1991. Also, Fordham, S., "Racelessness as a Factor in Black Students' School Success," *Harvard Educational Review*, 58:1, 1988; and Fordham, S. & John Ogbu, "Black Students' School Success: Coping with the 'Burden of Acting White.'" *Urban Review*, 18:3, 1986.

CHAPTER FOUR

Multicultural Education: Maintaining the Borders in Inner-City Schools

Introduction

We have a culture of ever-increasing diversity
and richness and a consciousness
dangerously intolerant of it. (D. Purpel, 1995)

At this point, it can be somewhat simplistically argued that there are two perspectives one might take as to urban schools. Certainly one possibility is that given the endemic racism in this country and the social and educational effects of ideologies such as *deculturalization* and *deficiency theories* that ground mainstream educational paradigms and practices, it is mere pollyannism to suggest that any meaningful change will or can occur. Certainly, given the American educational system's profound investment in positivism, meritocracy, and instrumental approaches to curriculum and pedagogy, it remains difficult to posit any hope for deep or significant change instead of the continued maintenance of urban marginalization and failure.

However, there are educators who have suggested that change for the better is possible within urban schools. Although comprised of several groups with different ideologies and purposes, an amalgam of educators perceives the root problematic as the inability of the current system (including its practices and theories) to facilitate understanding of the inherent diversity and differences of the people and cultures within these schools. Their vision, arising also out of the political and social demands of minorities, is of an educational schematic that would be multiracial, multigendered, multiethnic, i.e., multicultural.

In light of the continued failure of urban education's various practices (compensatory programs, the basic skills curriculum, etc.), educators have been searching for alternative theories and practices to reform inner-city schools, at least at the curricular and pedagogical level. Countering the Right's call for increased emphasis on basic skills and/or effectiveness or its ignoring of urban schools altogether, liberals and mainstream educators have attempted extensive curricular reformation derived from variations on a theme of "multiculturalism." The theoretical understandings and resultant curricular and pedagogical practices of multicultural education (also termed crosscultural, multiethnic, pluralistic) (Grant & Millar, 1992) have exhibited complicated mixtures of assimilatory, oppositional, reformist, and mainstream modes. In part, Chapter Four will describe and analyze the most prevalent (or at least the most advocated) approaches to multiculturalism as proposed as solutions to the current modalities of education within inner-city schools and their usual subsequential failure. I will argue in this chapter, that the great proportion of those multicultural approaches are or have become instead continuances of the very failure they were intended to reform. I will also argue that they fail because the implemented multicultural proposals have not sought connection to larger social issues, such as racism, or the educational problematics discussed in prior chapters. Instead they have been reduced within urban schools to the continued underwriting of educational irrelevance and failure. Instead of being promulgators of change, due to the unwillingness of most multicultural advocates in education to interrogate the mainstream value systems implicit within many of the approaches to multiculturalism, these approaches or concepts have become protectors of the status quo.

A very different approach to the possibility of change within urban education can also be loosely termed as multicultural. However, it derives from a radically different perspective. This view presupposes that the reasons for the tragedy in urban education does not derive from the schools but lies within the ideologies and cultural practices of the dcminant society. Therefore, in order to effect change in inner-city schools and/or communities, we as a society must change our basal understandings, theories, and knowledge. Although consisting of a broad grouping of multicultural approaches, the overall style of "critical" or "reconstructive" multiculturalism is based on its critique of general inequalities, framed within issues of race, class, and gender (or some order thereof!).

The critical proposals derive from feminism, postmodernism, critical pedagogy, and, although in general they have targeted broader social amelioration, they either have included specific notions as to education or can be tangentially implicated in changes for urban schools. In addition to their role in the furtherance of multicultural education, their concepts begin to set the groundwork for the ideas of change which are the topic of Chapter Six.

This chapter will first describe and critique the dominant approaches to multicultural education generally, then specifically in terms of how they have been incorporated into urban schools and classrooms. References will be made to the educational rationales and processes discussed in Chapter Two and the narrations of Chapter Three to illustrate how multicultural education has been subsumed and debilitated within the normative schooling practices currently configuring urban schools. Second, I will present and analyze critical pedagogy or social reconstructionism as it is applicable or not to inner-city education, although this is not intended as an in-depth explanation of critical theory. Even though the critical pedagogists, with some few exceptions, do not directly address inner-city schools (except as examples of American social injustices), their critiques certainly have framed this text, and their arguments do provide a salient point in which to analyze the societal rationales and cultural practices imposed on and/or defining urban education. At the same time, their implied recommendations for change contain the seeds of their own contradictions, which I will also address to again set the thematic frame for Chapter Six.

Lastly, because probably the most significant research and theorizing in education today is being performed within the transformative analyses of critical pedagogy, this chapter will attempt in abbreviated form to introduce the reader to the concepts of "border pedagogy," easily critical pedagogy's most profound and far-reaching theorizing on the topic of education and its relations to society and culture.

Inasmuch as a wide variety of approaches and programs, self-styled as multicultural, are increasingly being directed at all facets of mainstream and minority education, in order to critique their urban educational efficacy, an understanding of these various schema is important. The next section will explore several typologies representative of multicultural education and pose both explanation and critique in line with the issues set out in Chapters Two and Three as well as examine how they are articulated within inner-city schools. Where applicable, I will include references to practices of the school in which I taught as representative of aspects of multicultural education, although the reader is referred in general to Chapter Three.

Multicultural Educational Schemes

Currently the latest fad among educators seeking a politically viable stance to ward off growing public and political disenchantment with education and growing public fears of diversity (as witnessed by increasingly strident calls for narrower limits on racial minority immigration), multicultural education has been promoted as a paradigm of change for inner-city schools, at-risk students and as a panacea to the problem of diversity. However, where multicultural education is included in the curriculum and/or pedagogy of inner-city schools, it tends to be incorporated by or mandated on the schools under the continuing guise of State compensatory programs (Crichlow, 1990), thereby becoming simply a novel way to incorporate traditional values within a rhetorical theme of diversity, leaving the issues of possessive individualism, social class disparities, and status issues such as race and gender unquestioned (McCarthy & Crichlow, 1993).

Further, within many of the approaches to multicultural education utilized in urban schools is the same linearity between educational achievement and jobs based on similar unwillingness to appreciate the conditions of the local communities. The assumption that scholastic achievement through the emplacement of a more culturally sensitive curriculum leads into jobs for black and Hispanic youth is continually frustrated by the urban environment and the existing racialized practices in the job market (McCarthy & Crichlow, 1993).

Multiculturalism's impact in inner-city schools is ultimately minimal since the parameters of social understanding that have constrained and bounded urban education in the past are still omnipresent: the Right's efforts at "moral" issues masking inherent racism, mainstream positivistic meritocracy and assimilation based on its "deficiency" ideology, and the perennial blaming of the victim.

> Multicultural education is gaining state legitimacy as a part of the preparation of White teachers for culturally diverse classrooms.

However, in the process it often becomes rearticulated and depoliticized . . . a form of individualism, a way to teach "at-risk" children, and an extension of the ethnicity paradigm which suggests that through hard work, delayed gratification, etc., blacks and other groups of color could carve out their own rightful place in society. (Sleeter, 1989, p. 63)

Since multicultural education and its derivative practices are either advocated for or included within urban school state-mandated compensatory programs, it would seem that its practices and underlying theories should be relatively clear. However, there is significant confusion at all educational levels as to what constitutes multicultural education. There are a number of contradictory approaches which several authors have attempted to sort into typological schemes. The next two subsections will describe and critique two of the leading typologies and their connotations for urban education.

A Typology of the Status Quo

A number of varied approaches to multicultural education have been presented and to some extent instituted in urban schools (Sleeter & Grant, 1989; McCarthy, 1992; Nieto, 1995; Banks, 1991; Gollnick & Chinn, 1990; Tiedt & Tiedt, 1990). For example, in his 1991 textbook, *Teaching Strategies for Ethnic Studies*, James Banks outlines various multicultural education approaches, which he critiques on the basis of both purpose and practice: (1) Contributions, (2) Additive, (3) Transformation, and (4) Social Action.

The first, the Contributions approach, is according to Banks, one of the most common. It diversifies by adding ethnic "heroes" to the curriculum who are viewed favorably or have been sanitized by the mainstream perspective. The heroes are generally those who are interpreted as fostering culturally dominant values, for example, Booker T. Washington, Martin Luther King, Jr., etc. These heroes are usually presented in a nonconflictual light. They are used as models for appropriate behaviors and social attitudes, i.e., working closely with whites and emphasizing harmony and getting along tolerantly with others. Those figures who cannot be presented in such a context are not mentioned, usually because they are identified by mainstream educators as persons of color who challenged dominant value perspectives or the

American system, such as Marcus Garvey, W.E.B. DuBois, Malcolm X, all of whom are generally excluded. [1] One limitation of this style is that it maintains the conventional Euro-western narrative by naming only those individuals that are deemed proper. In a sense, the inclusions in the additive style are rendered safe (Cornbleth & Waugh, 1995).

During Black History Week as celebrated in many urban schools, figures such as Malcolm X, Louis Ferrakhan, the Black Panthers, W.E.B. DuBois, etc., are conspicuous by their absence. Martin Luther King Jr. is highlighted for his faith and work with whites; his struggles and denouncements of the overall system in this country are silenced. "Nice" stories are assigned or read to the children; they are not exposed to the social critique and anger of writers such as Dick Gregory, Angela Davis, Toni Morrison or Calvin Herndon. Much as is pointed out by Heath & McLaughlin (1993), urban schools proclaim multicultural education but reserve study of minority Americans for special days or weeks and then usually in a very limited contextualization. The irony of a school curriculum or multicultural celebration in a racial minority school that is reluctant to discuss the full history of minorities in the United States is self-evident.

The second style, Additive, does attempt to bring minority culture, concepts and themes into the curriculum but only within narrow parameters framed by mainstream interpretations. This approach would incorporate a few African American or Hispanic authors or perhaps a short unit on a particular group. However, it is limited to that level and constrained by its acceptability to the dominant concept of knowledge, social relations, and values (Grossman, 1995). In urban schools, Africa, its culture, literature, and art, is often reduced to the schools allowing the wearing for that week of "Afrikan" T-shirts and caps. In my own district, little of Africa or American black history was incorporated into the curriculum, and the movies *The Color Purple* and *Roots* were banned as being too inflammatory. This same truncated multi-culturalism is applicable to schools largely populated by other minorities as well.

Beyond the shallowness of their connection to difference and culture and their obvious purposes of assimilation and maintenance of the status quo, these two styles are intrinsically located within that combination of perspectives discussed earlier—deficiency assumptions and blaming the victim. Within that perspective, student success is attributed to individual merit and failure to personal inadequacy. When multicultural education fails in providing equality of outcome in schooling for marginalized groups of students, school administrators counter that they have made substantive changes and are justified in putting the blame upon the students (Levine-Rasky, 1995).

According to Banks (1991), the third approach, Transformation, represents a multicultural approach to curriculum and pedagogy that includes multiethnic materials. Banks, however, does not elaborate beyond that. This approach would, perhaps, attempt reformation of curriculum and pedagogy to include and/or be centered around ethnic history, experience, and knowledge. Unfortunately, more often the scheme is limited to a narrow definition of ethnicity and does not interrogate racial experience or meanings or examine pervasive issues of racism, ideology, or the American social investment in the maintenance of differential social benefits based on race, class, or gender. While acknowledging ethnicity, it fails to connect education to society, and Banks is too vague on this scheme to allow much critique.

The fourth category, Social Action, is preferable according to Banks and consists of adding the concept of social transformation plus what he terms individualistic-oriented socially cognizant decision-making. Banks argues that the ultimate goal of multicultural education is "to empower students to make reflective decisions on issues related to ethnicity and to take personal actions to solve ethnic problems" (Banks, p. 25). Although condemning overt racism, Banks' scheme is grounded in ethnicity theory excluding thereby student exploration into the social constructiveness of race and gender and fails to question how such socialization is culturally used to maintain dominant values (Omi & Winant, 1986). Although Banks argues that students should become involved in social issues, the emphasis is still positivistic in that it is tied to changing the consciousness of individuals (and then testing for change), rather than on collectively identifying underlying issues of differential power, cultural capital, or racism.

This approach avoids the concept of collective social change as the emphasis is still on the individual becoming enlightened and then acting as a change agent. Even if we assume some level of increased awareness and motivation on the part of students through the use of this approach, the result is often increased cynicism and despair as students, caught in an individualistic logic, perceive themselves as powerless. Thus, their personal actions are stymied and their decision-making, without a sense of the collective, becomes reproductive.

Banks advocates this last approach but fails to extend his vision to its failure of implementation. He misjudges the hegemonizing maintenance power of mainstream racial ideology (Omi & Winant, 1986) by failing to interrogate the nature of race construction in this society and targets his advocacy of practice toward suburban schools (incidentally begging the question as to whether he assumes multicultural education is for white middle-class students).

In any event, even if adequately argued by Banks, the latter two approaches are absent from inner-city schools, with the possible exception of schools operated by groups such as "The Nation of Islam" (Ladson-Billings, 1990; King & Wilson, 1990). In public schools, including those in urban communities, there is rarely any effort made to connect multicultural curriculum, lessons or programs to social issues, racism or even the local community.

Sleeter & Grant: A Typology of Diversity

In a more critical (in the sense of Left radicalism) effort to understand the strands of multicultural education promulgated in our schools, Christine Sleeter (1989, 1991) and Carl Grant (1987, 1989) have distinguished five approaches to multicultural education, each bounded by different conceptions of multiculturalism and purposes of curriculum and pedagogy. Unlike Banks, they have attempted to connect the various strands to deeper social issues. While calling for a generally reconstructionist approach, they have also been critical of whitening multiculturalism and have attempted to recenter multicultural education around the margins.

Sleeter & Grant note that the primary approaches to multicultural education all use the rhetoric and language of a pluralist style but are constrained by still being grounded in positivistic mainstream values (e.g., assimilation into Euro-western cultural capital, meritocracy, and individualism) and conditioned by deficiency theories for interpreting minority students' experience, behavior, and educational results (e.g., Grant, 1995; Sleeter, 1994; Sleeter & Grant, 1994; Sleeter & Grant, 1987). The identified approaches are:

1. Teaching the Exceptional and the Culturally Different
2. Human Relations
3. Single Group Studies
4. Multicultural Education (Cultural Pluralism)
5. Multicultural and Social Reconstruction

Before discussing each approach separately, a few caveats are in order. First, although many educational practices located under the rubric of multicultural education can be placed primarily in one category or another, there is also overlap in the sense that a particular program or process may incorporate concepts from more than one category. In actual curricular or pedagogical advocacy and practice in inner-city schools, the framing language is rarely specific. An adherent of assimilation does not generally and openly denigrate a racial minority; instead the framing language may sound like the rhetoric of another category (i.e., many assimilatory programs have mission statements that seem to advocate pluralism); however, the respective practices as actually played out are generally recognizable as belonging to one category or another (Sleeter, 1989). Second, not all categories are found at all levels of education, so discussion of one might not be applicable to all grade levels.

1. Teaching the Exceptional and the Culturally Different

This approach specifically targets the assimilation of students of color into the cultural mainstream (Sleeter & Grant, 1987; Sleeter, 1991) and is the normative frame for most ESL, bilingual and government-sponsored compensatory programs. The approach endeavors to "mainstream" what are perceived as "deficient" students (culturally and educationally) by inculcating dominant cultural values and skills through a process of acculturation. Predominantly these are skills and values (see Chapter Two) such as adaption to hierarchy, belief in meritocracy and competition, regimentation, minimal-level math and literacy skills, etc. The object thus becomes to teach children who are different to become as mainstream as possible so that they can share in social benefits. The problem is the assumption that such assimilation will have the best chance for eradicating poverty, unemployment, racism, sexism (Sleeter & Grant, 1994).

The majority of existing multicultural programs fall within this broad category and tend to emphasize pathology (e.g., the targeting of the culturally deprived "at risk" child), requisite value adjustments, problematic social relations, and the negation of social tensions associated with racial minorities (Gordon, 1990) such as discrimination. However, as to the latter, the underlying social realities (racism and poverty) are assiduously avoided, thereby masking any contradictions.

Inherent Eurocentrism is typically masked by the inclusion of a benign list of admirable men and women who are touted as a "credit to their race" or their gender. While supposedly democratizing the list increases the diversity of the players, it does little to insure that their voices, interests and perspectives will be included. It does little to remove the historical falsifications that are embedded in mainstream cultural perceptions (Crichlow, 1990).

Even where there is a concerted effort to include other racial experiences and perspectives within the curriculum, it is stabilized within educational paradigms and practices by a language of presumed universality and objectivity, making assimilatory education a central site for preserving a selective tradition that still demarks minorities as bearers of a deviant culture (McCarthy, 1990).

While assimilation is justified more often than not on the basis that it ensures the entry of blacks and others into the mainstream, it is dehumanizing at its core (hooks, 1989):

> Embedded in the logic of assimilation is the white-supremacist assumption that blackness must be eradicated so that a new self, a 'white' self, can come into being. Of course, since we who are black can never be white, this very effort promotes stress and pain. . . . Much of this pain is evoked by the effort to assimilate, which is a demand for self-negation. (hooks, 1989, p. 67)

The scheme ignores and/or denies issues of racism, sexism, and class and does not interrogate positivistic educational practices, nor is it usually relevant to the lives of the predominately black and Hispanic students of the urban ghetto. As Sleeter and Grant (1987) have pointed out, this approach attempts in the name of assimilation to equip marginalized peoples with the skills and cultural capital to compete in the mainstream. It fails completely to imply that whites should be taught anything about racism, classism or other groups.

Another critique is one that McCarthy (1990) outlines and I touched on earlier in this chapter, which constitutes possibly the central contradiction in urban schools' educational purposes. The assimilatory rhetoric stresses that a reformed school curriculum will enhance minority opportunity for academic success and better incorporation into the labor market [Note: in previous sections I have discussed how often administrative rhetoric links student behavior (studying, obeying) with successful job futures as well as the students' oppositional rejection.] This linear connection is, in fact, frustrated by the existence of racialized practices in the labor market—"racial and social connections, rather than educational qualifications per se, determine the phenomenon of better job chances." (McCarthy, 1990, p. 53-54) The purveyors of assimilatory programs ignore the inherent contradiction and do not acknowledge the subtleties and pervasiveness of racism that a black student who succeeds academically will face in his or her attempts to assimilate.

Assimilation education is problematic in inner-city schools due to inadequacies of means and practices, funds, staffing, and peer cooperation and the general irrelevance of its messages to the students themselves. Bilingual aides mandated by legislation are often last hired, first fired, and texts are almost nonexistent. Districts accept federal and state funds for multicultural purposes and divert the monies to cover other exigencies. The students are confused and reject textbooks showing few or no blacks or Hispanics. Many are frankly bored with repetitive references to sanitized "heroes" whose whitened language has no connection to their actual lives. The "linear connection" McCarthy (1990) speaks of between schooling and jobs flounders in the face of poverty, unemployment, gangs, and crime; yet the administration and many teachers unceasingly peddle the connection and make the mistake of assuming that student silence means consent.

This approach was used in several ways at the school which was typical of its district. One was the periodic special occasions such as Black History Week and its annual Black Heritage assembly and Cinco de Mayo. The other approach was a broader inclusion within the curriculum and environment (posters, signs, etc.) within the classrooms.

The former, which I have already described in Chapter Three, was effectively limited to two days in the school year. The Black Heritage assembly occurred usually in February and consisted of several skits and songs. It lasted about forty-five minutes and was held usually just before lunch. The principal repeatedly admonished the children to maintain silence except for applause and the students responded with rude comments and the inevitable "whoo, whoo, whoo" for their friends who were performing. The skits were always the same ones about Harriet Tubman or Rosa Parks, historically inaccurate, and, although mentioning slavery and civil rights, carefully avoided any reference to whites. The perpetrators of injustice were always invisible. Some of my students even thought that slaveholders had been black and had just finally let the people go. The songs were either gospel or thematic about freedom and love for all. Noticeably absent was the civil rights anthem, current rap music (which all the students delighted in creating and performing, even in the classroom) and any reference to racism, segregation, discrimination and social inequality. It was often after such assemblies that we talked in class about slavery, racial discrimination and conditions in the "hood."

The sad fact was that for most of these children, the promises made about studying hard, obeying the rules and getting a diploma and thereby ensuring "making it" in America were patently false but the assimilation script had to be followed.

The Assimilatory approach, although the primary approach in urban schools to the problems of control and diversity, which is successful in the sense of being abundantly utilized, ultimately fails due to its central contradiction—no matter how assimilated a student is in mainstream language and values (i.e., no matter how white), s/he remains black or Hispanic and subject to life as an Other in a racist society (hooks, 1992). Ultimately the approach deflects attention away from the majority group and how it perpetuates discrimination and inequality (Sleeter & Grant, 1994).

2. Human Relations

This approach emphasizes sensitivity training, the curricular conceptualization of self-esteem, and teaching that we are all the same in spite of our differences (Sleeter & Grant, 1987). It advocates a "color-blind" pedagogy, harmony, and interpersonal relations without interrogating how those arise differently within cultural constructs (Nieto, 1995). Teachers and administrators tend to see this approach as a methodology to reduce prejudice and tensions.

This advocacy of color-blindedness sounds fair and impartial, but in actuality it means refusing to see differences in value systems, cognition, what constitutes knowledge, and accepting the dominant culture as the norm. "It results in denying the very identity of students, thereby making them invisible" (Nieto, 1990, p. 109), which tends to increase the very tensions for which the approach was incorporated.

The approach emphasizes communication between people of different cultures without questioning the content; it does not raise issues of how social and institutional racism and sexism both silence and mask cultural communication, nor does it differentiate between cultural communicative styles. The emphasis is on the individual, thereby letting the dominant culture "off the hook" (McCarthy, 1992) and leaving issues of differential social benefits and power uninterrogated. It is essentially the Contact approach (Banks, 1991) by another title and assumes that by increasing inter-group familiarity, schools can decrease or minimize prejudice, discrimination, intolerance, etc. Similar to those who employ the Assimilation approach, practitioners of Human Relations place great emphasis on cultural artifacts, overt customs (dress, foods, holidays, etc.), and behaviors.

The Human Relations or Sensitivity approach places tremendous significance on the espousal and generation of feel-good educational methodology, both within and outside urban schools. An entire industry has grown up around providing schools with Sensitivity materials—lesson plans, films, training sessions, workshops, and conferences. It is typically the style underlying school rhetoric and practices regarding self-esteem promotions and lessons, whereby teachers are taught how to "give" students self-esteem—never interrogating the contradictions of implied power in the scenario of "giving" and the derivation of a sense of self from and subject to the power of others. This approach has been widely accepted within general education and urban schools and forms the core of urban schools' administrative rhetoric and communications.

Unfortunately, many teachers in and out of urban schools think multiculturalism is "human relations," which means having lessons in "getting along," claiming that the relational skills will dissolve discrimination and racism. Even if this is successful at the school level, it is impossible to be unaffected by the racism, sexism, discrimination, classism, etc., that is all too prevalent in the larger society. To expect schools to be an oasis of sensitivity in the midst of social stratification is unrealistic (Nieto, 1995). The approach is limited, not in its pervasiveness but because it fails to interrogate why discrimination exists: how does a notion of difference play a role in the formation of individual and social identity and how does it play out societally to sustain traditional values (Sleeter & Grant, 1994).

In inner-city schools, this approach is popular with teachers and administrators as it echoes pervasive community religious connections and values. Many classrooms and school libraries are surfeited with materials garnered from various community organizations (usually outside of the ghetto), film strips and tapes (which usually can't be used because of the lack of equipment) and there are even speakers who will come to the school to speak about harmony and "gettin along." These messages usually fail as frustrated educators attempt to disconnect students from "street" knowledge and behaviors, which are continually represented as being unacceptable (Yeo, 1992). Exhortations to resolve problems by talking seem irrelevant in the face of lives of violence, guns in the school, and turf battles within the hallways. Students regard such "teacher talk" as irrelevant and/or lacking "machismo." Much of the administrative and teacher rhetoric is couched in the language of this scheme (as well as the imperatives of individualism in the first approach) and is subjected to constant challenge by the students' own street rhetoric (Yeo, 1992).

Examples of this style of multicultural education were prolific at the school, some of which I have discussed in Chapter Three. Much of the various principals' communications over the P.A. system were of this style, emphasizing for students how important it was to get along, to be friends with everyone and respect the teachers. These broadcast admonishments often occurred after some particular incident, such as a fight at lunch or a teacher had left in the middle of the day. One example I jotted down one afternoon as it unfolded through student reactions to the principal:

> Principal [on the P.A.]: You all need to be good grown-up boys and girls . . .
>
> Student: That be some shit, Mr. Yo, how's I ta be growed up at thirteen?
>
> Student: Do I gotta be good ta Missus Brown too? She always be throwin me outa her room.
>
> Student: That's cuz you be cussin her ole booty, niggah!
>
> Student: Nah, its cuz she be light skinneded and ah be black!
>
> Student: Yeah man, black be beautiful.
>
> Principal: . . . be friends with everyone you meet, boys and girls. Be kind to each other and follow the school rules. That way, we can be proud of Washington.
>
> Student: How ya gonna be friends with the Bloods, they always wannna shoot yo ass?

Student: Ahm only gonna be friends wid mah homies, blood; dey be the onliest friends ah gots in de hood, man.

Implicit in the student comments is a rejection of the Sensitivity approach contained within the principal's remarks, which is quite simply irrelevant to their experience and lives. One interesting issue contained in these remarks represents a constant tension at the school. The students often reacted to the teachers and each other on the basis of a status conferred by perceptions of skin coloration. In what would seem to be a reflection of the stratification implicit within mainstream notions of race and color, students were aware of the "value" of color that more closely approximated white. Students whose color was very dark were often referred to in demeaning ways by other students whose skin tones were lighter. The issue of who was closer to being white gave rise all too often to schisms between students as well as being reflected in perceptions of self-worth by individual students. Teachers reflected both a concern for the issue and the Sensitivity approach in their attempts to bolster students' self-worth by telling students that we are all the same color under the skin or that black was beautiful.

This particular approach is undoubtedly well meant but masks the contradiction that we are NOT the same under the skin, particularly if we are black, Hispanic or Native American in a white, Euro-centered society that grants no credence to alternative cultural values or understandings. Remarks by students, such as the above, represent their fundamental disbelief in the approach based on their experience, both at school and in the community. Although it has been suggested (Sleeter & Grant, 1994, p. 117) that many teachers of color who have in the past advocated this approach subsequently have shifted to a more pluralistic style of multicultural education, in terms of the inner-city school this is wishful thinking. This style, in conjunction with the Assimilatory approach, constitutes the great bulk of multicultural practices in inner-city elementary and secondary education. In inner-city schools a tremendous effort of resources and administrative and teacher time is devoted to the pursuit of these two approaches. They form the basis of much of the school rhetoric (Yeo, 1992), including parent conferences, teacher-to-student talk, discipline, and the entire gamut of adult-student relations.

Despite its pervasiveness, however, both the rhetoric and the values of this Sensitivity approach are rejected in the main by students and parents due to the contradictions, the overt derogation of minority cultures, and the disconnection of the experiential realities of students' lives, which just do not connect with "feel good" admonitions (Nieto, 1995; Solomon, 1992; Yeo, 1992). As I have indicated elsewhere, there is additional contradiction as students struggle with alternative notions of education deriving from historical community and racial understandings and attempt to internalize educational messages that are sold as underpinnings of academic and future achievement.

3. Single Group Studies

This approach attempts to foster cultural pluralism by teaching courses about history, experience, and culture of distinct ethnic, gender, and/or social class groups (although less of the latter). It typically emphasizes ethnic division, e.g., Black Studies, Chicano Studies, and heterosexual genderization through Women's Studies. The literature pays little attention to overall goals and purposes, although Banks (1991) does say that it is to somehow help students make better reflective decisions. Authors within this approach emphasize teaching about the contributions and experiences of a group without necessarily raising awareness of nonsynchronous oppressions or the need for collective social action

> For example, a teacher might teach about American Indian cultural practices but not even mention their oppression today. Although there is value in teaching about cultures, the failure to address issues of current social stratification and social action ignores a major component. (Sleeter & Grant, 1987, p. 429)

Additionally, since the tendency within this approach is to emphasize only ethnicity or gender (not usually any combination), it ignores multiple forms of diversity and oppression (Sleeter & Grant, 1987) as well as differences within the labelled groups. Such courses as Black or Chicano Studies can and often fail to examine group internal problems of gender or social stratification and tend to portray monolithic views of a group. For example, texts on Chicano Studies replicate the patriarchal nature of much of Hispanic culture by generally emphasizing only males. While granting that there is an increasing amount of Latina writing, it is generally by women, about women, and avoided by men.

One of the criticisms leveled at this approach is its refusal to deeply interrogate the varied textures of the African American, Hispanic, or other racial minority cultures in this society. Although often presenting material from non-white groups, there is, in general, a turning away from any of what Cornel West calls "thick" opposition, that which critiques American society in terms of the maldistribution of wealth, power, and political/economic relations (hooks & West, 1991).

This approach is rare in inner-city education. Such studies as do exist of black or Hispanic subjects are subsumed within chapters of standardized American history texts or found in a lone title by a black author within a literature class. There is virtually no mention of the culture, history, or present problems of Native Americans or Asians. This approach is generally confined to universities and colleges and is rarely used in secondary education. The exception at the elementary or secondary educational levels is possibly in ethnic schools such as those sponsored by groups such as "The Nation of Islam" or in "home schooling" situations, but the latter is also rarely found in the inner-city.

4. Multicultural Education (Cultural Pluralism)

This model incorporates the goals of cultural pluralism and ethnic diversity although giving less attention to issues of social stratification, wealth distribution, and effects of state policies. The approach calls for curricular reform on the basis of diversity, alternative life styles, culture and social justice yet still lies within the framework of the dominant educational value system (Sleeter & Grant, 1987) in its emphasis on individualism, meritocracy, and positivistic approaches to knowledge and education. There is also virtually no reference to the nonsynchronous nature of sexism, racism, or classism (McCarthy, 1992) by which McCarthy means that neither individuals or groups live in realities contextured by just racism or sexism, etc. Since all of the various sources of oppression and alienation operate differently in different persons, we should not assume a monolithism to any particular pain nor that any particular group suffers similarly within itself. This approach unfortunately fails to incorporate that understanding.

As one of the most utilized texts in teacher education for multiculturalism, Banks' book, *Teaching Strategies for Ethnic Studies* (1991), argues strenuously for this particular style of multicultural education. Under what he calls "Social Action," Banks suggests a number of goals (Banks, p. 25-27) for the "pluralistic" approach: to develop decision-making and social action skills, to help students view historical and contemporary events from diverse perspectives, to develop cross-cultural competency, to reduce ethnic and cultural provincialism (to help understand their own cultures better and eliminate cross-ethnic racism, which presumes that any racial group can be racist), and to master essential educational skills (math, reading) in a multiethnic atmosphere. This approach places significant emphasis on equal opportunity for individuals of difference within society. Additionally, the advocates of this pluralistic approach argue that the curriculum should present diverse experiences and perspectives, especially those that society has traditionally silenced or omitted, including that of gender (Sleeter & Grant, 1994; Nieto, 1995; Gollnick & Chinn, 1990; Banks, 1991).

In contradiction, King & Wilson (1990) and others argue that because the pluralistic scheme, especially that represented by Banks, deletes and/or ignores any need to foster social change through a collective consciousness and/or becomes locked into a narrow vision of which "ism" is worse, autonomous cultural identity or pluralism is theoretically suspect. They point out that this format of pluralism has flaws similar to the liberal conceptualization of integration and desegregation which can foster what Cornel West calls an "illusionary inclusiveness" (King & Wilson, 1990, p. 14). Similar to the first two approaches, this pluralistic multiculturalism is framed within a rhetoric of cultural inclusion, but in practice is closely tied to the Human Sensitivity approach in its delegitimation of difference, whether we are referring to racial minorities, such as blacks and Latinos, or religious minorities, such as Jews, Moslems or others (King & Wilson, 1990). Within this approach, there is no intrinsic worth attributed to difference and/or diversity, except in a contributive notion.

Another problem is this approach's hinging of educational and social change on the reorganization of the curriculum to include more culturally and racially sensitive materials. This still does nothing to affect the unequal relations that exist in schools between whites and students of color; between teachers, students, and administrators; between textbook publishers and reformist demands, and so forth (McCarthy, 1990). McCarthy also argues that this approach, as well as the others, pays too little attention to the internal relation of competition and cultural selection in education that configures race with gender and class (McCarthy, 1990). He states that minority needs and interests are not homogenous or unitary, and often the intersection of these racialized, stratified and gendered interests in the unequal environment of the school are systemically nonsynchronous, which none of the multicultural approaches takes into account (McCarthy, 1990).

One problem with this approach, particularly in urban schools, is that most white teachers and many "of color" (middle-class minorities) do not think in broad terms of oppression, racial or otherwise, thus they miss connections between racism and power, economics, and/or politics. Cultural pluralism becomes harmonious integration in which color is rendered unimportant (Sleeter, 1994), which is what Sleeter found in her research on teachers learning about multicultural education in workshops. She found that most teachers still thought of multicultural education as individually oriented, not linked with a collective social movement aimed at redistribution of societal resources (Sleeter, 1994). "For them, it was a tool for addressing problems they saw in their classrooms; tensions among groups of students, boredom, and failure" (Sleeter, 1994, p. 251). The concept of social transformation, even if pedagogically present, is subsumed within an instrumentalist logic. Cultural pluralism becomes another way to solve issues of classroom management and assessment.

Lastly, this approach fails to theorize or strategize adequately about the State and its uneven and variable involvement in race relations and/or racial formations (McCarthy, 1990; Omi & Winant, 1986).The Pluralistic approach remains trapped by mainstream pedagogy; it fails to connect issues of the hidden curriculum and multiculturalism, school and systemic practices (tracking, meritocracy, standardized evaluation, etc.) to actual teaching (Sleeter & Grant, 1987).

In terms of inner-city schools, there exists almost no literature to suggest this approach's use and/or the results of any attempts at implementation, nor has this author seen the approach attempted or even discussed in any urban schools. Even if attempted in some fashion, it is doubtful whether districts would commit resources to its implementation given their relative scarcity.

5. Multicultural and Social Reconstruction

The last approach outlined by Sleeter & Grant is the least developed in terms of practice although the most radical theoretically in its stressing of student and teacher collectivity, language and cultural analysis, and the investigation and confrontation in schools of racial, gender and class issues (Sleeter & Grant, 1987). It is grounded in the notion that collective pedagogy can translate to social action and argues that multicultural education must be pervasive and that Eurocentric education cannot be changed by simply adding units or lessons here and there about African Americans, Native Americans, Hispanics or women. It is propounded as critical or transformative education, but often curricular or pedagogical models seem somewhat vague and/or set in theoretical language too obtuse for teachers to want to take the time to investigate.

Typical of the aims of this reconstructive multiculturalism are those set out by Gollnick and Chinn (1990):

> (1) To promote the value of cultural diversity; (2) to promote human rights and mutual respect; (3) acquire knowledge of the historical realities of U.S. society to understand racism, sexism and poverty; (4) to promote social justice for all; and (5) to promote equity in the distribution of income among all groups.

Or as succinctly stated by Sonia Nieto in an article in *Harvard Educational Review* (1994);

> Multicultural education should be basic for all students, pervasive in the curriculum and pedagogy, grounded in social justice, and based on critical pedagogy. (Nieto, p. 416)

The foundational argument of reconstructive or critical multiculturalism is that it can and should be transformative; that it can be used to empower collective action by students to delegitimize the structure and oppressions of school and society, although how this is to be accomplished pedagogically is left unclear (Sleeter & Grant, 1987) due to the lack of praxis-oriented writing and research.

Sleeter and Grant (1994) have responded to some of these critiques by arguing that although schools cannot be expected to change society, they can collaborate with other institutions in effecting change. This does bring up the issues of curriculum that would address issues of building collectivity—"little has been written or studied about how coalitions among diverse groups can be built" (Sleeter & Grant, p. 237).

This approach is problematic as to inner-city schools because of its basic assumptions: (1) that such reconstructive multiculturalism can envision and effect its political project within urban education and schools, and (2) that in some fashion this infusion of diversity and "celebration of difference" into the schools will connect to change in the surrounding urban ecology and in the greater society (Weiner, 1993). If the reconstructionists' political project is for broad social, economic, and political change, presumptively to a more just and democratic society, how will a multicultural curriculum in its most liberatory sense produce such pervasive societal change, particularly one grounded in inner-city schools? Given the pervasive State involvement in urban educational practices, it seems somewhat less than creditable that such a multicultural style can effect significant change at the sociopolitical level or extend from such marginalized schools to the broader society.

The assimilationist and the sensitivity trainer would remake ethnic minority students into white clones and the results of these approaches are evident in the continuing high dropout rates and school failures of urban education. The radical multiculturalist would remake ethnic minority students into reconstructionists of society without regard for whether they or their schools can gain the political and economic power to do so, or even have the desire to do so. Both camps are also basically integrationist, neither taking into consideration whether a particular ethnic minority group wants community with others (Peller, 1992). It assumes that minorities want to be part of the American mainstream, albeit in a transformed, more just society. While this may be the case for some members of minority groups, it is not for all unless we assume that monolithic presumption about minorities which McCarthy (1992) argues against. Within almost all minority communities, there is a dialectic over the issue of integration versus separation often polarized over cultural questions, not political or economic.

On this specific issue, a group of community workers meeting with one of my classes to discuss careers argued that integration was, in some ways, more damaging for black Americans than Jim Crow. In response to a student question, a black minister offered the following:

> Ya see, when the white man decided to let us join him, he took our Black children and sent them to those nice White schools. We got to have those nice White teachers, the books that talked about Whites and all their nice White ways that we had been looking at for years. When I was in school in Alabama and we integrated, I got to go to the White school. Gone were my Black teachers, my principal, my Black pictures on the walls, and my friends. The

White school put us in classrooms where we was the only colored person there. We couldn't talk Black any more, but still sat in the back. I think we lost more than we gained and that's the Lord's truth.

James Cone in *A Black Theology of Liberation* (1970) makes a similar point when he argues that the cost of integration was black culture and community. Latino and Native American authors have made similar arguments that integration is presumptively assimilationist and the result is always deculturalization for the minority group (Darder, 1991; hooks, 1992; Nieto, 1995; Jaimes, 1992).

In addition to the cultural issue is the political. One of the possible reasons that the reconstructivist literature has not connected multiculturalism to inner-city schools is because they are patently a poor base from which to reconstruct American society. It is difficult to suggest with a straight face that the reconstruction of the dominant ideologies of this country and their resultant social practices can be generated from the ghettos and barrios. In this thinking, even critical or social reconstructionist multiculturalism still espouses a liberal notion of integration, that the goal of education is to construct a democratic society for all—a scheme of integration in which somehow the dominant white, Euro-centered power structure will be convinced to share or diminish its hegemony. Within this approach, the goal of integration is rarely questioned, except by the minorities, and their political voice continues to be silenced even by those who claim to be interested.

This critique should not be interpreted to suggest that education, even within the borders of the inner city, is not or could not be important nor that multiculturalism would not be an effective vehicle for a more limited and/or localized vision of change. Instead of the panacea for all ills, a multiculturalized curriculum and pedagogy that recognizes, interrogates, and affirms the voices and experiences of these students and their communities could play a significant role in revitalizing the energies of the citizens of these communities. The focus needs to be on the linkage between school and community in order for both to change. The lessons of cooperation, constructive confrontation, realization of the factors of one's social and cultural history and the understanding of the structures of power within the greater society could be the "capital" for connecting the schools to the communities for the betterment of both. Reconstructive multiculturalism would be well advised to view integration as less of a goal than community engagement; community empowerment as the purpose of education rather than some wider national cultural revival.

To task schools with relevancy for their own clientele seems both more meaningful and hopeful than the implication that they should be responsible for the reconstruction of a white society to which they are virtually invisible and irrelevant. This is what minority writers mean when they speak about a pedagogy that reinforces intra-ethnic solidarity without promoting inter-ethnic antagonisms while at the same time providing strategies for coalitions with other groups with similar needs and interests (Lomotey, 1990).

However, as I will argue in Chapter Six, if we presume that there are spaces for change within the borders of urban schools to an educational stance that commits the schools to internal transformation and connection to the local community, then the reconstructive notions for empowerment and collective social action may well contain the seeds of hope for change through the empowerment of an emancipatory consciousness that can perceive both the need for social change and potential paths for it. In other words, multicultural and social reconstructive education may not provide for immediate and/or broad social and ideological change, but it could provide students with the critical insights to interrogate social inequalities and personal and social contradictions and relations of power, and experience acting collectively to foster change. This would thus provide the experience and mechanisms to effect change and the hope that their efforts could be meaningful. Certainly, if there is one thing that inner-city students often lack, it is hope that their education can be meaningful, especially within their communities.

Multicultural Education: A "Border" Pedagogy

The question of practice and connectivity is the Gordian knot for the social reconstructionists, since it should seem clear by this point that most multicultural education as espoused and practiced in American education has been mere lip service to minority demands, and even innocuous proposals have not been taken seriously (McCarthy, 1990). Further, it should be clear in terms of inner-city education that even the most radical multiculturalism is irrelevant through its absence and potentially oppositional to minority goals. Multicultural education as it has been institutionalized in the public school has been grounded in two principles. The first assumption is that perceptions about minority children of cognitive and affective deficiency has been used to dehistoricize and depoliticize issues of knowledge and educational attainment (McCarthy, 1992). Rather than understanding discrimination and prejudice as the product of the social construction of race, class, and gender, the various multicultural education approaches have individualized and abstracted it from social struggle (McCarthy, 1992). The second assumption has been to make the "other" visible but in such a way that the distance and boundaries between the "center" and the "margins" are maintained. It has not challenged an essentialist conception of identity and has limited itself to promoting tolerance (McCarthy, 1992, p. 18).

The problematic of multicultural education is that, for the most part, it is mired in substantiating mainstream notions of curriculum and pedagogy as well as furthering the dominant understanding about race which is configured by the permutations of ethnicity theory. For inner-city schools, therefore, it constitutes in the main nothing more substantive than a face lift, neither solving or ameliorating urban educational problems.

The Reconstructionists argue that if in fact we do desire to effect change in both urban education and by extension in the larger culture, then we must move beyond "benign" pluralism and/or the mere critique of mainstream programs. We must go further than the compensatory strategy of simply adding diverse cultural knowledge(s) onto the dominant curriculum (McCarthy, 1990; Nieto, 1995). This is where the social transformative educators wish to go—to redeem society as a whole through the reconstruction of education in light of new knowledge about identity, culture and consciousness, i.e., into a "border pedagogy" (Giroux, 1992, 1991b; McLaren, 1995, 1991; Steinberg, 1995).

Arising out of the social reconstructivist approach, Henry Giroux (1992, 1990, 1988) and others argue for an expansion of democracy's ideals as articulated though critical pedagogy or what he terms as Border Pedagogy (1992) through the agency of a radical multiculturalism. In this section I will briefly describe and explain the theory of Border Pedagogy, including a critique based on what I interpret as inherent contradictions for its problematic applicability to inner-city education. This is only an introduction to critical and/or Border Pedagogy, which are complex theorizations of the connections and implications of education, culture, economics, society, etc. with multitudinous permutations. 2

Situated within a social reconstructionist perspective of multicultural education, critical pedagogy's concern is that the United States appears to be reconfiguring its political, social, and cultural geography to deny rather than maintain a democratic community. Instead of engaging a politics of diversity, community, and democracy with respect to the principles of justice, equality, and freedom, the current trend seems to be about severing the links between democracy and political equality (Giroux, 1992b).

Giroux (1991) in responding to this concern argues that Western culture has ruthlessly expunged the stories, traditions, and voices of those who by virtue of race, class, and/or gender constitute the Other. In *Border Crossings* (1992), he contends that to cross borders pedagogically is to recoup these oppressed traditions through recognition of the experiential knowledge and culture that students bring to school and to teach to the multiple narratives suffusing classrooms.

To theorize this teaching, Giroux draws on concepts of identity, voice, culture, and a reconceptualizing of experience and identity by blending postmodernism, feminism and critical concepts of race and ethnicity, which he argues are the most important discourses for developing a cultural politics and pedagogical practice capable of advancing a politics of radical democracy within multiculturalism. As for multiculturalism itself, Giroux's concept is based on a proposed linkage between pedagogy and the imperatives of a critical or radical democracy that is socially, culturally, and racially inclusive and nonhierarchial. He argues for an approach that will reconceptualize the pedagogical struggle over race, gender, and ethnicity. Similarly to Sleeter and Grant's version of reconstructive multiculturalism, Giroux argues that multiculturalism must act pedagogically to reconstruct possibilities for "establishing a progressive vision that makes schooling for democracy and citizenship a possible reality" (Giroux, 1992, p. 137).

Border pedagogy represents a multiculturalism that is part of a discourse about an engaged plurality and the formation of citizenship in a democratic polity. This discourse stresses a notion of a lived community that is not at odds with principles of justice, liberty, and equality and that allows and/or encourages multiple and heterogeneous ways of life to come into play (McLaren, 1988a). Giroux calls on educators to prepare students for a style of citizenship that does not separate abstract rights from the realm of the everyday and does not define community as the legitimating and unifying practice of a one-dimensional [Eurocentric] historical and cultural narrative (Giroux, 1992). Additionally, the intent is to reject mainstream educational concern with instrumental techniques, skills, and objectives, which Giroux sees as masking questions of power, history, ethnicity, and identity. Further, critical multiculturalism proposes to interrogate how specific conceptualizations of difference held by dominant groups are sustained, specifically those in which minorities are seen as deficient, in which their humanity is either cynically exploited or ruthlessly denied.

Giroux's argument, arising out of postmodernism, is an advocacy of the recognition that difference is political and social in the way that it constitutes individual and social identity. Like race, difference is socially constructed, and is therefore fluid. Giroux implies that people can elect relations of both similarity and difference through the social construction of motile borders of identity. The aim educationally would be to help students become aware of their own individual and social borders, as well as those of others .

For those not familiar with it, in brief, postmodernism, as a general group of theoretical positions, rejects Euro-western tradition as the exclusive referent for judging what constitutes historical, cultural, and political truth. It argues that reason, science, and history can only be understood as part of a broader historical, political, and social struggle over relationships of power (Giroux, 1992). This postmodern critique leads Giroux and others to analyze how modernism has constructed paradigms and interpretations of difference that name, legitimate, marginalize and exclude the cultural capital and voices of subordinate groups in American society (Giroux, 1988). He asserts that by locating differences in a particular historical and social context, it becomes possible to understand how they are constructed so that we all know and understand culturally and socially our particularistic social and cultural terrains and the rules and regulations located within dominant social forces which either enable or disable any differences. Indeed, this is what the assimilationist multiculturalists propose—that difference needs to be first identified, presumed a deficiency, deculturalized to a mainstream norm, and minority children taught new normative social boundaries—a destruction of difference. This, of course, is as border pedagogy would predict, an unmitigated disaster in urban schools and communities.

Giroux, in his formulation of border pedagogy (1992), calls for educational formulations that would encourage students to be able to cross over into different zones of cultural diversity and form hybrid identities to rethink the relationships of self to society and self to other and to deepen the moral vision of the social order. At the same time, he is concerned for the postmodern dangers of the abandonment of commonality and community for the sake of essentializing difference and the denigration of those universals (in a moral and ethical sense) of political modernity, such as democracy, freedom and social justice. Increasingly for those involved in extending critical pedagogy's project(s), the issues of difference versus community, particularism versus universalism, and methods of teaching border crossing(s) have become the crucial matters.

The essence of what Giroux (1992) is proposing is that through border pedagogy we can come to perceive that reality is fluid, changeable, perhaps even malleable; that identity is not only not fixed, but it should not even be construed in such rigidity; that instead of seeing social construction as deriving concreteness, it should be perceived as underwriting change. Obviously both the teaching and classroom environments grounded in such assumptions would be profoundly different. Giroux argues that we need to come to the point where, unlike mainstream pluralism, we do not just respect borders of culture and identity but we can cross borders through a fluidity in identity. I have argued elsewhere (Yeo, 1995) that such border crossing is possible for teachers in an inner-city school environment and ought to form the core of teacher education as well as of urban educational pedagogy itself.

In attempting to answer the question as to the practice of such a theory, Giroux (1992) in some senses resurrects the Deweyan argument that the ultimate aim of education should be about democracy and community. Social justice and respect for identity (individual and social) must be the abiding foundation for any society and form the core of its educational institutions. He recognizes that if we seriously desire to have communities comprised of democratic citizens working toward resolving issues of social justice, then we need to educate for a radical democracy based on actual, but malleable, social agreements capable of reassessment or reconstruction depending on the needs of the community. A significant center for bringing citizens of such a democracy to recognize and cross the borders of knowledge, culture, and understanding is in the classroom—hence the need for a pedagogy (in an enlarged sense that includes both what has been traditionally defined as pedagogy as well as all aspects of schooling, schools, and education) that prepares citizens to be cultural workers and border crossers.

Of course, this conceptualization of pedagogy is in direct opposition to the theories and practices of current mainstream education and the dominant modes of multicultural education. Its strengths are in its connecting of school to community, the de-emphasis of cultural competition and hierarchy, and the recognition that not only is all cultural knowledge educationally valuable, but it is a prerequisite for the vibrancy of democratic society.

Border Pedagogy: A Critique

Much as any other multicultural schema, Border Pedagogy can and should be interrogated for its internal contradictions and assumptions, in particular for its implications for and applicability to inner-city educational conditions.

The latter is perhaps the primary problematic for the theory. Border Pedagogy needs to address the contradictions of a theory based on a professed concern for oppression and marginalization of the "Other," that lacks explicit connectivity to the domain of the inner-city school and community(s). The theory as an approach seems to also lack an understanding for the limits of possibility within bureaucratic and power spaces of urban schools and the existential realities of teachers' lives and relationships with fellow teachers and students.

The question must be raised, to whom does border pedagogy speak? Who constitutes (to use the language of border pedagogy) the lived audience? Does it address those peoples who live in and frequent the streets, convenience stores, police stations, and schools of the "hood"? Or the teachers buried in the welter of daily interactions, preparations, and paperwork of the inner-city school? Or other academics of the Left? This is not to fall into the heuristic trap of arguing the efficacy of theoretical language but to query whether the writings of those purporting to explain border pedagogy have not inadvertently fallen into a different trap—that which bell hooks (1990) calls the hubris of the white Left elite.

The problematic seems to be the implicit assumptions within the theory as to the nature of the often-mythical Other. Although castigating mainstream society for its marginalizing of race, class and gender, Border Pedagogy seems to imply that often taken-for-granted motif in multicultural education where one alludes to the oppressed and the marginalized but without naming, without facing, their humanity. Border Pedagogy and its interpretations seem at times to be so caught up in the search for new language that its advocates seem to have forgotten that the impoverished, the poor, the gang-bangers have names. There is a tendency to objectify, even reify, the oppressed as a faceless mass. This constitutes a weakness in the theory, a retreat from righteous moral indignation driven by knowing the oppressed, rather than an academic knowing of the oppressed.

To construct a project for the benefit of the Other within a "project of possibility" evokes appropriate cerebral responses but sheds little light on the identity, name, needs, or wants of the ubiquitous Other. Even more to the point, those of us who advocate critical and border pedagogy need to keep bell hooks' admonition in mind, when she warns

> Often this speech about the "Other" is a mask, an oppressive talk hiding gaps, absences. . . . Often this speech about the "Other" annihilates, erases—"No need to hear your voice when I can talk about you better than you can speak about yourself" (hooks, 1990, p. 151-152)

This is not to argue that critical theorists need to rush out and find themselves an Other to play with, but it is to acknowledge Sharon Welch's dictum that we cannot know the Other until we experience with the Other. She argues that in order to transcend our own social location with all of its acquired assumptions about others, we need to move away from Cartesian objectivity to understanding our own subjectivity and its constituencies of difference. Our subjectivity and its attendant understanding of others can only come by actual working with different groups (Welch, 1990). Welch argues that one does not naturally or intellectually have "experience" such as to underwrite a theorized Border Pedagogy. That is, one needs to acquire experience by experiential acts and engagements; i.e., experience should never be presumed or proclaimed. The aim is to construct shared understandings and sensibilities which cross boundaries of race, class, and gender to promote linkages of common commitments through shared experiences (hooks, 1990).

Welch (1990) suggests that in order to effect an understanding of another's difference and locate points of similarity, one must place oneself in a position to become the Other, although this too is inherently problematic if in so doing we assume to already know the Other. To effect a "politics of solidarity and difference" requires an understanding gained by experiencing 'Otherness' that allows for connectivity to those traditionally marginalized as the Other. Welch argues that one does not naturally or intellectually have "experience," such as to underwrite a politics of emancipatory democracy. Put differently, the contretemps is that to begin to understand the lives of inner-city children, for example, we have to in some fashion begin to experience it with them. Yet at the same time, we have to acknowledge the limitations of our own experience. The danger is that of arrogance and a lack of empathy in proclaiming that we know who they are when all we ever know (if we're lucky) is who we are.

The problem with Border Pedagogy is its implicit arrogance in proclaiming the needs of the Other without either experience or commonality. Even Giroux acknowledges that we can never truly speak as the Other, that we must instead work with diverse others so as to gain some understanding of the complexity of the tradition, histories, knowledges and politics that they bring to the classroom (Giroux, 1992). This requires an understanding of what it means to be marginalized beyond one's own experience and that one's experiences do not automatically equate with another's.

Ultimately it is the need to move away from academia and join what Cornel West calls the "camp meeting" (West, 1993a). Although there are a few critical theorists working and researching in inner-city schools, they are too few to effect the transformation that Border Pedagogy advocates. Unfortunately the educators who work toward effecting change in urban schools are generally of the mainstream variety, promulgating more of the same failure and blaming of the victim. As profound and potentially transformative as Border Pedagogy is, its virtual absence in inner-city schools acts to sustain the dominant multicultural modes of assimilation into a society that perpetuates racialized hierarchies and the deculturalization that it critiques.

Another issue has to do with the question of Border Pedagogy's potential efficacy with and for teachers. The theory seems myopic in its perceptions of its own potentiality with regard to the conditions and structures in which teachers work and interact. As Lois Weiner (1993) points out, critical pedagogy (and by extension, Border Pedagogy) assigns teachers and students political roles that transcend the classroom and perhaps even the school and local community. Rarely do critical theorists take into account existing school organization and/or practical actualities when arguing for educating teachers for "critical consciousness" or "emancipatory pedagogy," different terms for the same phenomena (Weiner, 1993).

Put another more practical way, assuming that one can change a white middle-class teacher's values and beliefs to accept the ideologies and praxis assumptions of Border Pedagogy, is it realistic or even fair to expect that teacher to actively attempt substantive changes in the values and practices of the school as an institution and/or as to the students themselves? Taking into account the discussion of whether a teacher can know what students want or need, is it even ethically right? The critical argument seems to cut against the grain of the exigencies of the daily routines and interactions in which inner-city teachers find themselves engaged. Perhaps it is a matter of expectations. It seems presumptuous to anticipate that a typical (surviving) inner-city teacher would be able to change the basic structures of the institution in which s/he works or effectively utilize components of the theory to transform the ennui and inertia of his/her peers or confront the principal over administrative demands for adherence to curricular, pedagogical, and evaluative standards, classroom adherence to behavior standards, and/or maintenance of test and worksheet quantity.

This is, however, emphatically not to argue against critical pedagogy and its extension of Border Pedagogy but to ask its interpreters to extend into the terrain of the inner-city school, which will be the purpose of Chapter Six. It is also to acknowledge the limits of critical pedagogy, particularly those conditions and structural or bureaucratic limitations that stem from the systemic characteristics of the urban school and within which teachers must work. Lastly, it is to affirm the insight of Audre Lorde (1990) when she warns that we cannot demolish the master's house with the master's tools, or of Liston and Zeichner who remind us that:

> We cannot create democratic school communities in an undemocratic society. We cannot build "tomorrow's schools" in today's unequal society. (Liston and Zeichner, 1991; cited in Weiner, 1993, p. 93)

or at least, it's damnably difficult to do so.

As a last critique of border pedagogy, I raise the question of its ethical efficacy. Border Pedagogy, like critical theory from which it derives, is an ethical/moral argument couched in political and economic language. Yet the ethical base is often muted in what resembles a curious mix of neo-Marxist economics and postmodern political language. One of the acknowledged problems with postmodern thinking is its flirtation with nihilism and the quagmire of irrelevancy (Burbules and Rice, 1991). Border Pedagogy thus inherits the same potential for being irrelevant as an argument for change. The contradiction is that although Border Pedagogy is obviously an ethical argument, its postmodern construction must disavow any moral stance as a dangerous universal or metanarrative. This leaves Border Pedagogy having to argue against its own ethical base. If one is making an argument for transformative social justice, which Border Pedagogy certainly does, one must perforce take a moral stand, which it tries to avoid. Critical multiculturalism is at its heart an argument for emancipatory education—a moral position Border Pedagogy needs to affirm. Ultimately, to initiate any form of bridging of differences, to transform mainstream education (and by extension, society itself) is a profoundly ethical project, not an epistemological one.

For all that I find to value in Border Pedagogy, the lack of an avowed ethical argument has its own criticality. Neither Border Pedagogy or Sleeter and Grant's (1994) social reconstruction model of multiculturalism are willing to grapple with "why" we should make the changes they advocate, why those changes are good, or why they are emancipatory for inner-city schools.

Ode to Another Direction

To a great extent, the question about audience posed to border pedagogy extends to all of the multicultural educational approaches—who is the intended audience? While we might hope that it includes the general public and maybe even legislators, the truth is that our audience of choice is teachers and those who teach teachers. This means, of course, teacher education and the institutionalized sites for the preparation of new and continuing teachers.

Certainly, multicultural advocacy is not new; its promulgation and practices have been around long enough and been successful enough that it has occasioned and engendered a sustained and vicious response from the Right. There are extensive libraries on multicultural theories and pedagogical practices, albeit operating primarily out of the assimilation and human relations approaches. Given that much of it is targeted at either pre-service or in-service teachers, in our discussion of urban education, we must take teacher education into account.

The next chapter will look at teacher education in its pre-service, formalized, and institutionalized formats. We will inquire into the ways in which the intersections of multicultural education and teacher education are constructed, the impact and effectiveness of multicultural education within teacher education, and how teacher education relates to and acknowledges urban schools, if it does. The next chapter will conclude with some thoughts as to the inculcation of changes within teacher education in regard to the specific preparation of inner-city teachers.

Notes

1. There has been a significant effort recently to sanitize Malcolm X through the machinations of consumerism and commodification (e.g., the sales of t-shirts, caps, textbook covers, etc.). The implied conclusion that has been media-generated and marginally promoted within the schools is that Malcolm X did not really blame white society, that other African Americans were the enemy.

2. Since there are a tremendous number of authors theorizing and writing within the broad categories of critical pedagogy and/or border pedagogy (and its derivative fields of feminism, postmodernism, cultural studies, etc.), only a few additional references are cited here: Giroux, Henry. (1992). *Border Crossings: Cultural Workers and the Politics of Education*, New York: Routledge. Giroux, Henry. (1988). "Border Pedagogy in the Age of Postmodernism," *Journal of Education*, 170:3. Aronowitz, Stanley. (1988). "Postmodernism and Politics." In Andrew Ross (Ed.), *Universal Abandon*. Minneapolis: Univ. of Minnesota Press. Darder, Antonia. (1991). *Culture and Power in the Classroom: A Critical Foundation for Bicultural Education*, Westport, CT: Bergin & Garvey. Kanpol, Barry, and Peter McLaren (Eds.) (1995). *Critical Multiculturalism: Uncommon Voices in a Common Struggle,* Westport, CT: Bergin & Garvey. Kincheloe, Joe L., and Shirley Steinberg (Eds.) (1992). *Thirteen Questions; Reframing Education's Conversation*, New York: Peter Lang. Lather, Patti. (1991). *Getting*

Smart: Feminist Research and Pedagogy within the Postmodern, New York: Routledge. McLaren, Peter. (1991). "Critical Pedagogy: Constructing an Arch of Social Dreaming and a Doorway to Hope." *Journal of Education*, Vol. 173:1. Purpel, David. (1989). *The Moral and Spiritual Crisis in Education*, Boston: Bergin & Garvey Publishers, Inc. Rosenau, Pauline. (1992). *Postmodernism and the Social Sciences*, Princeton, NJ: Princeton University Press. Purpel, David and Svi Shapiro. (1995). *Beyond Liberation and Excellence: Towards a New Public Discourse for Education*, New York: Routledge.

CHAPTER FIVE

A Vested Interest in Failure:
Teacher Preparation and Inner-City Schools

Introduction

Teacher education programs continue to prepare teachers to work in schools as they are, rather than as they ought or might be. (D. Purpel, 1995, p. 192)

One of the salient factors in any discussion about inner-city schools must be the teaching staff, their beliefs about teaching and their students, their expectations of both, and their training to teach, particularly their preparation to teach in an inner-city or urban school. In various points throughout the previous chapters, teachers have been introduced as a crucial element in the environment of an urban school. Much of what has been written has been in the nature of a critique suggesting perhaps to some that teachers are a substantive factor in the continuing and profound failure of education in inner-city schools. While certainly to some extent this is no doubt true, one should keep in mind that many, if not most, of the teachers in any urban center school arrive with little or no preservice preparation, and I would suggest that such criticism, in and of itself, is again falling into the trap of blaming the victim.

Why portray the inner-city teacher as a victim, particularly when it seems that most political and educational theorists represent the inner-city teacher as a villain? When one recalls the oft-cited results of instruction in inner-city schools (the abysmal standardized test scores, the seeming countenance of illiteracy, the dropout percentages, the students who graduate with math and language skills at elementary and/or middle school levels, the litany of failure), one could quite naturally assume (and perhaps in many cases should so presume) that the pedagogy in these schools is nothing less than mediocre. Indeed, when I have had college students read Kozol's (1991) *Savage Inequalities*, most are quick to condemn the teachers above all else. However, this rush to judgment ignores and renders innocent (or invisible) the institutional and the social. It also, in a more practical sense, ignores the conditions of teaching in these schools that few would deign or dare to work and teach in. The effect of day after day of attempting to cope with students who often have survival consciousnesses and come to school abused and/or hungry, the crowded classrooms of 40 to 50 students but desks for only 30, the lack of current (or perhaps any) textbooks, the stultifyingly rigid administrations, the decrepit (often unsafe) physical plants, the demands of district and administrators for dull, repetitive, mundane, noncreative classes, the broken doors, desks and windows, and the trash, broken equipment . . . I could go on, but the picture should be clear by now. These teachers, whom we are so quick to disparage, often struggle years under these conditions, often subjected to disdain from suburban colleagues and always one step from violence and burnout. Many do the best they can with the preparatory tools they were given—which leads us back to teacher education.

The lack of preparation for teaching in inner-city schools is a serious problem affecting all urban school systems. For example, the city system of New York estimated recently that over 75 percent of their elementary and secondary teachers are on emergency or temporary credentials with little formalized teacher training. In the district in which I taught for several years, while the district refused to release the statistics publicly, it was widely estimated among teachers that over 70 percent of the teachers were non-credentialed—to say nothing about the myriad of inner-city teachers who teach outside of their credentialed subject.

Accordingly, we should not be surprised at the subsequent high rates of turnover, the inability to relate to students and their communities, the frustrations over lack of resources and assistance, the survivalistic adherence to rigid lesson plans, routinized instruction and mandated curriculum and pedagogy (e.g., Basic Skills and Assertive Discipline), nor their retreat into ennui and projected attitudes of non-caring and non-motivation. To validate any critique, we must remember that many of these teachers arrive all too quickly at the point of mediating failure and feel helpless in the face of the conditions of their worksite.

Yet not all teachers come to these schools unprepared. Many, and this includes the administrators, have received training within formal institutions of teacher education. Additionally, these folks tend to influence the uncertified teachers to a significant degree, thus allowing us to trace the origin of many urban teachers' attitudes and values back to teacher education, not to mention the larger society. Many of the new noncertified teachers quickly become dependent on the certified teachers and administrators for guidance and counseling. Also, in some inner-city schools, principals do attempt various levels of training and explanation for new teachers, particularly the noncertified. Thus, again, to trace the linkage of knowledge of curriculum and pedagogy and the substrate values and beliefs, we end up at the doorstep of teacher education.

While it may be tenuous to assert any direct and/or intentional linkage between teacher education and urban education, given teacher education's proclivity for ignoring such schools, it seems clear that teacher education definitively influences those credentialed teachers and administrators who teach in inner-city schools. Thus, another factor that needs examination and analysis as to inner-city teaching is clearly teacher education, especially as housed and proselytized through formal institutions of teacher education.

There has been a great deal of criticism from all sides of the political spectrum written about teacher education, and it is not my intent here to replicate either the research or the analysis and critique of teacher education in general. Instead, this chapter will focus on two areas: first, the theories and practices teacher education inculcates in incipient urban teachers and, second, to investigation of the ways in which teacher education has responded to the issues of diversity introduced in Chapter Four, how it absorbs and subsequently transmits value judgments about various approaches to multicultural education. For that discussion, we will refer to the typologies of multicultural education explicated in Chapter Four, particularly as they are related to issues of urban education.

Additionally, and for the record, while I am loath to place significant responsibility at the doors of urban teachers, I am not reluctant to blame teacher education and teacher educators. Thus, I intend to assert the direct culpability of teacher education for the styles and results of teaching in urban schools. This chapter can and should be taken for a candid condemnation of mainstream teacher education, which plunges into the twenty-first century while fervently, almost religiously, believing in the efficacy of the common school tools of the nineteenth. Teacher education still remains, of course, committed to positivism and ethnicity theory as the rationales for its unswerving maintenance of instrumental ideologies, adherence to protestations of neutrality and objectivity, refusing to recognize the need to theorize about teaching practices, democracy, and diversity, and blind faith in the ultimate triumph of the American middle-class way of life through assimilation and deculturalization:

> Possessive individualism and instrumental rationality establish a belief in a meritocracy and a consensus of goals in a society that is, in fact, culturally, ethnically, and economically differentiated . . . current social theories are not only used to create consensus and perpetuate the social order, but also to perpetuate institutional pedagogical practices. (Popkewitz, 1987, cited in Trueba, 1993, p. 209)

The Urban School as Symbol

The issues surrounding diversity and teacher education's reactions to it bear directly on urban schools and the efforts of teacher education to prepare teachers for that environment. To a great extent, how teacher education relates to and copes with minority students underscores how the hidden (and sometimes not so hidden) curriculum of teacher education sustains dominant mainstream educational history, ideologies, and practices, even in the face of student and community resistance and rejection occurring in urban and inner-city schools. It also illustrates how teacher education reacts and/or relates to diversity, difference, and the minority student. The implication here is that how teacher education reacts to the students of racialized difference within teacher education itself has a direct bearing on how teacher education typifies whiteness as a norm, as an ontologic and epistemic frame for its perceptions of minorities outside the programmatic concerns.

The narrative sequences of Chapter Three can easily be interpreted to represent the dominant values, attitudes, and ideologized practices asserted by teachers and administrators, many of whom are products of teacher education. It is the personal and individual incorporation into personal value structures of such conceptualizations about reality, knowledge, and Others that is the main thrust of teacher education, albeit perhaps unconsciously as to individual teacher educators. Another explanation is that a more profound, albeit hidden, agenda of teacher education as to Others is the production and furtherance of a set of understandings, of cognitive and affective perspectives, within the consciousness of its students about the act of teaching, about knowledge, about students, and for our purposes, about students who have been racially ascribed. This includes the confirmation of students' common-sense notions about ethnicity, minorities, traditional ideas of success and who deserves it, and the legitimacy of institutional hierarchies.

The problematic for teacher education is and has been (and surely will be) that this effort of value incorporation and/or enhancement has been relatively easy as to white, middle-class preservice teacher students, presumptively because they come to teacher education with similar values and with rationales already intact. However, minority students remain the Stranger (Greene, 1992), the unknown, even when they may have parallel value systems. But the spreading diversity in public schools in this country is another matter entirely. Generally resolved in the minds of teacher educators by the adoption of additive multiculturalism, there is a subsequent dualistic operative motif that affects, often directly, the minority student. First, recruit and send forth ("back") minority teachers, and, second, ignore the exigencies and virtually the existence of urban teaching altogether and thereby influence education students to not only ignore the existence of urban schools but minority students in future classrooms as well. Teacher education will often utilize texts and films that create the impression in the minds of its students that urban schools, like city centers, are dark, forbidding, and dangerous places. The implication is that urban schools represent metaphorically the Other and the situs of the Other, not a site of knowledge and success for whites (teachers). The specifics of the "sending" of black and Latino students "back" undergirds the understanding in white students' minds that urban schools are fit and apt places only for racial minority students. Teacher education, while willing to use the images of the urban school in a symbolic sense to maintain mainstream formulations of race and ethnicity for white students, fails to otherwise connotate such schools, leaving pre-service teachers with confirmed, if vague, notions of urban blackness and alienation. This has been brought home time and again in classrooms in educational methods classes, where mostly white, middle-class students evidence shock and surprise after reading Kozol's *Savage Inequalities* (1991)—this after three prior courses in teacher education that include in their syllabi issues of multicultural education. The shock and surprise are engendered very simply because they have never been confronted (even vicariously) with the knowledge or experience of urban schools. In their papers, they reiterate their horror over the conditions of such schools yet never wonder why they were unaware or resort so quickly to a blame-the-victim rationale.

As I noted in Chapter Two, the breadth and amount of ethnic diversity in schools today is increasing (Sleeter, 1994; Nieto, 1995; Banks, 1991; Darder, 1991). It must be staggering and somewhat ominous for white new teachers or white students in preservice teacher programs to contemplate the future breadth of demographic differences in American schools. At the same time, the ethnic diversity of teachers, both currently teaching and in teacher education programs, is decreasing. At the present time, fewer than 4 percent of all new teachers come from culturally different backgrounds—different in the sense of being non-white, non-Euro-American and non-middle class (Cannella & Reiff, 1994). Or to put it somewhat differently, as noted earlier in the book, by the turn of the century, the 25 largest districts in the country will have a majority of minorities. By the year 2010, non-whites will become the majority in many states and in most schools. Yet at the same time, it is estimated that for now and the near future, around 96 percent of new teachers are and will be white, and most will be middle-class and female.

Perhaps worse and of more concern is that this trend of a widening ethnic and cultural chasm between students and teachers seems to be self-sustaining. When one looks at the demographics of those students now enrolled in institutional teacher preparation programs, most (81%) are female and white (92%); fewer than 3% speak another language, and very few (9%) would choose to teach in an urban school (1991 *ATE Report*, cited in Cannella & Reiff, 1994). One can only assume that the percentage is even lower regarding their willingness to teach in an inner-city school. A number of studies and articles have addressed this issue of the lack of minority representation in teacher education (Hood & Parker, 1994; King, 1993; Haberman, 1989; Sleeter & Grant, 1991) and denoted a growing problem—the dearth of minority pre-service teachers contrasted with the increasing diversity of students. My own conjecture is that this represents only part of the problem; the other part is the perception of minority students harbored by teacher educators and the concomitant issues emanating from the unmediated understandings of difference which informs the practices of teacher education.

Minorities within Teacher Education

One of the problems with much of the research on minority representation in teacher education is that it is generally constructed around the unfortunate assumption that minority students should be encouraged and prepared to "go back"—to return to the urban schools from which it is presumed they originated. Several problems emanate from this assumption and the ways in which teacher educators interact pedagogically with minority students in their preservice certification programs.

This assumption assumes a normative mainstream understanding about minority students and teaching—that minority students are all from inner-city, or at least urban, schools. While certainly allowing for the minority students who come to colleges through programs such as HEOP, many, if not most, come from middle-class or working class families and suburban environments. Many come from racially mixed parents and do not perceive themselves as being Hispanic or African American. These students have little or no connection to inner-city or urban schools and communities, and their being "of color" is of no relevance except to teacher educators. In talking to many of these students they often do not identify with black or Latino campus issues or organizations and claim to perceive little discrimination in their lives. Whether their interpretation of their own lives is real or imagined is not the issue. What is at issue is how they are perceived by teacher education, which is by the assumption by which mainstream teacher educators understand and guide most students "of color." This exemplifies the general mainstream teacher education understanding and use as a basis for curriculum and pedagogy of ethnicity and race as being monolithic and perhaps even genetic versus socially constructed. This understanding will be discussed again later.

The assumption also presumes that urban and inner-city schools are where minority teachers belong—itself a view fraught with racist overtones. Hood & Parker in their 1994 article note particularly how minority students, many from urban schools, are conflicted by the prodding they receive from teacher educators to "return." Teacher education exerts a continual pressure on minority students to "go back," even if in error, using racially skewed language in the guise of being sensitive about students helping "their people." It functions as an ironic and debilitating contrast to teacher education's usual representation of "color blindedness." One result is to dissuade and/or discourage minority students from continuing in the program or to limit them to urban schools for experience.

If the further assumption on the part of teacher educators is that only, or predominantly, minority students should be prepared and sent to urban schools, they fail to recognize both the widespread need for teachers in these schools and the demographic implications that even if all minority students were to teach in urban schools, there simply would not be enough of them to answer the teaching needs of these schools. Even urban and inner-city schools reflect the "whitening" and feminization of teaching.

The effect of this assumption(s) which lie at the heart of teacher education's understanding of minority students (including preservice minority teachers) is to maintain the scourge of discrimination and racism through the implicative imposition that minority students will not and could not succeed in suburban schools and, worse, do not belong in suburban schools.

Thus, and importantly for our analysis of teacher education, by equating minority students with urban schools, teacher education facilitates and deepens the understanding of non-minority preservice teachers that preparation for and attention to the special knowledge and experiences required for teaching in urban schools are irrelevant and/or applicable only as lower status pedagogy and curriculum for minority students. As we will see, this attitude frames a critical part of the hidden curriculum of teacher education and extends to the broad unwillingness of institutional teacher education and teacher educators to address and confront issues of diversity, urban school teaching, and, ultimately, multiculturalism itself.

Teacher Education & Urban Schools

Recently, the Regents of the university system of New York State, in which I presently teach at a small private college, issued a call for schools of education to more actively address the issue of preparing teachers for urban schools. Ostensibly, this represents the university administrators' recognition and awareness of the growing gulf of diversity within education and the need for trained teachers in urban and inner-city schools. The problem lies, at least in New York, in the fact that most public and private university- or college-based teacher education programs are located out of those urban and/or inner-city environs AND many of their prospective preservice teachers come from similar environments. Thus, most of these smaller city and suburban teacher education sites have either tended to continue in their current ignorance of urban and inner-city teaching and schools or adopt an additive style multicultural education curriculum and assume that the job is complete. Even in the Capitol District of Albany where there are some five or six college-based teacher education programs, only the SUNY department has courses in urban education (and theirs is for graduates only, not preservice teachers). For most then, it remains business as usual. According to current research on teacher education, this is also true around the country.

> The subject matter, content, and nature of the experiences offered in preservice courses have undergone little change, especially in comparison to the clearly unmet needs of urban students and students of color. *Schools of education, although clearly aware of the changing demographics in urban schools and the failure of their graduates to successfully teach students of color, have done little to meet these challenges* [emphasis added]. (Grant, 1994, p. 1)

It should be noted that teacher education's responses to demographic changes and the minority students in certification programs derive to a great extent out of their own perception of the relative success of their programs with suburban schools. To be sure, critical pedagogists, neo-Marxists, feminists and critical multiculturalists have for some time been criticizing that perception of success (Giroux, 1992, 1988; McLaren, 1989, 1991; Lather, 1991; Shapiro, 1990; Purpel, 1989; Kanpol, 1992; Kincheloe & Steinberg, 1992; Darder, 1991; Weis, 1988; Nieto, 1995; Simon, 1992; to name only a few). However, mainstream (the great majority) teacher educators in general seem content with what they do for preservice suburban teachers. There is an attitude that, first, if it's not broke—don't fix it; and second, the instrumental logic that pervades teacher education suggests that an additive to the curriculum—a new test and more forms–are or should resolve the problem as to urban schools as it has so successfully in the past been perceived to do for suburban schools. Without getting into the question of whether in fact that is true or not, the typical response of teacher education of being content to add multicultural information to current course curriculum of teacher preparation is insufficient, ineffective, and potentially misleading—even damaging (Grant, 1994).

This might be construed as overly cynical. However, given that current educational reforms, such as Schools of Choice, Goals 2000, and Schools of Excellence (which have been heralded as constituting substantive reform in education), constitute for teacher educators little more than extensions of current curriculum and pedagogy, the cynicism seems warranted. Additionally, it needs to be remembered that many teacher educators have a vested interest in the status quo. A comment by Donaldo Macedo (1995), although referring to teachers in general, seems particularly on point here as to teacher educators:

> Their [educators'] naivete is never innocent but ideological. It is ideological to the degree that they have invested in a system that rewards them for reproducing and not questioning dominant mechanisms designed to produce power asymmetries along the lines of race, gender, class, culture, and ethnicity. (Macedo, 1995, p. 75)

Part of the problem is, as Purpel and Shapiro (1995) have noted, that schools and, parenthetically, teacher education departments have been extraordinarily successful at what they do—reproduction of mainstream values and knowledge, maintenance of hegemonic competition and hierarchialization, and assimilation or devaluation of difference. So when the call is issued to shift targets from suburban to urban schools, teacher education responds in like manner to calls for reform of suburban schools. The result is continued reproduction and transmission of those same concepts and the values that go to rationalize them within students' worldview. While for many this may seem simplistic, it needs to be understood that many, if not most, mainstream teacher educators perceive that what they do is instrumental, not ideological.

So what can we say about teacher education's connections to urban and inner-city schools beyond the issue of avoidance? Certainly teachers who have undergone formal preparation and teach in urban schools connect and link teacher educational understandings through the influence they and similarly trained administrators have on the internal curricular and pedagogical structures and rationales of the school as well as on the attitudes and practices of other teachers. The understandings, values and beliefs promulgated by teacher education are thus carried over into urban schools, including the perceptions as to the adequacy of additive forms of multicultural education.

To answer the question suggests two areas of further inquiry: first, the values and practices teacher education inculcates in prospective urban teachers, and second, the attitudes and perspectives with which teacher education perceives not only urban schools but also the students who are to be educated in those schools. The latter takes us into the realm of diversity and multiculturalism which we will take up later in this chapter. I will now turn to the question of teacher education's ideology, values and practices as they impact on urban schools.

Teaching Teachers to Teach

> The eyes do not see; they only record while the mind sees. To the extent that the mind can be ideologically controlled, it filters in order to transform what the eyes record . . . (Macedo, 1995, p. 80)

The above observation by Macedo is significant to our analysis of the connections between teacher education and urban schools, because it suggests that we only "see," comprehend, and understand that which we already have the capacity and/or experience to see, which itself is shaped by pre-existing ideological frameworks. Thus, teacher education students can and will only begin to comprehend urban teaching if they are provided the experience and ideological frameworks to do so. However, one of the major understandings that has come out of the critical or Left research on schools and teacher education over the past two decades is that schools function to reproduce the dominant ideologies of the society in which the school is located (Apple, 1982; Bowles & Gintis, 1976; Anyon, 1980; McLaren, 1989; Giroux, 1992, 1988b, 1983; Purpel, 1988; Shapiro, 1990; Kanpol, 1992) and in this regard teacher education functions similarly, thereby effectively limiting the seeing and/or the understanding.

That same research represents that the dominant values shaping that reproduced ideology are, to name a few, a belief in the inherency of meritocracy and the social hierarchy resulting from it (Giroux, 1988b, 1983; Kincheloe & Steinberg, 1992; McLaren, 1989; Apple, 1982), the intrinsic rightness of positivistic values such as neutrality of knowledge, objectivity, and Cartesian instrumental logic (Giroux, 1992) and a faith in the intrinsic superiority of Euro-American, western ethnocentrism and the need to ameliorate difference (Darder, 1991; Purpel, 1988; Purpel and Shapiro, 1995). Along with other side effects or nuances not necessarily concerning us here is the importance placed on an instrumental, cognitive approach to learning and the need to assimilate or nullify difference, specifically cultural, ethnic, and ideological differences.

All of the foregoing tends to reduce the curriculum of teacher education to that which can be routinized, sequentialized, and memorized—and, of course, objectively reduced to a test-based assessment of predicted learning. Teacher education is still wedded to the behavioral objectives of Tylerism and the concepts of developmental learning of Piaget and Bloom (Purpel, 1988; Weiner, 1993), which are deeply ingrained to the point where even class syllabi are prepared and presented to students with pages of course objectives. Prospective teachers are thus taught the schemata of such adroit pedagogical successes as "Bloom's Taxonomy," Assertive Discipline, "Hunterisms," and so forth. Recalling Macedo's (1995) quote above, preservice teachers learn through a combination of lecture, modeling, and acting out to incorporate these values and the pedagogical practices they rationalize. In addition, they interpret those experiences through the values (ideology) that they have already acquired through years of education under cognitive regimes of similar value structures and ideologies. This coincides with one of the purposes of mainstream schooling, to reinforce the reproduction of knowledge and experience by rationalizing both into existing truths.

> Most mainstream teaching practices, therefore, could be characterized as "membership-oriented" pedagogy which requires that teachers assist students in acquiring those necessary interpretive skills and forms of cultural capital that will enable them to negotiate contemporary zones of contest. (Sleeter & McLaren, 1995, p. 6)

Sleeter and McLaren's point, while accurate, it would seem, in illustrating the effect of teacher education on its clientele—future teachers—fails to note that to a significant extent teacher education students do not arrive in teacher education in a *tabula rasa* state. Instead they are in teacher education, a collegiate activity, because to a significant degree they have already acquired those "skills and forms of cultural capital" by being successful in their prior experiences at schooling. In other words, teacher educators and their students to a great extent are predeterminatively matched. Teacher education extends and confirms the rightness of their interpretations and cultural capital by furthering their investment in a value system which has seemingly rewarded them for accepting its validity in the first place.

My own teacher preparation was virtually useless, if not dangerous, for teaching in an inner-city school, and should be familiar to most teachers. Although couched in humanistic (human relations to use Sleeter & Grant's [1994] terminology) language, courses were grounded in the beliefs of manipulative meritocracy, objectivity, and instrumentalism. One learned that students can and should be manipulated, motivated and evaluated objectively, thereby negating the human empathetic impulse, which ideal caused many of us to enter teaching in the first place. There was a distinct emphasis in favor of emotional distancing and alienating hierarchial relations linked to strategies of control and authority. The predominant construct of teaching was psychological bolstered by the partial import of recontextualized phenomenological theory. Control techniques took precedence over a concern for transformation and student understanding of their own power. "Knowledge" and "learning" in the cognitive sense became signifiers for content and skills and concerns for process and effectiveness took on meanings extrinsic to context.

Many teacher education courses still contain exhortations to exercise effective classroom management framed around actual or some variant use of Assertive Discipline (Kanter & Kanter, 1976), which emphasizes the implementation of pyramidal threats and intimidation. The presumption is that the teacher is the authority and collaborative, communal or democratic approaches to discipline are untrustworthy. Not only were these contradictions not questioned, the implicit problems of classroom utility never arose. Method courses often have as their center the construction of behavioral objectives, which promotes the objective quantification of both teaching and assessment often propounded against the background of a "mythic norm" (Lorde, 1990) of student experience, culture, and knowledge. And, of course, prospective teachers come to such preparation in the expectation that teacher education will be an extension of the styles of teaching and learning that they have experienced for years. Clearly teacher education doesn't disappoint them:

> The life experiences of most teachers demonstrate their allegiance to the ethic of vertical mobility, self-improvement, hard work, deferred gratification, self-discipline, and personal achievement. These individualistic values rest on the assumption that the social system works well, is essentially fair, and moves society slowly but inevitably toward progress. (Sleeter, 1994, p. 257-258)

Given Sleeter's (1994) insight, it is little wonder that preservice teachers with all their emotional baggage and anxiety about teaching and professional success begin to think in ways that reproduce normative values about education and schooling as well as potential relations with peers and students.

Unfortunately, the result of teacher education is to produce eager, sincere new teachers who have incorporated the lessons of teacher education or expanded their pre-existing understandings and value structures by and through teacher education's hidden curriculum and are now prepared to complete the circle imbued with what Giroux (1988) has called a "technocratic rationality." Instead of becoming reflective transformers of consciousness and knowing, preservice teachers have been reduced to little more than mere technicians of particularized practices. In effect, their experiences in teacher education have deskilled them rather than the reverse (Kanpol, 1992). Instead of empowering teachers to develop a critical understanding of their purpose as educators, most teacher education programs foster a dependency on predefined curriculum, outdated classroom strategies and techniques, and traditionally rigid classroom environments (Darder, 1991). The result is a continuance or perpetuation of similar classrooms to those from which they came and/or experienced throughout their personal histories. This reproduction occurs to such a degree that few are able to envision teaching outside the scope of barren classroom settings, lifeless instructional packages, bland textbooks, standardized tests, and the use of meritocratic systems for student performance evaluation (Darder, 1991).

So how does this connect to urban education and/or pedagogy in inner-city schools and classrooms? If we refer to the descriptions of inner-city curriculum and pedagogical styles in Chapters Two and Three, the prevalent teaching methodologies and rationales prevalent in urban schools should seem similar to the practices advocated by teacher education. Teacher education places the same emphasis on preservice teachers learning through concretized steps, routines, and specified control approaches, which are accurately replicated in urban classrooms. Urban pedagogy is highly structured around transmittal [or "deposit" to use Freire's (1970) term] teaching, routines that rarely vary from day to day, and teaching that predetermines recall styles of evaluation, with an emphasis on cognitive learning approaches toward material that is usually irrelevant to the students and their lives in their communities. Peter McLaren in his 1989 text, *Life in Schools*, discusses his discovery of this contradiction of pedagogical irrelevance which affirmed my own struggle to reconcile what I was to teach and what students disclosed were the dynamics of life in the "hood":

> In the streets, knowledge was "felt," classroom knowledge was objectified and often sullied by an inflated rationalism, . . . In the street, students made use of bodily engagement, organic symbols, and intuition. Students struggle daily to reconcile the disjunction between the lived meaning of the streets and the subject-centered approach to learning in the classroom. (McLaren, 1989)

There are a significant number of similarities between the practices taught in teacher education and those pedagogically found in urban classrooms, not to mention suburban ones as well. In teacher education, as in inner-city schools, material is generally taught within a cognitive approach with rare use of affective engagement. It is often esoteric and seemingly irrelevant to the experience of the prospective teachers. There is a tragic irony in the realization that as a result of teacher education, teachers in inner-city schools expend time and energy teaching material that is equally irrelevant to them and to the students. Similarly to the classroom management techniques found in urban classrooms (and too many suburban classrooms as well), teacher education engages in a substantive use of deferred gratification schemes as a form of extrinsic motivation (combined with the fear of poor grades) through the promise of control over classrooms and the increased potentiality of jobs if success in teacher education has been earned by the student. Both grades and future employment are the carrot for adherence to the rules and practices of teacher education and of the urban classroom. Knowing that for inner-city students the equation is worthless, an interesting query would be whether there is any similarity in perspective to preservice teacher education students. Or have they already invested so much that the equation needs to be true?

The issue of control and power, known euphemistically as classroom management (prospective teachers are usually tested and graded on their acquisition of so-called skills), is a major, if not the major, theme in teacher education. Students are taught routines and procedures virtually guaranteed to impose order in any classroom. They are also taught a mediating interpretation that allows for mitigation of teaching failure. That is, if these rules and practices prove insufficient, they should look for an external cause, i.e., to the student, his/her parents, community, race, etc:

> The teachers were generally unwilling to attribute a student's lack of success to a characteristic inherent in the child or to their own instructional programs. They therefore moved outside the classroom to find the cause of the student's problems. These cases most often rested on their students' home lives and parents. (Sleeter & Grant, 1994, p. 48; citing a study by Richardson et al., 1989 on teachers attributing causes of risk)

So, too, in inner-city classrooms is discipline and control over students highly regarded. Administrators of urban and inner-city schools are consistently more solicitous toward teachers who exercise a high degree of classroom control and order, not the teachers who emphasize creativity and student-centered learning, which can lead to somewhat more energetic and expansive learning situations.

At Washington Middle School, it was often the teachers whose pedagogical styles were stultifying, unimaginative and geared toward rigid classroom order who were publicly referred to by the administration as being the better teachers. Interestingly, the teachers at the two extremes, in the sense of combining creativity and order, were marginalized by the administration at the school. Teachers whose classroom demeanor entailed significant order but who invoked creativity in their teaching and those whose classrooms were rowdy but functioned as learning centers were equally ignored by the office. One example of this that stands out in my recollection had to do with the teacher who routinely allowed no more than twenty-five select students, sending the other twenty or so to float the halls. A common, often daily, occurrence for a number of us was to have these kids from Mrs. Brown's class knock on our classroom doors, begging for admittance to avoid being caught and suspended by the assistant principal. The knocking and pleading would start about five minutes after classes started and continue for about fifteen as kids found shelter. The entire process both increased the number of children in our rooms and effectively disrupted the classes. Given the preselected number of students (most of whom were in the GATE program), her classes tended to be disciplined and quiet. One year during the annual selection of the "Teacher of the Year," the committee (four teachers who volunteered) selected a young teacher whom we felt was extraordinary. However, when we met with the principal she advised us that our choice was unacceptable because Miss Davis's classes were too noisy. She said that Mrs. Brown was obviously the better teacher since she had such quiet classes and would be the choice despite some rather vociferous disagreement on the part of the committee. Mrs. Brown was given the award by the principal two years in a row at graduation.

A premium was placed by the administration on order, quiet, and discipline, in many cases even where it was at the expense of student learning. This should not be too surprising, except perhaps in its extreme degree, since classroom management is a primary theme of teacher education. I have heard too many teacher educators and cooperating teachers proclaim that "good discipline yields good teaching" too many times to believe otherwise.

It should be kept clearly in mind that these techniques and approaches are intended for use in suburban schools, since as previously discussed, teacher education pays little heed to the needs, conditions and exigencies of urban schools. Ironically, the result of teacher preparation is a teacher admirably suited ideologically for teaching in an inner-city school. Equally ironic, however, is that teacher education refuses to acknowledge issues of culture and society which causes the same teacher to not so admirably fail in an inner-city school.

One might argue that the above approaches to pedagogy and their respective rationales (values) as instilled and/or confirmed by teacher education are successful in suburban schools, although very few in this country from any particular political persuasion seem to regard American schools as successful. However, the same argument must acknowledge the consummate failure of urban and inner-city schools, a failure which perforce must include the teaching and the teachers.

One significant reason, among many, is the preparation given by teacher education which has effectively acted to narrow the range of curricular and pedagogical choices available to prospective teachers. This subsequently acts to narrow the ontological possibilities by which they can come to grips with the conditions and cultural differences they face in an urban classroom. Macedo (1995) argues that teachers, like most specialists in many fields, have accepted the dominant ideology reducing them to technicians of instrumental pedagogy and curriculum. He notes that teachers, by virtue of the specialized training they receive in an assembly line of ideas and aided by the mystification of this transferred knowledge, seldom reach the critical capacity of analysis to develop a coherent comprehension of the world (Macedo, 1995).

While I generally agree with Macedo here, it seems to me that on one point, that of a lack of a coherent worldview, he is being too simplistic and structural. Teachers, even young teachers, have a coherent view of their world; however, that worldview, while perhaps narrow since it is based only on an unmediated interpretation of their experience in schools, has been further confirmed and desensitized by the experiences and teachings of teacher education.

Simplistically, these young teachers fail in droves in inner-city schools because they do not have the reflective experiences (or skills, to use teacher education's terminology) to broaden their horizons and include and work with the differences they face in an inner-city school environment. For all the rhetoric on reflective practice to be found in educational textbooks and teacher education literature, reflection and critical thinking are still confused by teacher education with memorization and mathematical or logical problem solving.

Throughout the entire process, whether because of the ideological investment of its actors or the hegemonic impact of mainstream value structures, teacher education effectively rejects self-analysis, questioning of its own value systems, and analysis of the social structures in which it and schools are embedded. Again, although Macedo is writing about education in general, his comments are equally applicable to teacher education:

> Seldom do teachers require students to analyze the social and political structures that inform their realities. Rarely do students read about the racist and discriminatory practices that they face in school and the community at large. (Macedo, 1995, p. 80)

Practitioners of teacher education assiduously maintain this atheoretical stance. Few courses or teacher educators attempt to pierce the technocist, instrumental veil of teacher education's configuring ideology to tell students that the social structures and value systems of education are not fixed but social (i.e., human) constructs. Much of teacher education's practices reconfirms for students what they learned in their own school years—that knowledge and experience exist outside of human effect or control—and disaffirm that the curriculum, subject matters, and practices of teaching or schooling always emerge out of a humanly (that is to say, socially) matrixed interplay of human conceptions of the social order (Greene, 1993a). Teacher education students find it disturbing or unsettling to struggle to understand the concepts of identity, values, ethnicity, race, gender, or even history as being socially constructed rather than fixed or transcendent. They resist coming to terms with how historical depictions of human nature have configured historicity of education and schools, even their own.

The result is often that the tautologies of teacher education leave them little room for understanding that which is not similar or understanding how others can truly be different in more than degree. This leaves new teachers dangerously deficient when they are thrust into coping with the conditions and variables of cultural values, experiences, and knowledges of an inner-city classroom. They have only the certainties of teacher education to fall back on, which derive from how teacher education as an institution and individual teacher educators perceive minority students, whether in suburban or urban schools.

Teacher Education & Theories of Difference

Teacher education, being a part of education, which itself forms a spoke in the social mandala, is, of course, rationalized and justified by the same paradigms as the greater society. Rarely has it found it necessary to step out of that character to act as an agent of radical social change. In a society of constants, teacher education has to be seen as intrinsically conservative and a bastion of the status quo. Certainly this should not be too surprising given that throughout the history of the country, education has served to maintain the dominance of the mainstream through assimilation and deculturalization (Spring, 1990; Kliebard, 1992; Karier, 1986). For our purposes, this means that the same value-laden cultural meanings as to racial minorities that are found in the mainstream form the basic understandings and conventions of teacher education. The culture of education mirrors that of the larger culture insofar as teachers and students willingly and unwillingly situate themselves within a highly politicized field of power relations that is constructed of unjust race, class and gender relationships (Sleeter & McLaren, 1995).

The significant impact of deficiency theory in construing dominant understandings as to racial minorities is additionally skewed by the attitudes about the urban that Stephen Haymes (1995) noted. While appalled by the conditions of ghetto and barrio, mainstream Americans (including most students of teacher education) interpret them as self-induced. That conclusion resonates within the systemic ideological messages about hard work, the vitality of individualism and competition, and implicit confirmations of white superiority. Thus, in general, scholarship on urban schools provided teacher education students generally focuses on either the deficient (i.e., "at risk") attributes of the children of those schools as representative of community values or the conditions of the schools themselves (Weiner, 1993). Somewhat more complexly, the conditions of the schools are blamed further on the perceived deteriorating values and cultural behaviors of those same communities. Factors such as the State, social value systems, and racialized segregation are rarely introduced, much less seen as determinative.

The prevalence of ethnicity theory allows the curriculum in teacher education to deny the significance of visible, physiological marks of ancestry and of the history of colonialization and harsh subjugation that Europeans and Euroamericans extended over other peoples (Omi & Winant, 1986). In so doing it denies white social institutions any complicity in the subordinate status of people of color. White teachers of students of color need some way of understanding why people of color have not done as well in society as whites have (Sleeter, 1993), and this is found in the combination of ethnicity and deficiency theories. These underwrite the practices of blaming the victim and not the promulgator of victimization.

For example, much to my chagrin, I recently required a class of student teachers to read Kozol's *Savage Inequalities* (1991). The reaction by the students was almost uniformly that the conditions of the schools described by Kozol were appalling and shocking. However, their ideologically grounded reactions framed their questions about causation: "Why do those people allow it to stay that way?" "Why don't the parents care?" "What is wrong with them?" The last question clearly connotes that, although the exact "wrongness" was unknown to the students, something was definitely not-right with the families of the communities. In their analysis, they argued that the conditions Kozol reported were due to urban families (a misapprehension in itself) having poor values, that they are lazy and content to be on welfare. They made no connection to the greater society and resisted connections to racialized structuring of cities, neighborhoods, schools and teaching. While granting that the societal and institutional causes of such schools are perhaps outside their experience as generally white, middle-class folks, it was equally apparent that their only frame of reference was from within a deficiency theory that made it seem logical and natural to blame the victim.

In explanation, Lois Weiner (1993), perhaps in consideration of Kozol's 1991 text, suggests that most influential depictions of teaching in city schools are those by persons who write exposés of what transpires there—a tradition which serves to generate blame rather than explain recurrent patterns (Weiner, 1993). Additionally, she confirms that the encompassing ideological frame is one balanced on understandings of deficiency. She notes that the scarcity of scholarship about how conditions in urban schools affect learning reinforces the proclivity to study student failure using student- and teacher-deficit paradigms (Weiner, 1993).

To begin to apprehend the intertwined social construction of race, poverty, and urban education as described by researchers such as Kozol (1991), Michelle Fine (1991), Lois Weis (1988), and others, new teachers must develop a critical understanding of the intricate and profound complexion of race, ethnicity, ideology, gender, ethics, and similar issues that schools and teachers of education neglect to address (Macedo, 1995). Such an understanding might begin with the deconstruction of the configuring force of ethnicity and deficiency theories in education and, in particular, within teacher education courses.

The reaction by my students to the matter of racial bias and discrimination after reading Kozol (1991) corroborates Sleeter's (1995) study on white teachers in a workshop on multiculturalism. She noted that most of the teachers interpreted race and multicultural education through their understanding of ethnicity theory (Sleeter, p. 160) and, although clearly operating out of a deficiency ideology, insisted that they interacted with racial minority students as if they were the same as white students, i.e., "color-blind" (Sleeter, p. 161). Sleeter's descriptions of the participants' reactions are enlightening.

Trying not to see what is obvious (color) and to suppress the negative and stereotypical imagery with which one is bombarded requires considerable psychological energy. Education about race conflicts with many white teachers' strategies of denial, compounding the psychological energy they must expend to continue being "blind" to color . . . since they did not perceive that there would be anything worthwhile to learn about African Americans and Latinos, or about racism, and since constant and direct attention to these groups brought their own negative associations, as well as white guilt, to the surface, some of the white teachers stopped coming. (Sleeter, 1993, p. 162-163)

My own students insisted adamantly that they, too, were colorblind and that the presence of the one black student (who had by the way been assigned by the department to student teach in an urban school) in the class represented progress, justifying both their assertion of color-blindness and their usage of deficiency and ethnicity theories to which they clung for understanding. Although, as I noted earlier, this belief structure forms a contradictive prevalency in our culture and teacher education, the attitudes of Sleeter's (1993) teachers and my own students exemplify the profound grip of both theories on education. It is through the respective lenses of these two theories that prospective and new teachers diligently incorporate the lessons of teacher education as to racial minority students. These same assumptions, as well as teacher education's notorious aversion to both theoretical discourses and ethnography (or other forms of qualitative research excepting only the ubiquitous "case study"), resist practical and pedagogical inclusion of sociology and social research. It is thus no accident that educators fail to apply social science research about the characteristics of urban schools to teacher preparation. This has been due to the hegemony of an ideology that analyzes student and teacher performance, and consequently teacher preparation, without reference to broader political, social, and economic developments or conditions in schools (Weiner, 1993).

Teacher education's maintenance of the preeminence of these two theories as explicative of urban school failure has profoundly and deeply marred its incorporation of two decades of research on race, diversity, and cultural interactions. In the face of changes in racial demographics in all schools, teacher education departments have adopted what is loosely termed as multicultural education. Yet this, too, has been shaped and contorted by both ethnicity and deficiency theoretical understandings. The result has been a shallow and instrumental applicability of multicultural knowledge in the form of cultural adaptations and contributions to teacher education.

Teacher Ed. & Multiculturalism: A Limited Partnership

In order to extend our analysis of the linkages between teacher education and inner-city schools, and within teacher education's justification of its level and practices of preparation of students for teaching in those schools, we now turn to examine its incorporation of multicultural education, which is predictably foreshortened from multiculturalism's range of possibilities. The incorporation of multiculturalism is also contextured by being within the scope of teacher education's ideologized relationship to minorities, race, and theorization of social structures. One should keep in mind that the only reasons that teacher education includes multiculturalism at any level are academic and governmental pressures and its dim awareness of the demographic changes in schools. However, even those pressures have not been enough to engage teacher education in any more than a perfunctory, truncated version of superficial multicultural education, still framed and grounded within teacher education's ideological value systems. Typically treating multicultural education as either supplemental or as curricula specially suited for students of color, teacher education programs fold multicultural concepts and knowledge into patterns similar to its meritocratic school practices that explain school failure by attributing it to individual (or cultural) deficiencies (Densmore, 1995).

Akin to how the public schools and education in general have processed and limited the potentials of multiculturalism, teacher education tends to incorporate assimilationist and human relations modes of multicultural education. These formats of multicultural education tend to be delineated within teacher education only in terms of the additive contributions of minorities deemed appropriate for student teachers learning about the learning and behavioral characteristics of specific minority groups. This formatting maintains and confirms the white recognition of minority deficiencies (Weiner, 1993). This results in the retention by student teachers of certain assumptions about what those labelled as minorities should learn.

In 1994, Hood and Parker published their research on how well and/or thoroughly teacher education was incorporating multiculturalism. They found that many teacher education programs were paying scant attention to diversity and multiculturalism, that multicultural concepts were relegated solely to foundations courses and/or electives and that "no course really dealt with issues of power and authority in minority schools except for the foundations course" (Hood & Parker, 1994, p. 167). They noted that the teacher education preparation courses had a decided white middle-class focus and that the courses failed to prepare students in any serious way to deal with diversity in the public schools. Their conclusions are indicative of the profound failure of teacher education to face and grapple with the issues of race, sociocultural studies and/or the social ideologies of diversity. Hood and Parker reported that minority students perceived a general lack of sensitivity on the part of the majority white teacher education faculty and that faculty and students often held racist assumptions about how to teach students of color (Hood & Parker, p. 168). In the study, minority students perceived that their teacher preparation programs were deficient with regard to racial diversity and that many efforts to change teacher education faculty with respect to diversity have failed. Not surprisingly, these students felt that faculty and the teacher education curriculum are divorced from the racial and cultural realities of students of color (Hood & Parker, p. 169).

In the teacher education departments that I have been involved in over the last few years, at both small private colleges and medium-sized state universities, none offered or required a course in multicultural and/or urban education as part of the credentialing process. Even where the college or university itself listed such courses within other departments, teacher education students were discouraged or precluded from taking such courses by education faculty. The rationales for the preclusion were various but always involved assertions as to students' limited time within the credentialing sequence of courses mixed with disparaging remarks as to the practical efficacy of such courses. These courses were often perceived by teacher education faculty as being too academic and insufficiently practical, that they concentrated on theory and not pedagogy, as if the two are and should be oppositional. The result is predictable; student teachers are generally multicultural illiterates. At some colleges, teacher education departments do include what they euphemistically term "multicultural material" within foundations or methods courses. This material is almost entirely of the contributive variety and framed by perceptions of minority deficiencies. Additionally, teacher education departments claim to have met any needs for experiencing minority differences through the requirement of student field observations and experiences. It is to these and the question of their ability to affect student teachers' perceptions that we now turn.

The Question of Field Experience & Difference

In final avoidance of the issues of racism and social dysfunction that lie at the heart of multiculturalism, teacher education's adoption of an abbreviated multiculturalism has become a fictional substitute for sustained relationships on the part of white, middle-class teacher education faculty and students with the socially oppressed in a society that retains many of its historical practices of apartheid in schooling (Roman, 1993). These attitudes also account for the disturbing results of preservice student reactions to field experiences, which teacher education has used for some time as a methodology to immerse a student in a classroom (euphemistically referred to as the "real world," connoting that the students' worlds are not "real" or valid), and simultaneously immersing them into the values and ideological understandings and practices of the cooperating teachers at the selected school site. Within teacher education the rationale for the field experience has come increasingly to be situated within the human relations (or "human sensitivity") modality of multicultural education. The immersion experience is justified by claiming that it will provide awareness of difference, knowledge of diversity in others, appreciation for cultural (meaning ethnic in the sense of ethnicity theory) distinctions, linkages to the real world of classrooms and students, and other similar rationales.

The typical field experience is generally a course requirement that the student visit a school site, shadow a teacher or spend time in a classroom, and write some form of report or journal describing the experience. Anecdotal evidence suggests that these students find the back of the room and observe, hardly an immersive experience. Similarly, the journals and reports tend to be limited to descriptive chronologies with little, if any, reflective and/or analytic material. In my own experience and from talking to other teacher educators, the reports contain little reflection, poor linkages to foundational course issues, even less connection and analysis of the dynamics of relations within the classrooms observed, and little critical deconstruction of issues of race, gender, power, authority, or ideological contexts. Thus, little immersion and even less contact with the Other occurs in field experiences despite teacher education's claims to the contrary. More often, or so both anecdotal and formal research suggests, the notion of the "fictional substitute" operates to further student notions of white versus the minority student Other, accounting for the lack of attitudinal and belief changes among pre-service teachers. Farber & Amaline (1994) reported that approximately 99 percent of teacher education departments use some form of field experience and that these experiences are generally considered to be positive and valuable for future teachers. However, Farber and Amaline (1994) noted that a number of educational researchers over the last decade have reported that early field experiences seem to promote simplistic utilitarian perspectives on teaching, including an entrenchment of authoritarianism, rigidity, and impersonalism with a decreasing emphasis on the humanistic impulse. Journals, reports and classroom discussion confirm that very few students undergo any significant modification of the views they held prior to the field experience. If anything, their understandings about teaching, students, hierarchial relations within the classroom, discipline, and what constitutes learning and knowledge are substantiated by the experience. Very few seem able to make connections from theoretical perspectives presented in the preservice course to events and interactions they observe in the field. They are relatively noninterrogative as to curricular and pedagogical assumptions, teacher relations, the interplay of power, minority relations to the school and teachers, and issues such as tracking, tests, stultifying lesson presentations by teachers, and evaluation. They do write detailed descriptions of classrooms, teacher interactions with students, and the roles of various participants. However, it is rare to read a journal that questions either the interactions or the relationships.

The problem with teacher education's solution of immersion (field experience) in urban schools is the ideological and cultural baggage by which the students interpret the experience without any alternative inquiry or critical reflection being provided by the faculty. The experience is still filtered through the norms of the dominant mainstream white value system. In terms of their observing minority students, the students operate within an understanding that being white is an entitlement, a form of raceless subjectivity by which they interpret the relationships between minority students and others. "That is, being white becomes the invisible norm for how the dominant culture measures its own civility" (Sleeter, 1993, p. 167).

Christine Sleeter (1993) noted along, with Martin Haberman (1992), that often teaching white students about racism results in tenacious resistance against notions of societal complicity (as opposed to blaming the victim) causing field experience students to reject lasting changes in white-oriented prerogatives. Haberman observed that students generally use these field experiences to selectively perceive and reinforce their initial preconceptions (Haberman, 1992). The effect of teacher education then is to reinforce, rather than reconstruct, how white students view children of color according to Sleeter (1993). She added that although some studies on field experience of preservice teachers evidenced some swing in attitudes, most of the research results represent that white students incorporate no significant or permanent changes in values or behaviors. None of these results should be surprising given the tendency of multicultural education as incorporated within education to "celebrate diversity" without adequately analyzing social power differentials positioned by racial categories and their consequent inequalities; even the phrase "people of color" still implies that white culture is the hidden norm against which all other racially subordinate groups are measured (Roman, 1993, p. 71).

However, in spite of teacher education's reluctance to engage fully in a critical or reconstructive multiculturalism in courses or as part of a reflective field experience, the conclusion of many researchers on student teaching is that extended experiences in culturally different schools and communities are essential (Grant, 1994; Haberman, 1992). The recommendations of several such researchers is that such immersion needs to be as totalized as possible. For example, several studies (Cooper, Beare & Thorman, 1990; Mahan, 1984; Nava, 1990; cited in Grant, 1994, p. 8) reported on projects in which student teachers actually lived in the communities where they taught. Unfortunately, while this sounds promising, we can only speculate on the results from the students' perspective since the reports were couched in the nominal language of teacher education.

> The opportunity to teach in Texas with its exposure to another culture appears to generate among participants an articulated willingness to *demonstrate multicultural competencies.* (Cooper, Beare & Thorman, 1990, p. 3) [emphasis added]

> Young teachers immersed in the local culture make culturally oriented adjustments in their *teaching strategies and styles.* (Mahan, 1984, p. 109) [emphasis added]

It is unfortunate that the researchers could not move themselves out of their mainstream technocratic analysis as they were expecting the students to do. We have only conjecture as to what "multicultural competencies" might be, but the overt language is again representative of those membership skills to which McLaren (1995) referred. If nothing else, the reports suggest how difficult it will be to articulate significant change in teacher education to relocate it out of the instrumental paradigm. Put differently, while the reports suggest that possible changes occurred in student perceptions and attitudes, the reporting language itself presents two conclusions: first, that it is difficult to ascertain any potential for change given the authors' use of objectifying techno-speak, since the language suggests that the writer immersed in that paradigm would in all likelihood not recognize a potentiality for critical change; and second, that assuming change in student understandings and behavior did occur, the ideological structure of teacher education represented by the language will effectively channel it into normative mainstream ways of understanding change, thereby limiting any critical potentialities arising from student experience.

On the other hand, what should be recognized from these reports is the potential for preservice students to adopt a broader, more transformative understanding of minority students and inner-city education as a result of teacher education's adoption of a more immersive format of field experience. However, the problem regarding field experience and teacher education is similar to that of multiculturalism and teacher education. Given teacher education's infatuation with instrumental practices, its atheoretical stance, its grounding in positivistic logic and its justificatory reliance on state mandates and regulations, field experience, like multicultural education, is likely to remain defined by form rather than substance. This seems to be true of both student teaching itself, as well as introductory course field experiences.

Conclusion

The efforts of these last two chapters have been to interrogate from a multitude of sources the nuances, meanings and practices of the connections between urban school teaching, multicultural education and teacher education. At the risk of seeming too cynical and perhaps simplistic, one can't help but conclude that for the most part, all three remain deeply entrenched in what Sleeter & Grant (1988) reference as business as usual. Rather than make any serious attempt to interact with inner-city schools and populations to effect change toward a democratically diverse society, including education, one that embraces a political and economic system that is not supported by the vested interests of segregation, racism, and inequalities, teacher education chooses to maintain its technocratic aloofness. Even its adoption of the language of human relations with its emphasis on sensitivity and empathetic care has not construed for teacher educators another mode of perceiving students and classrooms. Even where teacher educators and departments adopted basic prescriptions of multiculturalism (such as assimilation and/or human relations), they adopted only those components that preserve instrumental competencies and skills and their underlying value-based rationales in the defense of white monoculturalism. Within teacher education, multiculturalism has become acceptable only when it is reduced to a pedagogy of transmission (Giroux, 1995).

As Giroux argues here, teacher education needs to rethink the issues of diversity and multiculturalism as part of a more significant attempt to "understand how issues regarding national identity, culture and ethnicity can be rewritten in order to enable dominant groups to examine, acknowledge, and unlearn their own privilege" (Giroux, 1995, p. 108). This demands an approach to multiculturalism that not only addresses the context of massive black unemployment, overcrowded schools, a lack of recreational facilities, dilapidated housing and racist policing, but a concerted attempt to view most racism in this country not as an issue of black lawlessness but as an expression of white supremacy (Giroux, 1995).

However, as imperative as Giroux's vision is, it runs headlong into those vested paradigmatically fueled interests of teacher education and the greater society where privilege is intertwined with that "mythic norm" (Lorde, 1990). To rewrite identity and culture in such a way that the dominant groups are willing to allow their own unprivileging seems naive in the face of terrible righteousness, ethnocentricity and outright privilege. So long as America's elite can convince the rest that the social pie is finite and only competitive, meritocratic individualism can obtain a portion, then we will continue to see racially based human triaging in this society. Until such time as that paradigm and its constituted social practices and behaviors begin to cause serious economic, political, and social discomfort for whites, and what Macedo calls the "Big Lie" is undercut in legitimacy, the politics of multicultural democratic subversion will continue to be marginalized.

On a similar note, in their 1994 article for the ATE journal report on diversity in teacher education, Canella & Reiff (1994, p. 37-44) argue that through the incorporation of social reconstructionism into teacher education "prospective teachers can be given multiple opportunities to critique and deconstruct their own social beliefs, the beliefs of others in society, and the conditions of schooling within society" (Cannella & Reiff, p. 42). Yet, the contretemps still remains—"schooling can either become an avenue for collaboration between multiple realities or a vehicle in which particular realities are imposed" (Cannella & Reiff, p. 42; citing Liston & Zeichner, 1991).

Unfortunately, like most critical pedagogists who must struggle against despair and cynicism, I believe that teacher education and education in general, particularly where it intersects with inner-city schools, will choose the latter course as it generally has in this country. Perhaps, as Cornel West suggests, there are other winds blowing; the social pressures are building for radical paradigmatic changes in how we as a society generate hope and vision (West, 1993). The key argument for unlocking that vision, West believes, is that we are a democratic society built and fabricated by immigrants—by generations of Others, albeit skewed by a market, positivistic mentality, racism, and narrow concepts of what it means to be human. But its rhetoric and a particular vision of the society's history are part of its ideology as well, and the struggle becomes to tap those notions in a manner both subversive and truth-telling by appealing to its own ideals (West, 1993a). One arena for such subversion is that of urban education and teacher education.

The next chapter will address those issues within the original venue of inner-city education in an attempt to respond to West's (1993a) seminal questions—what is the moral content of one's identity? What are the moral and political grounds for this vocation of teaching? Within the notion of what constitutes the moral, I believe there are spaces through which an agentic pedagogy as advocated by critical multiculturalists can increase democratic possibility within localized points of urban schools. Recognizing that social movements for profound change, conservative or radical, are grounded not in political or academic argument, but in emotions and connected notions of the ethical, Chapter Six will argue for a vision framed in the ethical components of critical multiculturalism within the inner-city schools.

The argument will not be made that such a possibility can or will drive greater social change nor will I presume to argue that one concept will be applicable to all urban schools. However, I do believe that there are possibilities within the spaces of teaching within inner-city schools that can effect a border pedagogy that will nurture change for these schools and their communities. Critical pedagogists argue that education and social relations represent sites of struggle, politically, economically, and ideologically (Shapiro, 1990; Giroux, 1992, 1983; Darder, 1991; hooks & West, 1991; Purpel, 1987; Kanpol & McLaren, 1995), and while I do not dispute that concept, as I have noted before, all too often the potentials for change are muted by the breadth of the arena in which we seek to struggle. Given the questionable hope for broad social change in this country as to race and the limited impact on that change that can be effected by inner-city education, the next chapter will argue for localizing sites of struggle in both the micro and macro senses. By that, I mean that perhaps all we can truthfully hope to change is inner-city education itself in localized terms and conditions, and through that change effect a similar change in some levels and purposes of teacher education. Although that view might be interpreted as a limitation, I will argue that instead it frees us to advocate and practice a democratic possibility within a specific terrain of struggle; one that can be ethically based and represent dynamic change in inner-city locales.

Notes

1. Recently there have been a number of excellent substantive texts written on urban and inner-city schools, both from the descriptive and from the analytic or critical perspective. In particular are the following: Fine, Michelle. (1991). *Framing Drop-Outs*, Albany, NY: SUNY Press; Kozol, Jonathan. (1991). *Savage Inequalities; Children in America's Schools*, New York: Crown Publishers; Solomon, R. (1992). *Black Resistance in High School*, Albany, NY: SUNY Press; Weiner, Lois. (1993). *Preparing Teachers for Urban Schools: Lessons from Thirty Years of School Reform*, NY: Teachers College Press.

CHAPTER SIX

The Search for New Connections

> There have always been newcomers in this country; there have always been strangers. There have always been young persons in our classrooms we did not, could not see or hear. [M. Greene, 1993a, p. 13]

Reprise

Up to now, the purpose of this text has been to examine urban education and its justifying and constructing paradigms and practices, and as it is affected by the larger society and teacher education. I have attempted to peer beneath the curtain drawn by mainstream education's rhetoric and rationales, statistics and compensatory programs, and to explore the cultural ideologies and educational practices that have countenanced the continuation of the conditions and results of inner-city schools in this country. The text has drawn from a number of sources—ethnography, critical multiculturalism, postmodern notions of identity and difference, and even liberal theorizing on urban and teacher education in a venture–not to ponder the "how-to's" of teaching in an inner-city school, but to theorize on the current dominant constructs of urban education and to decipher the connections between teacher education and the quandaries of multiculturalism.

Chapter One delineated the statistics representing American urban educational and social failure—the poverty, the dropouts, the economic alienation of millions of people of color. Central to this chapter (and the entire text) is the assertion that present urban social and educational conditions derive from and are rationalized within the historically constructed moral sickness of *racism* that has long been justified by the dominant culture. This sickness frames normative understandings of those who appear and are different from the Euro-American white norm, the dominant economic and political positions in regard to minorities, immigrants and the urban, and mediates the debate in this country as to who deserves and who does not.

Chapter Two outlined the current and historical mainstream responses to urban education and discussed how cultural values such as racism, Eurocentrism, and rational empiricism all construct, shape, and further the particular curricular and pedagogical practices of inner-city schools. Chapter Two also attempted to give the reader some understanding of the evolution of modern segregated schools, urban communities and the context in which teaching occurs in these schools. Additionally, the chapter introduced the reader to the styles and justifications of curriculum and pedagogy in inner-city schools.

Chapter Three used a phenomenological lens to open the reader to the exigencies of educational practices within inner-city schools. Framed by the narrative of my own experiences as a teacher, I wanted the experiences of teachers and students to evoke an awareness of the profound need for change in urban schools and to convey that the immediate accountability for the conditions within them rests within the practices of mainstream education. However, the primary purpose of the chapter was to invite the reader to vicariously share the atmosphere, the language, the frustrations, the purposelessness and the bitter-sweet joys of a special place.

Chapter Four described and critiqued the current educational panacea for urban and national demographic concerns, i.e., diversity or multicultural education. Through the use of multicultural typologies, it was argued that the "new" multiculturalism has become entrenched in urban schools as an additional compensatory program within already failed older models through a curriculum based on blaming the victim and profoundly influenced by ethnicity theory. I also delineated and critiqued the reconstructivist proposals (typified by Giroux's notions of Border Pedagogy), albeit with sympathy for their advocacy of democracy, social justice, and economic equity. One purpose of this chapter was to display and dissect the various approaches to multicultural education and ponder on their involvement in maintaining the status quo in inner-city schools. The argument was made that while multiculturalism may have potential for effecting change for the better in these schools, all of the formats are debilitated either by internal contradictions and lack of connection to the urban (as in the Left's critical version) or by its incorporation within already existing formats of assimilatory education that are designed to further urban school failure.

In Chapter Five, we examined the role of teacher education in furthering both the dominant hegemonic social ideology as to race and racial minorities and the inept pedagogies teacher education sustains in urban schools. The chapter illustrated the way in which teacher education has reconfigured a proposal born in the struggle for civil rights, multicultural education, to maintain its pedagogical and ideological control over education. I made the argument that teacher education is significantly responsible for maintaining the marginalization of both minority students and minority teachers, thereby discouraging the former from entering the teaching force.

This final chapter will address the possibility of change, particularly democratic change, in inner-city education. There are two chief problematics in any discussion of such change. One is the inability of urban communities to effect the state agencies that govern their schools in any significant manner. Thus, when discussing change, we must presume that the lack of resources, the poor quality of administration, and the dearth of funding will continue to occur. We must also assume that state education bureaucracies will not only continue to maintain their advocacy of outdated skills curriculum, but will actively resist any attempts to remove the schools from their purview or any attempt to significantly change the curriculum. The second major stumbling block to transformation of inner-city education is ideological and goes to the values and understandings of the teachers, students, parents and others involved in these schools. As I have already discussed in earlier chapters, urban educational justifications and practices are deeply rooted in mainstream value systems, albeit somewhat conflictorily. That conflict is derived of the actors' awareness of the irrelevance and paucity of what is essentially a white education foisted on minority communities. The conflict is also derived from the historical ambivalence of racial minorities to mainstream education, which mistrusts white structured pedagogy at the same time valuing education for furthering communal and individual aspirations. Lastly, the conflict is framed by the historic influence of the black church whose influence is an integral part of the black community, as other religious influences are part of other minority communities. This influence imbues many minority communities with a sense of the spiritual that is antagonistic to mainstream thought and practices.

Given these understandings, this chapter will attempt to present what I feel are potentialities for change in inner-city education. As I stated at the outset, I do not intend to set forth specific pedagogical practices; it was never my intent to write a methods textbook. Instead, the text explores alternative rationales in which such practices might be developed. Further, each urban community differs in what it needs to educate the children and a practice applicable to one may well be inapplicable to another. Instead, the balance of this chapter will address two issues: first, the crafting of an alternative ideological framework that will justify a different pedagogy and curriculum. It has been mine and others' argument that missing in critical multiculturalism is an ethical foundation capable of energizing a populace to effect social transformation. When Cornel West (1993a) speaks of the necessity for a "camp meeting" to coalesce a transformative resistance, he means for the language to be primarily ethical, moral, not political and economic. What this chapter attempts is a beginning discussion of what sort of ethical matrix we may be developing for that meeting. Second, and more in the practical sense, it is my belief that urban schools must frame their educational efforts within the boundaries of the communities to which they belong. That is to say that as I have noted before (Yeo, 1995) one of the problems with critical theory is in its visualizing the school as a site for societal democratization. Perhaps that might be possible in suburban schools (although there too it is doubtful), but definitely not in the inner city. Here the concerns are too trenchant, the needs too immediate for much more than localized transformation. Thus, in part, this chapter will sketch the parameters of an educational approach attuned to both the borders and the interior of the urban.

Preamble

The crucial educational question must be how a vision of change for inner-city education can be fashioned and empowered in the midst of social value structures which continually disaffirm our redemptive hopes in the name of a particular Eurocentric distillation of the past. Cultural traditions which might provide a vision for radical social change have virtually disappeared in a welter of staticism, technocracy, pervasive corporate-consumerism, and the fearful alienation of a ritualized individualistic conformity (McLaren, 1991). Education has increasingly come to play a role in the maintenance of the dominant mainstream paradigm, of limited means entangled within an even more limited vision of what it means to be a democratic society. Education has become the leading edge of "the sickness of our age; the failure of conscience" (Heschel, 1965, p. 15). Teachers all too often find themselves having to justify conscience in the face of administrative technocisms and instrumental rhetoric. This is no less true for inner-city schools than anywhere else in the country. There is often no place in the educational lexicon for matters of conscience; ethical concerns are displaced by a need for objective justification and the dead hand of testing.

As if that were not enough to undercut redemptive dreams and hopes, there is the melanoma of racism eroding the polity, propelling what Cornel West terms "the nihilistic threat to its very existence" (West, 1993, p. 12). Urban schoolchildren, their families and communities must cope not only with economic deprivation and political powerlessness but also with the "profound sense of psychological depression, personal worthlessness and the social despair so widespread in Black America" (West, 1993, p. 15).

The continued promulgation of mainstream contentions that the urban schools' problems are economic, political and/or structural is tragically superficial. Even in the face of human tragedy, loss, and despair, we as a culture have continued to stay the course of neglect, marginalization, and oppression towards those who are different racially, ethnically, and sexually, particularly those whose mediated identity is derived or associated with the urban. This represents a critical choice to refuse to critique the cultural issues associated with the continued hemorrhaging of democratic liberal ideals. It represents the choice by millions of Americans to continue to benefit from racialized injustice while paying lip service to equality, compassion and democratic ideals. In Kozol's research for *Savage Inequalities* (1991) he documents how white middle-class students attending suburban schools claim concern for the less fortunate but are adamantly opposed to sharing when equalization of school funding is proposed. These students, in their unwillingness to accept a lesser share of the societal benefits (and even that is not a certainty), represent a microcosm of America's infatuation with self-aggrandizement, greed, and lust for materiality. Their tunnel vision is a mirror of mainstream values in this society.

In my own teacher education classes, students will react time and again with horror and righteous indignation at the images Kozol paints, but equally repetitively and fervently argue their right to hold onto their portion (and even expand it), even if that territoriality is to the detriment of others. Most of them see no connection between their life-styles and those of the poor and/or the urban. While legitimately appalled at the conditions of inner-city schools, they are unable and/or unwilling to consider some of the funds that support their schools being used for others. They blame the victims and suggest that welfare, teen pregnancy, teachers, drugs or some combination is to blame. Even when confronted with the results of social triaging and misery, they cling to their choices.

One of the problematics for many who desire deep change in our social and educational institutions is a profound cynicism in the face of such sociocultural choices. Reflecting on my own urban teaching experience, I have become convinced that the human tragedy in our cities exists because the great majority of Americans elect and affirm these choices. Additionally, when one contemplates how deeply entrenched and vested education and teacher education are in the rationalizations of such choices, cynicism leads all too quickly to despair. While granting that there are schools attempting change, much of that is driven by corporate determinations of market needs and the relegation of minority and poor white students to the lowest labor pool in the name of a global economic meritocracy. Where an attempt is made in urban schools to infuse a more critical notion of education, it is rendered invisible, reduced to academic writing or subverted eventually within mainstream pedagogies.

Janis Joplin once sang, "freedom is just another word for nothing left to lose," which could suggest that in that despair we have nothing left to lose but the freedom to contemplate a refashioning. Yet we must also face squarely and boldly a few facts. The current mainstream understandings of race and difference in this country have a long and sordid history and cannot be expected to change, at least in the short run. Writers such as Derrick Bell (1992), bell hooks (1992), Peter McLaren (1995), Christine Sleeter (1993), Audre Lorde (1990), and others argue correctly when they point out that whiteness is based on and requires blackness as an inferior oppositionality. Derivative of that necessity is that the country is accelerating its move to a more conservative political, economic, and social stance while hope for broad-based change in the ideology of racism seems less and less likely.

In terms of the conditions of life in inner-city communities, there are no indications other than wishful thinking that serious political and/or economic initiatives are in the offing to alleviate life in the ghettos and barrios of America. Before we can begin to work with these communities for reform in the schools, we are going to have to accept the fact that state monies will continue to be limited, that federal monies will be increasingly curtailed, and that the resources and conditions will continue to be abysmal. To be blunt, in the current political and economic climate, inner-city schools and communities will continue to have no other resources but their own, as limited as those may be. To suggest otherwise, in my belief, is pollyannish and self-defeating.

Education in general and teacher education in the specific have, despite years of criticism from the Left, maintained and furthered dominant cultural values and educational practices from within and/or behind a plethora of reforms that have been superficial at best and more deeply entrenching of mainstream techno-rationality at worst. There are few, if any, indicators of profound and liberating change to that stance. Even the potentialities of multiculturalism have been muted and minimalized, when not directly absorbed. Therefore, in contemplating change in inner-city education, it is unlikely that the mainstream population of America will do anything more than it does now and inner-city communities are thusly on their own.

The underpinnings for these facts, as well as the seeds for change, lie in the nature of the socio-political arguments made by various political and ideological adherencies that form the overt discourse of politics and the more subtle configuration of belief in this country. These are formulated through the interpretations of the challenges people see in everyday life and the choices they make for safety and resolution justified by the dominant values and icons of this culture. In the next section, I will briefly discuss those choices in terms of how they act to maintain the current social policies and educational practices, and their internal contradictions that simultaneously provide the fractures in which we might envision different purposes, curriculum, and pedagogy in inner-city schools.

Choices and Challenges

The current cacophony of voices arguing for change in education, including the somewhat muted advocates of urban education, unfortunately does not divide neatly into discrete channels. However, at the risk of some essentializing, there are some basic components: the mainstream, the Right (particularly the religious Right), and the Left. Each has a dominant voice and a number of subtones; however, since it is the former in each that frames the respective educational practices, it is to those that we turn. Within the discursive strengths and weaknesses of each, I believe, are not only the continuing justifications for current social practices but also potential linkages that could energize an opening for change in urban education. The following subsections will briefly discuss each alternative to examine its particular advocacy for continuation of current social and educational practices and its respective potential for seeds that cumulatively might germinate a different consciousness beyond mere critique of mainstream fallacies and which would effect significant social and educational possibilities within the urban school.

The Mainstream: Choices for Inertia and Failure

The educational and social mainstream has been relatively successful at the promulgation and emphasis of a particular value structure consisting in chief of the ideologies or understandings of empiricism, positivism, and educational neutrality (Giroux, 1992, 1998; Kanpol, 1992; McLaren, 1992, 1991). Specifically, the focus for mainstream education has been to constrain public and professional discourse within a technical realm, rather than on social, political or moral issues (Purpel, 1989; Giroux, 1988). Yet it also constitutes a profound and ultimately debilitating ethical failure in its callous disregard for the poverty of lives, resources, and social empowerment (Kanpol, 1992; McLaren, 1991; Shapiro, 1992); and further by its relegation of people of color to the margins of society, to communities of hopelessness, violence, and nihilism (West, 1993; Marable, 1992). Mainstream-configured schools represent a powerful force for the continued structure of social, intellectual, and personal oppression, the rationales for which represent a number of deeply held cultural values in this country, for example, the profound American beliefs in hierarchy, Eurocentrism, conformity, materialism, and social control (Purpel, 1989; Giroux, 1995). In terms of this book, the ultimate mainstream immorality is the racially framed contention (explicit or oblique) that it is the victims of those policies and ideologies who are to blame.

Within education, a mainstream institution, the whole pedagogic paraphernalia of objectivity, ethical and political disengagement, dispassionate subjectivity, the belief in the social efficacy of testing and tracking, the deskilling of teachers, and the disempowerment of minorities (including those who are different by virtue of ethnicity, race, and language) reinforces and replicates the forms of cultural hegemony which elicit increasing levels of alienation, cynicism, and dwindling levels of public legitimacy (Shapiro, 1991).

Mainstream education has become a force in the United States for maintenance of the racial and ethnic status quo, the furtherance of corporate marketing and popular consumerism, and the justification of that most powerful of beliefs within American social life—individualism—which breeds such terrible alienation. Tinkering with the system within its own milieu has and will continue to prove to be futile, except for those few it benefits. What is required for significant changes in the schools amounts to a fundamental transformation of the culture's consciousness, according to David Purpel (1989), yet there is little sign that such a transformation is either underway or that there is any potential to do so.

Against such staticism, arguments for change have been made for alternative visualizations within our cultural mosaic; specifically the religious Right and certain groups within the Left. Each, in a different manner, has increasingly attacked mainstream public and educational practices and beliefs, albeit neither has been very successful for various reasons inherent in their respective critiques which I will delineate in the next two subsections.

The Choices of the Right

The political and religious Right has vociferously attacked mainstream institutions and ideologies for their respective reliance on technicity, empiricism and moral neutrality. Although not monolithic, the Right in general calls for increased emphasis on an ethics of piety, obedience, hard work, personal and social responsibility, and a narrow definition of community. The Right's use of an ethical text with an emphasis on certainty, personal accountability, community and religious rituals has struck a strong chord within American culture. The Right's arguments for piety and social Darwinism are often denounced by others as appealing to self-aggrandizing emotions, simplicity, and security, but there can be little question that they have energized millions of people in this country to mobilize for social, political and educational change. These dogmatic arguments for social conformity in the name of institutionalized religion represent powerful traditions in the American culture, which has seen religious-based cultural revolutions in previous eras. Many of the current distal Protestant churches have evolved from earlier revivals which invariably preached similar messages.

At its heart, the religious Right represents a rejection of Western modernism's value preferences centered on materialism, science, individuality, and consumerism (Purpel, 1989; Cox, 1984). It interprets the current social crisis within a specifically moral ideology that paints the picture of beliefs gone astray, values betrayed, and lost meanings (Shapiro, 1991). Its discourse articulates the alienation, indignities, and frustrations felt throughout society within a visualization contextualized by a certainty in morality, a stable religious community, and an assertion of the politicized nature of education. This certainty is buttressed by the transmission of an ethical discourse which conveys a belief in a moral universe that is unambiguous, catechistic and beyond public and rational dispute according to Shapiro (1991). The religious Right's discourse of unswerving certainty in its own righteousness has fueled powerful influences within many institutions in this country, with education being both the most noticeable and the most affected. Thanks to modern media, all of us have seen the religious pickets, received the misanthropic literature, heard the pronouncements about public officials who have not been "born again," and had cultural history uprooted in the name of religious censorship. Rare is the school district or textbook publisher who has not been subjected to the diatribes of the certain faithful. Although most noticeable perhaps in the so-called "Bible Belt" of the South and Midwest, the movement has powerful influences in all regions of the country. Whether or not it is founded on personal insecurities and intolerance, as critics claim, ultimately does not matter given its popular strength, its reformative agendas, and its influential rhetoric. It has become a powerful force for a particular understanding.

However, the weakness of the Right is its paradoxical reliance on a particular religious frame and a failure to see beyond its own understandings of individual human experience. The paradox is to be found in its religiously-based rhetorical emphasis on love and humanity contradicted by its justification of prejudice and racism driven by its political and social fear of difference and diversity. The contradiction is found in its notion of conditional care and compassion supposedly based on a faith that scripturally argues for the unconditional. It is located in its ethnocentric visualization of its own central spiritual figure—the historical Jesus—portrayed as a white, middle- or working-class male upholding the virtues of a puritanical, rigidly Victorian society. Hardly a figure to appeal to the oppressed racial minorities of the inner cities. Within the conversation and rhetoric of the religious Right, there is a fear of change, of where the world and our society is going, of what the changing faces of diversity mean for whites, and what are the new social mores developing in our society:

> It is a discourse that rages against social life but offers little resistance to the *systemic* roots of human suffering and degradation. It has little to say about . . . the commodification of human relations, about corporate responsibility, about racism, sexism and the widespread pauperization of women and children. (Shapiro, 1991, p. 15)

Additionally, the Right's propositions for social change are framed by an emphasis on white racial superiority, ethnocentricity, static social hierarchy, and patriarchy. The Right's failure to disconnect itself from racism, Eurocentrism, sexism, and corporate-consumerism ultimately increases the very social alienation it desires to ameliorate (Shapiro, 1991). While it powerfully responds to individual morality, its failure to extend its understandings to social and political morality relegates the Right to mere stridency in the face of mainstream intransigence. However, I argue that is also within those notions of morality, community, and spirituality that may be found the possibilities for a rhetoric of reform when combined with the Left's notions of difference, identity and social justice. Put differently, while both the Right and the Left vociferously attack the dominant values and practices of the mainstream, it is the Right alone that has successfully attracted millions of adherents and forced change on the center. While granting that the Right's message is terribly flawed, we must admit that its ethical and moral context has tremendous cultural power to motivate for change. The next section will explore the Left's visualization, its similarly flawed promulgation, and its possibilities.

The Discontinuities and Possibilities of the Left

As noted in the section on critical or border pedagogy in Chapter Four, the Left has fractionated itself virtually into immobility and irrelevance as to the public at large. I believe, as do others on the Left (Shapiro, 1991; Kanpol, 1992; West, 1993; McLaren, 1992; hooks, 1992; Simon, 1992; etc.) that the influence of postmodernist theories, while opening up Critical Pedagogy's (the Left's predominant educational critique) reliance on neo-Marxist analysis (Giroux, 1992; Burbules & Rice, 1991; McLaren, 1991), has also caused it to lose sight of the purposes of change and hope within endless deconstruction. The Left's current preoccupation with difference acts to reduce its political discourse to the clamor of a warring tribalism (Shapiro, 1995). It offers an image of a world divided into an endless proliferation of those who claim some history of oppression and exclusion, a politics that divides people and emphasizes our separation (Shapiro, 1995).

Postmodernism's rabid avoidance of affirmation and ethical value preferences (due to their implicit power connections) and the insistence on unending relativism (bordering in some cases on nihilism) has resulted in the Left's inability to construct a moral vision capable of mobilizing a collective will to engage in emancipatory democratic social change. The Left in general, and critical educators in particular, have suffered from the effects of their own successes as relentless deconstructors of transcendental truth claims and demystifiers of natural knowledge. The very stuff that constitutes moral visions and languages of possibility is blasted by our own critical discourse (Shapiro, 1991, p. 24).

The postmodern Left suffers from its own message in the sense that if one totalizes the concept of uncertainty and argues that all positions are discursive positions of alienating power and therefore to be avoided, then what position for social change can be taken? The answer is ultimately none, which creates a quandary when it comes to advocacy of social reform. "You cannot mobilize a movement that is only and always against; you must have a positive alternative, a vision of a better future . . . " (Giroux, 1992, p. 6). As certain as the Right appears, the Left is immobilized by uncertainty, divisiveness and internal bickering. There is a sad irony in the Left's criticism of the Right's righteous claim of epistemological verity flawed by the contentiousness of the same claims made by all of the various subgroups within the Left. Each group pronounces (usually set within a rarefied academic discourse intended only for other members of the same group) its truth-claim and denigrates other Left discourses for some infraction or another. Avoided are connections to the commonplace, to urban realities, rural impoverishment, and the everyday tribulations of outrageous fortune. As Cornel West notes, the Left suffers because it really doesn't have a developed tradition of thinking about crucial cultural institutions in civil society—like family or neighborhoods, or church, synagogue or mosque (West, 1993a). Yet, the Left, especially the critical pedagogists, still, I believe, poses a serious challenge to the mainstream and the Right, arguing for the extension of democracy, social change, and connectivity to the margins of society. Derived from feminism and postmodernism, the Left has argued for a certainty within uncertainty, that all epistemes represent truth, that universal should be inclusive, not exclusive, and that identities themselves represent potentialized representations rather than closed products of socialization or genetics. Although conflicted by its own brand of competition and hierarchy, the Left recognizes in general that historical constructs are narrative discourses, including those of identity and ethnicity, thereby broadening the range of individual and social possibility. Put another way, it is the critical Left that has recognized that we are the stories we tell, that history is constructed for the justification of our own narratives (Karier, 1986) and does not rest on some transcendent truth, which is itself another narrative. There is a certain irony in it being the Left that expands the possibility for individual knowing and experience versus the Right's claim to individualism which is narrowed by its contra-emphasis on conformity.

Although the weakness of the Left is its own self-defeating divisiveness combined with its reluctance to move literally and figuratively into the streets, the ghettoes, and the barrios, at the same time the strength of the Left's argument is that it holds the potential for furthering traditional ideals of pluralism, individuality, community and democracy. As noted earlier, its most serious flaws are its dearth of a compelling moral vision and, for our purposes, a lack of direct connection to inner-city education.

The Challenges of Vision

The implications of the foregoing are that the critical potentialities of the Right and the Left offer us clues for the visualization and implementation of change. The issue, however, is how does one generate an ethical practice and governing ideology from both repressive individualism and the critique of any universals? The answers are neither easy nor clear but must be teased from the predominant themes outlined within each major text.

In answer, one argument suggested as an ethical framework is the elimination of "unnecessary human suffering." However, I believe this doxology to be definitionally specious. It begs the question of what constitutes "unnecessary" and situates us within the problematic of the political determination of care wherein once again the distribution of power will delineate both the definition and the application of deserving. If suffering is determined to be "necessary," it implies a justification for an aloofness and distancing all too compatible with modern mainstream and Right individualistic ethical arguments that negate compassionate solidarity in favor of parochial community. To a great extent, the care-giving of AIDS sufferers has fallen into this conundrum. Within the arguments swirling around the subject of AIDS, the suffering of the afflicted individuals has all too often been presumed as deserved or "necessary." They have become the modern lepers ostracized and damned by all but a few, and like the leper of old, their suffering is often interpreted as resulting from sin. It is the same logic of blaming the victim that we have seen before in the relegation of the children of the inner city to the margins of society. Our society seems to have a number of "lepers."

Considering the argument of an ethical imperative of "unnecessary suffering" further, perhaps it could be argued that if we have the power to alleviate another's suffering then by definition it is unnecessary. There are two problems with this proposition, however: first, it reduces caring and service to others to a question of resources and power. Second, it places the responsibility and concomitant power of defining "help" with the donor, not the beneficiary. As Sharon Welch (1990) notes, the incorporation of hierarchically based "help" and "care" systems are exploitative when the caregiver presumes the determination of suffering without understanding one's own implication in its causation or being open to the specificity of the needs expressed by the sufferers (Welch, 1990).

This brings us back to those earlier "facts" and the choice that has been implicit throughout the discussion. It seems pointless to pose ameliorative recommendations for inner-city education that either rely on mainstream largesse or are connected to an equally futile scheme of broad ideological and cultural change, resting on the disempowered for power. Yet to continue in despair is to be complicit in the present cultural and social triaging of difference and poverty. Therefore, if we choose not to allow the disablement of despair, we are left needing to find some fractures within the other alternative, which I believe are to be found in a connection of the seemingly disparate potentialities within the Right's conceptualization of locating the political within the ethical and the Left's notions of celebrating difference and the social construction of culture and identity. This leads to two broad statements that could begin to frame a different sort of discourse about inner-city education.

First, that those of us within education, and specifically teacher education, must, while continuing our critique and deconstruction of dominant values and practices, begin to couch that critique within a search for and implementation of personal within social moral arguments, even perhaps spiritual (Purpel, 1989; Simon, 1992), and ground our advocacy of change unabashedly within the moral. The basis for such an advocacy does indeed lie within the Right's conceptualizations of the ethical, but we need to lift it out of their truncated, fearful idolatry, racism, patriarchy and economic nationalism. One of the critiques that is implicit in liberal and critical recommendations for urban education is a moral-political question of "to what end . . . ?" Or are we to assume that the recommended pedagogical practice is an end in itself? Since that ultimately circles back into what already exists in urban pedagogy, any project needs to be able to help propound an answer to that seminal question. Since it is an ethical inquiry, then before we can address the pedagogical, we need to address the moral basis for our teaching. As noted previously, the failure of inner-city education is intrinsically an ethical or moral failure from which the political, economic and educational failures flow. Thus the need is firstly to fashion a new moral foundation, not a political or economic argument, before beginning to craft a curricular or pedagogical frame for inner-city teaching.

Second, we must acknowledge that the only change we can effect within urban schools and their communities is that within localized place and space. Put differently, we must begin our efforts for pedagogical and curricular change with the acknowledgement that if we want to help change the conditions of the Other, then we must not presume to dictate the place or style of that change. The site of the struggle is in the schools, the streets and the "hoods." We must reject the hubris of the intellectual and understand that the struggle worth making is the one that is possible. Perhaps overly cynical, I am convinced that neither the State nor the mainstream population in this country will, in the foreseeable future, change their respective relationships to the urban or to inner-city education. Therefore, if change is going to occur, it must do so from within those locales targeting reform only therein and not as a base for changing the white middle-class society as too many of the Left would have it.

Based on the first statement, as to the need for a transformative ethic in which to frame an agenda to a different approach to inner-city education, the next section represents what I would like to think is an initiation of that process. It is unfinished and should perhaps remain so, as with any conversation. It is an attempt to reconcile the experiences teaching in my school with the question, "to what end?"

The Choice of a Moral Covenant for Inner-City Education

> All we can do is speak with others as eloquently and passionately as we can about justice and caring and love and trust. (Greene, 1993b)

An ideology represents how we see the world and others, how we perceive reality through taken-for-granted notions and understandings (Giroux, 1992; McLaren, 1989; Eagleton, 1991). Yet it is also a sense, a faith, of what is good, what constitutes the "right"; i.e., at its heart, an ideology in constructing social and individual consciousness must rest on an ethic of what constitutes good. Therein lies the rub, for in that conversion of ethic to ideology and ideology to praxis, much confusion and mis-connection occurs. For example, although most might agree that individual autonomy is good, the contortions of individualism within capitalism's notion of competition can and have become synonymous with alienation, personal anguish and social dysfunction. Most would agree that studying is good but not when used in repetitive rote models of teaching to insure classroom order. We might even be able to agree that education in the general sense is good, but not when we fail to connect it to street lives and dysfunctional communities and use education to justify social triage.

What is needed instead is a different moral framework in which to situate an individual's or a society's understanding of the world and relations to others. At the same time, this new framework must be capable of energizing connectivity amongst individuals and communities to effect the expunction of such social ills as gender violence, poverty and racism. This means that it simultaneously must be simple in its clarity yet capable of a broad scope of social implementation so as to be applicable and natural within and across a range of individual and social differences. I believe that the constructing elements of such a framework are found in the contemplation of the ethics of difference, compassion, awe, and hope. Each of these already forms the advocacies and belief systems of both Right and Left, although differentially interpreted and argued. Although fully cognizant that no group representative of a particular set of sociocultural values and attendant advocacy is monolithic, for the purposes of discussion, I will regretfully resort to the use of terms such as the "Left" or the "Right," also assuming that the following will give the reader better ideas to critique than a putative reductionism. In this section, I will define the four "ethics" as I have chosen to term them and their respective potential for energizing social transformation and then will suggest how such a moral stance might be practicalized in inner-city schools within the framework of critical pedagogy.

Difference as an Ethic

> Lacking in America is any sense that the nation is a collectivity of difference, that the human community might indeed be enriched by the experience of the Other, of that which cannot be rendered transparent. (McLaren, 1988a, p. 60)

The concept of difference, itself a major problematic for the mainstream and the Right and a potential source of both emancipation and nihilism for postmodernists, is touted through a pluralistic rhetoric which has significant ideological and social resonance. The country, or at least the white-dominated part, acclaims and believes itself to be a melting pot of difference. Yet the practices of difference as an ethic within mainstream autocracy suggest that individual and/or ethnic differences are better sublimated beneath a particularistic western, Eurocentric rationalistic conformity. According to Welch (1990), this tendency is manifest in the contemporary American proclivity to see pluralism and complexity as problems to be solved rather than constitutive elements of social organization. Thus, as with many such ethics in this culture, there are conflicting nuances that generally tend to obscure potential for change and instead produce severe social dislocations and individual alienation all too often disguised as autonomy.

It is the alternative view of difference evident in Giroux's concept of Border Pedagogy that I want to redefine and expand. Difference needs to be viewed both as a positive possibility and an absolute necessity as the foundational ethic for a radical democratic polity. We must move away from the construction of difference in the dominant hegemonic view in which we posit a generalized Other, who is assumed to be fundamentally the same as Self within the framework of conformity. Instead, what is needed is a consciousness of a particularized, or "concrete" Other (Welch, 1990) in which individuals and groups are recognized as discrete with a specific (not generalized) history, identity(s), and affective understandings. To construct such a consciousness requires that the ethic of competitiveness and hierarchy be redefined culturally, which could be generated by the second constitutive plank of a new social compact, compassion.

Compassion: An Ethic of Action and Sharing

As an existent ethic within our culture that could potentialize radical change, compassion has instead been mainstreamed into irrelevance, which has reduced all of us to victims (Fox, 1990). The issue is no longer who (or which group) has a corner on oppression and marginalization, for without suggesting that there is equivalence in the forms of pain and oppression, we need to recognize that there is no privileged bearer of oppression or suffering in our society. As Shapiro (1995) notes, there is not a simple duality that distinguishes people as either those who dominate, exploit or inflict pain on others, or those who are its recipients. Put differently, all of us are inflicted as we inflict; we are oppressed and oppressor. It is this notion of there being a broad reservoir of personal pain and alienation within our society that the religious Right has so successfully responded to (Shapiro, 1995, 1991; Kanpol & McLaren, 1995).

Although compassion exists as a concept within the religious values of this culture, as an ethic it has unfortunately been increasingly displaced by sentimentality; our concern and care of others has been so truncated that we have reduced caring to a Hallmark card. Our modernist language of rationality, disconnection, and objectivity has corrupted the meaning of compassion, so that we confuse it with pity and/or indulgence. As Michael Fox (1990) has written, in our replacement of compassion with pity, we have failed to realize that pity connotes condescension, which in turn implies separateness. Pity connotes that the object of its regard is not only suffering, but is also weak or inferior. Compassion, however, derives from an understanding of our awareness of shared weakness. It is the ethic underlying the popular phrase, "there but for grace, go I." The root of the word compassion means to suffer with, to undergo with, to share solidarity with (Fox, 1990, p. 3). Compassion springs from the awareness that there is a shared mutuality, of hurt, of mortality, of simple need. Compassion is based on an act of solidarity; it is a joining-with to relieve shared suffering. It is the energizing force required to combat the ugly ego-centricity that has become a pathological state in our culture.

Compassion combined with an empathy for plurality and difference would connote an act of celebration, an act of sharing, both of what we are and what we are not. Sharon Welch (1990) points the way to effect this combination. First, we need to recognize that we are both in pain, that we are both oppressor and oppressed, that we all participate in the human drama of experience where we are disempowered and disempower, we are victim and victimizer. Second, one must place one's Self where one can experience as the Other, experience Otherness. To use Giroux's (1992) term, it is to cross borders of experience and identity. While Giroux does not give us an ethical framework to cross these borders, I would contend that the possibility for doing so lies in acts of compassion laced with celebration of difference, keeping firmly in mind that compassion is a reaching out for solidarity and kinship without control or manipulation. I think Sharon Welch again states it well, that we can transcend the blinders of our own social location, not through becoming objective, but by recognizing differences by which we ourselves are constituted, and by actively seeking to be constructed by work with different groups. (Welch, 1990, p. 151)

Awe and the Ethic of Celebration

A third possible ethic that needs reconceptualization is that of the concept of awe, which, while axiomatic within much of the religious doxology in this country, has become truncated in its meaning and practice. In fact, it is a word rarely used outside of certain fundamentalist religious circles and certainly never graces the pages of educational journals. Awe is a concept whose meaning and use as an ethic has become politicized and disconnected from its power to effect change. It has been reduced to cartoonish trite expressions indicative of low imagination and intelligence; i.e., "awesome, dude!" The fundamentalist Right speaks of the necessity of awe within a stylized and political notion supposedly affirming the sanctity of life, particularly in terms of opposition to issues such as abortion. Yet it sees no contradiction in the death penalty, poverty or starvation. The mainstream suggests a rather oblique perspective of awe for objectivity and Truth, while perceiving truth in numbers instead of within the limitless numbers of truths. The postmodern Left contends that an ethic of awe, whether spiritual or otherwise, connotes equivalency between presumptive universals and oppressions, thereby obviating the issue by equating awe with language used only by institutional religion. Awe for the Left connotes universalism and power differentiation which is to be avoided. The Left's absence and the Right's contradictoriness leaves only the hegemonic construction, wherein awe and its concomitant, celebration, have been reduced to a transitoriness, a patina of awe over technological moments. The dearth of what Heschel (1965) refers to as "radical amazement" or awe is at the heart of our losing the power to celebrate, especially as to each other. As we enter the world of virtual reality, we presume that "virtual" equals "real" instead of "near." The cyber-age elides reality for that which is quasi- or virtually (near) real. Through the increasing impact of corporate marketing, we are being distracted by that which emulates reality instead of confronting our own and others' notions and understandings of what is real.

   The essence of awe is the acceptance and appreciation that the world of phenomena, of stable objects, which we seek to understand and control does not constitute all of reality. In contrast to mainstream notions framed within scientific empiricism, awe is an intuition or an understanding, not a knowing; it is a realization of the ineffability of life and reality. As Heschel argues, awe is more than an emotion; it is a way of understanding, an insight into meaning greater than ourselves (Heschel, 1965). Awe is at its essence the act of celebration, but if so, what do we celebrate? The latter term is certainly used in mainstream multicultural curricula, but does not answer the question. For example, we celebrate Martin Luther King Day, we celebrate diversity, we celebrate Cinco de Mayo, we celebrate contributions by minorities, but do we ever celebrate difference? The answer is unfortunately a resounding negative; instead; we have made an icon of conformity and reduced incommensurable difference to the educational psycho-babble of deficiency and being "at-risk." All too often, to celebrate means a day out of school or superficial lessons couched within the contributive or human sensitivity versions of multicultural education.

To celebrate truly is to find joy and inspiration but there is little joy in the marginalization of millions of minority and poor children, in the anxiety of testing and grades, in mindless repetitive lessons hunched over worksheets or the crumbling classrooms of inner-city schools. The sad truth is that there is very little joyful or inspirational about education. Rare is the teacher who helps children find joy in being Puerto Rican, Cherokee or Vietnamese or inspire children to understand their Lakota heritage or find joy in being African American. What we do as teachers is ameliorate difference and diversity, not celebrate it. Yet I believe that within a project of social reconstruction, while such a repositioning of the ethical seems daunting, virtually impossible, "virtual" means nearly impossible, not impossible. In order to move to a celebration of difference in an inner-city classroom, we require one more ethic, that of hope.

Hope: An Ethic of Transcendence of Possibility

The message of social construction and social contingency is one of hope. It is hopeful because it also suggests that there is no objective necessity or rational principle to justify the way things are, to legitimate the hierarchies of wealth, power, prestige and freedom. (Simon, 1992, p. 301)

Hope is arguably the primary ethic of the four for without hope that our efforts will have both meaning and fortuitous results, the balance becomes irrelevant. There is no need for awe, compassion or celebration without the hope that meaningfulness exists. Without hope, life becomes drudgery excited only by the illicit and/or immoral. Hope has, along with fear, all too often become a survival emotion for inner-city children, a fact of life of which too many teachers are ignorant. Hope is the acknowledgment of openness to all possibilities for human attachments and the hopeful person acts upon that possibility by loosening the hold that ideologies and routines have over imagination (Simon, 1992). Hope is the antithesis of the Right's wistful nostalgia for a golden age of white supremacy, the Left's cynical critique, and the mainstream's inertia. In our increasing confusion of hope with cyber-dreaming (McLaren, 1988a) or the wishing for a supposedly perfect past by the Right, or the prohibition of dreaming at all by the mainstream architects of techno-objectivism, we have forgotten or deluded ourselves into a cynicism where "Murphy's Law" explains the loss of possibility, not its gain. As Simon notes, the metaphor of possibility stands empty. Accused of meaningless rhetoric, it can only be rescued from the dismissal of cynicism by developing its substance (Simon, 1992, p. 13). In our restricted human condition framed by dominant paradigmatic modes, we have come to fear possibility in any sense other than the next amusement or disaster. Mainstream ideological rhetoric and educational cynicism have profoundly limited access to human hopes for a good life (with its concomitant danger of people acting thereon) through the label of "utopianism," the presumption being that if some hope of change is utopian, it is impossible, irrational and specious. However, as Giroux proposes, a language of possibility does not have to dissolve into reified utopianism; instead it can be developed as a precondition for nourishing convictions that summon up the courage to imagine a different and more just world and to struggle for it (Giroux, 1990, p. 41).

Hope provides the linkage binding awe, compassion and difference into a gestalt without which the capacity to imagine social alternatives is a headgame, lacking force and true self-engagement (Wexler, 1987). If the Right relies on fear of the future to mobilize for social and educational change, we on the Left in order to progressively propound our vision of social, political, and cultural justice must argue vociferously that the future is grounded in hope and possibility: that perhaps it is the past and security that we must fear.

An Ethical Compact of Possibility

Many of us have had to struggle personally and professionally with the profoundly alienating cynicism that seeps from the wellsprings of our culture as well as with the frustrating efforts to engender a critical and multicultural agenda within education. Such cynicism occludes vision, insight, and possibility and forms the basis for the attrition of critical approaches to educational reform, especially as it undermines our attempts to teach in inner-city schools. The current morality maintained by dominant ideologies in this country is a travesty of being human against the world in which we live, and results in dehumanized communities, families, and individuals. The alternative proposed by the Right, while publicly resonant, is fearfully narrow and through its apocalypticism confounds possibility (Cox, 1984). The basis of a critical morality contexted within a world of marginalized difference, of suffering, of human tragedy, is to answer the penultimate question of human solidarity. Where are the bridges that connect the suffering of one group of human beings to another? *Who speaks for humanity?* (Shapiro, 1995).

The obvious answer, denied by virtually the entire current social and political spectrum but simultaneously haunting the community, is that the bridges desperately need construction. I believe a political agenda akin to "border pedagogy," grounded in the proposed reconstructive ethic, can do this. Within such a revitalized ethic, education would take on a profoundly different countenance and role, necessitated by a society more concerned with the practice of humanity, not human practices. The argument is essentially that if critical pedagogists truly want to effect a democratic pedagogy, it must be framed in an ethical stance that people will agree to and struggle to support. That stance must resonate within the hearts of a broad spectrum of society, whether born-again Christian, Black Baptist, liberation theologian, Jew, Gentile or feminist, to name a few. To paraphrase Giroux (1990), it must be an ethic that will engender courage to struggle for democratic and educational possibility, to truly celebrate difference within our individual and social mix, and to sustain that struggle in the face of fear and uncertainty.

To answer Shapiro's question within the current sense is to acknowledge that all too few of us are willing to speak for humanity. To ponder the question within a reconstructive ethic is to suggest that we all do. While that answer has the onus of an obvious simplicity, it equally has the simplicity of being an obvious answer. Simplistic or not, the fact remains that the dominant educational (and social) ethic in this culture underwrites and maintains increasing human suffering, social triaging, and personal and communal alienation, none of it necessary. We are a society that has in the main replaced human presence with K-Mart presents and confused human possibility with economic opportunity. Particularly within urban education, the dominant ethic is nothing short of destructive and dehumanizing. It is the antithesis of hope, destructive of possibility, and results in furthering nihilism and personal meaninglessness (West, 1993). To build bridges is going to require a new social ethic, one that will bring about a sea-change in our understanding of what's good. The proposal of what I have termed as a reconstructive ethic is meant to argue for both the context and the initiation of such a building project. It is also to argue that without a profound ideological change, there will not and perhaps cannot be any significant change in urban education that is at its least more democratic and more humane.

As we begin to explore the implications of implementing a reconstructive ethic within the boundaries of inner-city education, one of the sites of resistance will undoubtedly be teacher education. In the next section, I will explore more specifically these institutions as representing one place where we must struggle caringly within a dialogic sense of difference to overcome and describe what a reconstructive vision might mean within inner-city pedagogy and curriculum.

Teacher Education and White Resistance

> Education either functions as an instrument which is used to facilitate the integration of the younger generation into the logic of the present system and bring about conformity to it or it becomes "the practice of freedom," the means by which men and women deal critically with their world and creatively with reality and discover how to participate in the transformation of their world. (Freire [1970], cited in hooks, 1989, p. 50)

One of the most problematic areas for urban educational reformers has been and is teacher education. In addition to being a bastion of systemic resilience in the face of changing themes and demographics and one of the primary places where dominant understandings of the nature and purposes of education, puerile comprehensions of culture and identity, and pedagogical instrumentalism are promulgated, there is the issue of the resistance of its clientele—the generally young, white, often female, middle-class suburbanite pre-teacher. Given that they have had fourteen or fifteen years of formal schooling, it is not surprising that they are resistant to proposals underscoring difference and privilege, such as critical multiculturalism. It is to be anticipated that both they and teacher educators will be highly resistant to accepting and implementing a reconstructive ethic. Given teacher education's current attitudes and dismissal of inner-city schools as valid sites for education and teacher placement, we can anticipate an even greater resistance to any change framed by concerns for urban education.

Ensconced in ethnicity theory's engendered perspectives, white pre-teacher students deflect both notions of social responsibility for minority predicaments and of their concomitant white privilege. To acknowledge these ideas would be to recognize the differentially beneficial nature of white status. This they are reluctant to do because it focuses on the connections between difference and power (Roman, 1993) which their education has denied exists, and on how they are directly and indirectly inequitably privileged thereby. Christine Sleeter (1993) argues that to even attempt to redress racism through white teachers is inadequate and potentially futile. She makes the rather salient point that to solve racism by educating white students is to locate racism in biased individual actions, which are assumed to stem from psychological assumptions in individuals, such as prejudiced attitudes, stereotypes, and lack of information about people of color. The assumption that, if we as critical educators can change what is in the heads of white people, then they in turn will create significant changes in institutions is the basis of the great bulk of multicultural education in this country, particularly the assimilation and human sensitivity varieties (Sleeter, 1993). Or as she rather pungently puts the matter:

> White people's common sense understandings of race are ideological defenses of the interests and privileges that stem from White people's position in a structure based in part on racial inequality. A structural analysis of racism suggests that education will not produce less racist institutions as long as White people control them. (Sleeter, 1993, p. 158)

Sleeter goes on to argue that the solution to the problem of teacher education's approach to urban education requires more educators of color because they are "much more likely to bring life experiences and viewpoints that critique White supremacy than are White teachers and to engage in activities that challenge various forms of racism. They are also less likely to marginalize minority intellectual discourse" (Sleeter, 1993, p. 169; citing Ladson-Billings & Henry, 1990 and Gordon, 1990). Although in general I would agree, instances of minority teachers being less than challenging to racism and less than respectful to minority student intellectual discourse abound in the hallways of inner-city schools, and whatever rationale we choose to justify that phenomenon, it is a fact of inner-city school life that we must expand our analysis to encompass. To maintain credibility and face an unpleasant factor in creating the dynamics of a critical multiculturalism in urban schools, we must recognize that in these schools far too many minority administrators and teachers have become perversely vested in the maintenance of a structure and system of beliefs and practices through assimilation of dominant mainstream values, even though that very social system devalues and marginalizes them. It must be recognized that the defensiveness of that interest will have to be as dialogically confronted as will white student defensiveness in teacher education. To argue otherwise is to fall into a scheme of mystification and reifying of those folks which is an attitude as dangerous to a critical agenda as any other.

Sleeter argues that a second necessity must be to reeducate white people "by forcing them to examine White privilege" (Sleeter, 1993, p. 169). The problem here is self-evident—such an approach within teacher education, no matter how it is justified, would increase white resistance, give grist to the mill of conservatives and the mainstream alike, and result in the negation of the program. Her advocacy of structured immersion experiences suggests Grant's (1994) ideas of encouraging field experience in teacher education, but the use of the word "encourage" is of a very different moral tenor than "force." It is the very use of such terms that causes others interested in urban education to presume an autocratic bent to critical multiculturalism and reject its potentials. White defensiveness is certainly real enough; any critical educator who has introduced multicultural issues, such as racism, to an educational foundations class of incipient teachers knows this phenomenon all too well. However, so is the prospective teachers' idealism which emphasizes qualities such as compassion, justice, equality, and communication. Rather than "force" understanding, which is a mainstream tactic in any case, dialogue with students in which contradictions can be deconstructed and connections made to issues of social justice within education and society is far more efficacious and on sounder ethical ground. The use of the student's own rhetoric provides the basis for beginning to open up defensiveness to acceptance and sometimes even commitment.

We should also be deeply concerned with the ethical contradictions within any such proposal that either "force" an ideological and/or methodological change or start with the assumption that a group of students (here white incipient teachers) is presumptively deficient or hopeless. To do so is to fall into the hegemonic trap of mainstream thinking where individuals are perceived as marginalized because of their identification within a certain group, itself labelled as deficient and marginal. While I understand Sleeter's frustration, having felt it myself, to react by advocating a scheme of automatic rejection in favor of another group is both violative of a reconstructive ethic and makes the favored group uncritically monolithic. While I absolutely agree that the numbers of faculty and students of color in teacher education must be dramatically increased, we should avoid the presumption that they alone can teach in urban schools and that such schools are where they belong, an assumption buried in Sleeter's proposal. The concept is symptomatic of teacher education where modelling falls short of rhetoric. It is in that same line of thinking as teacher educators lecturing students on the necessity of teaching being interesting and to use a variety of pedagogical approaches. To presume that white students, because they are white (which they may not be) and middle class (which again they may not be), are deficient and somehow worthless as potential agents of change in urban schools is to blame another victim. It presumes that these students have been in control of their own education and do not also feel alienated, confused, and disempowered. Instead, we need to affirm their idealistic notions while helping them to deconstruct their contradictory notions of order, culture, and teaching. Instead of criticizing, we need to model compassion for others, hope for change, and the celebration of difference, including theirs. This is not to say that we need to affirm their values but rather to avoid wholesale denigration by entering into a dialogic community with students that challenges them to realize the implications of their presumptions and beliefs, thereby affirming their voice, if not the words.

Additionally, given the demographic trends of teacher education, we must work with what we have, and that means working assiduously, but affirmingly, to find the fractures in the walls of white defensiveness, not simply deriding it in the hope of colorizing teacher education. To argue otherwise is to categorically assume that white students cannot become cultural workers or border crossers (Giroux, 1992; McLaren, 1995). Just as Sleeter (1993) argues that we must be careful to avoid the tendency to reify the oppressed, so, too, must we avoid essentiallizing whites. Unfortunately, this is one of the ethical and epistemological problematics that have led other advocates for inner-city school reform to reject critical pedagogy.

An "Ecological" Approach to Urban School Reform

In her excellent book on urban schools, Lois Weiner (1993) makes a cogent argument against critical pedagogy in favor of an "ecological" model proposed by Liston & Zeichner (1987, 1991). The basis of the critique is twofold; first, that critical pedagogy "assigns educators the task of transforming society through their classroom function . . . a political function that transcends classroom borders" (Weiner, 1993, p. 88-89). Weiner, it seems to me, is correct in her understanding that critical pedagogy (including Giroux's conceptualization of what he terms as border pedagogy [Giroux, 1992, 1988a]) assumes inordinate influence on the part of the classroom teacher, disregarding the structural and institutional conditions limiting their potential as change agents. Secondly, she links critical theory to its Marxist roots, claiming it argues for a Soviet-Leninist approach to ideology and educational practice which is incompatible with democratic ideals. She bases this accusation on the connections between many formulations of critical pedagogy and Paulo Freire's writings, such as *Pedagogy of the Oppressed* (1970). Here, she exhibits a lack of understanding of the maturation of critical theory, particularly in its format as critical multiculturalism, where it has been profoundly influenced by feminism, postmodernism and cultural studies, and misappropriates academic hubris for incipient totalitarianism. While I have previously noted my own problems with critical pedagogy, particularly as to inner-city education and its ethical problematics, critical theory, including border pedagogy, is too inextricably linked to a Deweyan notion of democracy and social justice through education to be the object of such an accusation (McLaren, 1995, 1992, 1991).

The preponderance of Weiner's criticism of other forms of urban reform is, however, insightful, in addition to being one of the few texts that directly interrogates the connections between societal structures, teacher education, and inner-city schools. She notes that other reform proposals generally focus on teacher and student attributes within a continuation of a "deficiency" understanding of urban education. These other advocates for mainstream-oriented reform either place too great of an autonomy on urban schools or focus on compensatoriness. Weiner correctly argues that while urban schools can provide the skills students need to be able to compete in the job market and to be citizens who know how to define and execute their social and political responsibilities, they cannot by themselves change the external conditions that subvert students' economic and political progress (Weiner, 1993). Put differently, urban schools can be made capable of teaching skills and dominant notions of social responsibility, but those efforts are and will be undercut and made futile by the social forces, such as discrimination and racism, that maintain the marginalization of the students and their cultures.

Weiner's advocacy of what she terms an "ecological" approach (Weiner, 1993, p. 106) contains much that mirrors both critical pedagogy and the reconstructive ethic. Citing Liston & Zeichner (1991), Weiner argues that teacher education must help incipient teachers come to understand urban students' perspectives, interrogate how the school's institutional structures inhibit teacher and student success, and examine "the entire social context of schooling" (Weiner, 1993, p. 91). Liston & Zeichner's social constructionist approach, on which Weiner's propositions are based, calls for an educational goal of social democracy couched within an analysis of what they term the "synergistic web of relations" that construct an urban school. Weiner suggests that it is the use of such an inclusive analysis, the "web," that makes the approach ecological. The emphasis throughout the analysis is on the critique of the social means and intents that formulate the educational rationales for urban educational practices.

While there is much to recommend the approach for its perspective and insight, there are also several problems with the ecological approach as a form of analytic construction. First, both the ends and the means resemble closely the critical pedagogy arguments and goals advocated by theorists such as Giroux (1992), McLaren (1995, 1991), and others. However, within the ecological approach, unlike critical multiculturalism (as a subset of critical pedagogy), there is insufficient attention given to issues of race, gender, class, and the sources and distribution of socio-political power and to the nonsynchronicity in which people live and move (McCarthy, 1992). Second, similarly to critical pedagogy, there is an undefined ethical basis for the proposals. While concern for the social structures that frame schools and education is obviously vital to understanding urban education, so too are the ideologies and/or values which provide justification and legitimacy to those structures. Without understanding the moral basis by which dominant social structures make sense and are sustained, it would seem arguably difficult to propose counterhegemonic structures that can be sustained as a public movement.

Weiner's description of the structurally caused incapacities and limitations that affect urban teachers and her call for changes in teacher education to address assisting teachers in understanding and crossing the chasm of difference (or becoming "border crossers" in Giroux's terminology [Giroux, 1992]) is both valid and problematic. It is valid in the exactness of her descriptions of the impact of urban conditions on inner-city schools and the history of educational reform as it has failed to ameliorate either the conditions or the deadliness of urban education. It is valid in the contention that multicultural education is a failure as presented in teacher education as implied preparation for teaching in urban schools and equally so as a pedagogical reform within those schools. It is problematic in that, like critical pedagogy, there is a need to struggle with the question of "to what end?" within the respective analysis.

As discussed at length previously, Weiner's point is equally valid as to the limitations of basing urban reform on teacher education:

> Teacher preparation cannot substitute for the political and social movements that are needed to alter the systemic deficiencies of schools . . . it cannot alter the systemic characteristics of urban schools. . . . (Weiner, 1993, p. 102)

She argues that teacher education can and should participate in the reconstruction of relationships among, parents, teachers, students, and citizens and additionally, that this transformation is essential if urban schools are to succeed (Weiner, 1993, p. 101). According to Weiner, the ecological approach can be utilized not only for analysis but also to help prepare teachers to overcome the obstacles that urban school systems and social and economic forces set before them (Weiner, 1993,

p. 106).

However, it is exactly within the foregoing argument that a crucial failure is to be located for most urban educational analysis—what do we mean by "to succeed," what does it mean "to overcome obstacles"? Overcome obstacles to accomplish what? What does or should count as success in an inner-city school? Granting the validity in the proposals, both ecological and critical, that teacher education must teach and urban teachers must practice an understanding of difference to be able to make a difference—what is the difference they will make? These are not facetious or contentiously academic questions; they are the ultimate questions that any proposal for urban educational reform must address and answer. Without struggling with these overtly ethical questions, any proposal for reform will either be shelved by practitioners as inappropriate and too academic or be reduced to another of the long list of compensatory programs that compound rather than ameliorate the failure that is inner-city education. Weiner and other urban educational researchers correctly argue that there is little an urban teacher can do to effect much significant change in the institutional or social forces bearing down on the urban-minority student and teacher, which leaves us little better off than before the analysis. In fact, the net effect is an ultimately increased cynicism, despair of or for change, and teacher withdrawal. To what end should one understand difference, if it makes no difference?

In the next section, I will present some responses to those questions that I believe will, when and if incorporated within a reconstructive ethic, prove more efficacious for inner-city education than either the ecological or critical approach. Perhaps a better way to put it is that while both of these approaches offer significant insight and possibilities for change in inner-city education, their internal contradictions debilitating their respective proposals can be cured by the incorporation of a reconstructive ethic.

Teaching Critically as Educational Subversion

Weiner (1993) does leave us a clue as to an approach for change, even if not followed fully through. She notes that the problems and the resolutions are grounded in the moral and that teaching is chiefly about beliefs, not about cognition.

> To work in these [urban] circumstances, teachers should understand
> what their own values and beliefs are, and how they have been
> shaped by social conditions, so that they can contend with
> institutional pressures to interact with students in ways that
> undermine their purposes. (Weiner, 1993, p. 114)

In a nutshell, I believe that statement to include several critical
points about inner-city education. What teachers do and can do is
essentially grounded in the moral—their values and beliefs, which
suggests that a starting point for teacher education must be the
construction and implementation of a reconstructive ethic to undermine
current beliefs about the appropriateness and rightness of current
practices in inner-city education. To undermine is to subvert, and thus
the purpose of teacher education and parenthetically of inner-city
education becomes the instillment of a subversive ethos aimed at
fracturing the systemic ideologies, structures and practices that define
and implement urban school failure. As Geneva Gay has noted:

> As pedagogies of difference, resistance, hope, and possibility,
> multicultural education and critical pedagogy are inherently
> revolutionary and transformative. (Gay, 1995, p. 181)

Given that urban education and its students and practitioners arguably do
not have the social and/or political power to influence the values of
mainstream society, to succeed then is to educationally (and with the
involvement of the constituencies of an urban school) locate the spaces
for local change, to come to an understanding of the social and political
forces that block that change, and to subvert those forces within a
localized context. The definition of success becomes change, not its
degree or breadth, but simple change. This may well, and no doubt will,
include the teaching and learning of the skills that mainstream education
now is limited to. However, there is an additional critical purpose
grounded in an ethos of a community, subversive in nature and acting
to undermine mainstream purposes for its own reasons and its own
transformation, not that of the greater society.

While perhaps open to the accusation of being simplistic, the ethos
of this proposal is no stranger to either the urban black or Latino
communities. It is the essence of the 1950s and 60s civil rights
struggle, the movement of La Raza in the California agricultural fields
and a host of other experiences that grew from a subversive collectivity.

Sonia Nieto (1995) confirms this exact point when she describes an effort in an urban middle school to connect math and science learning within a multicultural context. The program was grounded in a "pedagogy derived from the civil rights movement using aspects of the Mississippi organizing tradition: the centrality of families to the work of organizing, the empowerment of grassroots people and their recruitment for leadership." (Nieto, 1995, p. 204). As she further comments—"one must organize in the context in which one lives and works, using the resources found in that context" (Nieto, p. 204). So too must any educational program for the change of inner-city education be founded on the human resources living in the community in which the school is located and not look to the greater society for assistance that will only be denied or linked to such an array of conditions that will destroy any possibility of school and community change.

The pedagogical should equally be obvious in its practice. How do we recover what Sharon Welch (1990) and others have called "dangerous memories"? Those memories are historical and available through narratives, biographies, remembrances, songs, and witnessing. They are found in the oral stories and traditions of every racialized minority in this country, often to be located in religious centers or community places of gathering. Inasmuch as mainstream myths and stories are used to teach history, English, reading, and physical education classes (although presented as facts and social representations of what constitutes knowledge), so too could these dangerous memories be used to teach the same classes. Teacher education can easily spend less time on lesson plans and schemes of classroom management and more on showing students how to recover such memories, including their own. Students of education would be better served by less memorizing of steps to so-called teaching effectiveness and more reflection on understandings of ethnography and personal experience. In schools, the collection of those memories can go hand in hand with community service with the elderly, often the communal repository for such recollections. Instead of teaching incipient teachers the art of imposing values through a hidden curriculum, reconstruct "values clarification" to help teachers model and engage students in coming to understand their own and others' values and beliefs, the understandings of historically informed cultural rationales for social and educational practices. Instead of the endless relativity of the "Human Relations" multicultural approach that spirals into acceptance of dominant rationales, teach how to investigate the construction of social attitudes and knowledge.

Science and history can be used to teach the value of an ecologically balanced community, and the underlying assumptions of socio-political systems such as democracy and market-based consumer capitalism. From there it is a small leap to student recognition of those market forces that sustain racial and cultural marginality and/or justify racialized notions of human deficiency and the hierarchialized determination of the division of social benefits. Math can be used to learn how to gather data to be used to support subversive arguments and student projects can be linked to community's efforts to improve life for its citizens. These can be linked to the interrogation and collective organization of students and community around issues of local concern and context. Equally subversive to the urban schools' isolation and administrative intransigence is the creation of connections to the local community and its concerns, including basing curriculum and schoolwork on the articulation of strategies for how teachers and students can work with and learn from diverse community members in working toward common concerns (Densmore, 1995). As Densmore aptly argues, "there is a tendency for educators to define academic curricula, even multicultural curricula, as properly distinct from engagement in solving social problems. Yet the impact of these problems (e.g., poverty) on the students in our classrooms means we must confront them if we are serious about educating the students we have." (Densmore, 1995, p. 413)

A subversive pedagogy is not difficult once we begin to unleash our own and students' imaginations, to agree to be honest and open in our critique, and to establish a model of shifting authority as learning and growth occurs. My own failure, illustrated in the incident with the principal over Malcolm X, was in not realizing the potential for change that the one small incident held. Although I had established a relatively good relationship with parents through an open-door classroom policy that aggressively asked them to visit, assist, and critique at any time, I failed to mobilize that support because I was not thinking either subversively or collectively. Not too surprisingly, I had earlier in life learned the power of a white male to get things done but had not learned how to develop a critical community. That incident was ripe with potential for the creation of a critically subversive community to join together to recover a dangerous memory for the students, and who knows where it might have led?

Incidents of similar potential occur constantly in any school, but in an inner-city school, particularly, they provide subversive moments.

Even though, as Weiner (1993) points out, the urban bureaucracy was designed to be insulated from parents and the community, that insularity is also a fracture point susceptible to any sustained pressure that holds the moral high ground. Urban principals are both powerfully authoritative and simultaneously politically insecure. The very insularity that provides a facade of power is an Achilles heel because they are often also without higher administrative support and thereby vulnerable to community pressure helped and targeted by a subversive faculty. While one of the problematics in urban schools (as well as any school) is the internal alienation of teachers from each other which makes it difficult to create a faculty collective, it does not take more than a few individuals working together within a reconstructive ethic to begin to impact the rest. Secondly, that alienation also derives from a sense of autonomy which can be utilized as another fracture point for teacher collective empowerment.

Even the turnover in teachers is or can be judiciously used as a fracture point. Teachers in inner-city schools who teach year after year, who return to the classroom every day, who arrange with students to share in classroom management so that few of their students appear in the office, who build cooperative understandings with other teachers, students, and parents *can* gain the freedom to locate and move themselves and their community within systemic fractures. One strength that I learned early to rely on was that the teachers who could be counted on by the principal to be in their classrooms day in and day out and who seldom sent or took students to the office for discipline were allowed considerable latitude in how, what, and where they taught. Many of the outside activities that I used to enhance my students' learning and interest occurred only because I learned to make use of that latitude. This in spite of my encouraging students to question and assert themselves against administrative contradictions through the school newspaper. Teachers who had established what amounted to an attendance consistency (note that this does not connote anything about their teaching) often were allowed by the office to operate with considerable freedom. For the most part, their instructional content and methods were subject to minimal, if any, office scrutiny. They involved students in fund-raising for pet projects, acquired equipment and books (which were usually guarded jealously), contracted with outside speakers and groups for presentations, and were usually the most vocal critics of the school administration. All of this was normally without office oversight or approval. Unfortunately, they also tended to be quite insular regarding new teachers and rarely extended their operational freedom to include other teachers or to make significant changes at the school. All too often, their insularity was directed at parents and relatives as well. The freedom gained, while often benefitting their students in some fashion, was generally used to procure a space free of bureaucratic control, not to create any collective or transformative agenda. Although a few of us assiduously used that freedom to gain space for what we believed was better teaching, in retrospect we failed to grasp the opportunity to come together with students and the community to create possibilities at the school. In part, this resulted from an understanding that change needed to be systemic and/or broad, a variation on the theme that you can't fight city hall. This understanding worked to convince us that since we could not change society, teacher education, or even the district policies by which the school was governed, any argument for transformative change was doomed to failure—so why exert ourselves? What we failed to understand was that we could have effected localized change at the school by coming together with the community to create a partnership to work for change in both. Therein lies a lesson for teacher education, whether pre-service or in-service, that it is possible to change at least the lives and conditions of the localized environment, particularly when connected to and within a reconstructive ethic. Once that process is underway, possibility becomes the impact of that transformative location on other sites in the web, although the goal is the local, not the system.

The actual pedagogies and classroom practices of a critical, democratic multiculturalism are not unknown. Numerous authors within the realms of critical pedagogy, multicultural education, bicultural education, and even within the boundaries of liberal pluralistic multiculturalism have sketched out the specifics of what teachers can and should do, and to recapitulate those efforts has never been the intent of this text. However, there are statements of perspective and purpose within which we can begin to construct a critical multiculturalism in the inner-city classroom. Often included in the texts cited in this book, these statements all need to be viewed from within the understanding that, ultimately, critical multiculturalism is about subversion and celebration, conflict and community, and the hope of social redemption.

All of these are eminently possible; however, there is one caveat: critical teachers in any school, including an urban one, must recognize what is doable and what is not. The old homily says that a long journey starts with one small step, and that is equally true of broad, fundamental systemic change. To conceive that one's subversion will lead to systemic change, to a social and educational transformation, is fraught with ego, not ethos. It is a plan for failure and cynicism, not change and hope. As I argued earlier, to contemplate the basing of broad social and cultural change in urban schools and upon urban students and teachers is to contemplate failure, and it is within that failure that despair and cynicism run rampant. Instead, the goal, the measure of success is incremental change; the transformation of a class, a day, a lesson is the alternative assessment to be invoked.

Conclusion

> As teachers we are always implicated in organizing the future
> for others and hence our actions always have a moral and
> political dimension. (Simon, 1992, p. 15)

The role of the educator must be to personally effect and assist students in a struggle for a more compassionately just and moral system capable of sustaining the diversity of human beings, a diversity not proposed as a solution to securing reciprocal equity within a social contract but as a fundamental condition of human dignity (Berger, 1981; cited in Simon, 1992, p. 23). Such an articulation would stress the plurality of human meaning-making, be it cultural or individual. It would call for educating for individual autonomy and community within a synergistic web of individual freedom and social justice. Additionally, we must engage students in both the heritage of their (and ours and others') cultural traditions and the difficulties and complexities that arise from the values inherent in the same narratives.

Here is the connection with Giroux's (1992) notions of Border Pedagogy; the concept of acknowledging and crossing borders to effect educational and social change can only occur within a mythos capable of energizing and sustaining human passions for justice, love, and mercy. It means that the educational institution must contain opportunities for the legitimate expression of diverse views and/or truths while being compassionate as to the partiality of their construction within nonsynchronous relations of gender, race, class, age, etc. (Simon, 1992; McCarthy, 1993). Those of us who have thrived on crossing borders in urban schools are also terribly conscious of the grim prospects faced by "our children." We are aware that no matter how successful they are personally or academically, these students face lives tragically limited by racism, ethnocentricity, and their status as the Other. We share a terrible, faceless cynicism, frustration, and anger at a social system that would intentionally, or worse perhaps, negligently condemn these children to ghettos and barrios of violence, drugs, and poverty and would do so all the while blaming them for the very conditions that society prescribes. If, in fact, we desire to effect a resolution of these conditions and a reconciliation between communities within and without urban centers, we must somehow replace that soul-less cynicism with hope and possibility. The anger and alienation is too great a burden to ask any human to bear.

I started out this text intending to expiate some of my own anger and guilt over the conditions and exigencies of one inner-city school. In essence, I intended an academic diatribe against the continued nihilistic impact of racism and ethnocentricity in this society in general and in education specifically. I found myself caught between the rocks of desiring profound possibilities of change through the vehicle of radical pedagogy and theory and the shoals of despair and cynicism engendered by the lengths and depths the dominant groups and forces of this society will go to maintain racial segregation and oppression. I found myself discouraged by the Left's unwillingness to address the ghettos and barrios except within a language of hyper-theorizing that obfuscates rather than enlightens, a symbolic discourse as removed from the classrooms of East St. Louis, Watts, South Chicago, Harlem and elsewhere, as are mainstream understandings and educational practices. I knew from experience that the mainstream concepts of compensatory education were an abysmal failure, that so-called multicultural education was a travesty convoluted by good intentions and terribly wrong-headed practices. The Right simply does not speak to the marginalized of our society, and the Left speaks about, but not to them. Experiences of human failure and institutional malfeasance have become a stock of cynical tales and war-stories to tell teacher education classes, overlaying a powerful anger that even students recognize and shy away from.

On the other hand, in the course of my research for this book, I found possibilities of hope within notions of border pedagogy when filtered through ideas about dialogue and solidarity. Like Sharon Welch, I realized that it was possible and indeed energizing to be in community with those that society perpetuates as victims and that what was needed within the Left's pedagogical theory were those elements of personality and ideals, the ethical constructs, as it were, that allowed for connections across borders of race, age and class within the grotesque confines of an inner-city school classroom.

It was the realization that these elements were not esoteric or symbolic but human and living that suggested that if they could be distilled, such a rarefied notion as border pedagogy could indeed be actualized. If, as so many point out, America is a land of the alienated and our schools and communities are haunted by individualism, angry ethnocentricity, dysfunctional families, rigid disempowering institutions, and social disintegration, then the sources of that anger and alienation must be faced head on in righteous indignation and denial. If education is not to represent our failure of conscience, according to Heschel, Simon, Purpel, and others, then it must *become that conscience.* As for the question "to what end," the end is the personal courage to denounce racism in all its formulations, to teach openly and unashamedly about love, joy, compassion, and human meaning and ultimately to summon the courage, individually and collectively, to demand that this society live up to its rhetoric in the advocacy of generosity, justness, and democracy. It is to acknowledge my own personal share of our collective shame and model the kind of teaching I desire in others.

If nothing else, it is my hope that I have made it clear that the American dilemma as to race, the dialectic that grounds our politics, ethics and morality, economics, and social relations, is at root level a matter of ethical choice—and that choice in terms of teacher education and urban education has been clearly and well put to us by Maxine Greene:

> It demands the identification of deficiencies in the world around (the addictions, the illnesses, the abandonments, the devastations) and a shared effort to repair. . . . Given what we see—the neglect, the cold carelessness, the rampant greed—it will take outrage if we are to succeed in education. It will take a new kind of hope, a new shaping of possibility, a new venture into the unpredictable. But, then, utopias are never predictable. We can only choose for ourselves something caring and humane and daring. We can only begin. (M. Greene, in Kincheloe and Steinberg, 1992, p. 292-3)

Appendix

Washington Middle School—Public Report Card
A Profile for the Community
1989-90 School Year

Note: The following are excerpts from the above entitled annual "Report Card." Sections are numbered as they are in the actual document, and the exact wording has been duplicated with the sole exception of the name of the school and the district. I have added commentary where I felt it necessary to describe the contradictions between the report and *actual* conditions as they occurred at the school.

Section 1—California Assessment
Program (Cap)

Each year, Washington Middle School's sixth and eighth graders take the CAP Survey of Basic Skills. Results are shown below (with the state average being 250).

8th Grade CAP results for the past 3 years.

```
        0    50   100   150   200   250   300
Reading *---*----*
        +---+----+-|
        #---#----#-|
```

```
Writing  *---*----*-----*              1987-88: *-----*
         +---+----+-----+---|          1988-89: +-----+
         #--#-------#--|               1989-90: #-----#

Math     *------*--------*-|
         +------+--------+---|
         #-----#-------#--|

Soc Sci  *------*--------*-----|
         +------+--------+--------+|
         #-----#-------#-------#-|

Science  *------*--------*--------*--|
         +------+--------+--------+-----|
         #-----#-------#-------#-------#--|
```

Section 4—Class Size

Schools throughout the district are staffed on the basis of one teacher per 30 pupils. Middle and secondary schools are assigned two additional teachers to further reduce class size.

****

Comment: *At no time in three years did I or any other teacher have fewer than 40 students assigned to a class. It was not infrequent to have as many students as 50 in a period. The lower ratio was derived by factoring in Resource and Administrative personnel who did not teach.*

Section 5—Teacher Assignments

Classes are staffed with teachers who hold the appropriate credentials. Several teachers in the district are employed on full-time emergency credentials.

****

Commentary: *At any one time, approximately one-half of the teachers who had credentials were teaching subjects for which they were not credentialed; e.g., I was credentialed for Life Science but taught Physical Science, Computers, 7th grade Math, 8th grade History and Algebra. In general, 50-60 percent of the teachers on staff, not "several," were on emergency credentials.*

Section 6—Textbooks

_____ Unified School District sets a high priority upon ensuring that there are sufficient textbooks to support each school's instructional program. Textbooks are purchased to coincide with the State curriculum cycle.

****

Commentary: *At no time in any classroom were there sufficient texts for students to be able to take books home for study and/or homework. When the State of California mandated a new Social Studies Framework in 1989, the District advised all schools that they would have the new text and workbooks for every student for the 1990-91 academic year. We had one copy of the new workbook and the teachers personally paid for ten (10) copies to be made for each Social Studies classroom; no additional copies were ever forthcoming from the district. The Science textbooks were copyright 1957, were variously broken or missing pages, and in my classroom they had been glued together by the water used to fight a fire in the next classroom; we used them as legs to hold up tables. Ergo, for several years Science was taught without recourse to any form of a textbook.*

Section 7—Counseling & Supportive Services

Students at Washington Middle School receive full-time services from non-instructional support staff.

Support Staff include:
-Counseling
-A School Nurse

-A Guidance, Welfare & Attendance Counselor
-A Speech Therapist
-A Psychologist

****

Commentary: *There were NO full or part time counselors on staff, although the Vice Principal doubled as an ad hoc counselor. There were no guidance or welfare counselors at the school and Attendance Counselor was the title given to the part-time attendance clerk. Although there was a district speech pathologist, she made only two trips in three years to the school; there were no full-time services of such a professional. There was a full-time nurse my first year, however, she was terminated, and we shared the services and time of a Nurse's Aide with two other schools. Injuries to students were usually treated on the spot by teachers or by telephoning the county paramedics. The district psychologist made four trips a year to the school to participate in IEPs with teachers and parents with a referral rate of less than 25 percent of the students seen.*

Section 10—Teacher Evaluation

Teachers are evaluated on an ongoing basis. Permanent teachers are evaluated no less than once every two years. Teachers found to be in need of improvement are placed in programs for professional improvement through school and district inservice programs.

****

Commentary: *At no time during my teaching at this school was I ever observed or evaluated by any administrative staff person, principal, vice principal or department chair. Nor was any other teacher of whom I was aware.*

Bibliography

Anyon, Jean. (1980). "Social Class and the Hidden Curriculum of Work," *Journal of Education*, 162, pp. 66-92.

Anyon, Jean. (1984). "Intersections of Gender and Class: Accommodation and Resistance by Working-Class and Affluent Females to Contradictory Sex Role Ideologies," *Journal of Education*, 166:1.

Aoki, Ted Tetsuo. (1988). "Toward a Dialectic Between the Conceptual World and the Lived World: Transcending Instrumentalism in Curriculum Orientation." In *Contemporary Curriculum Studies*, Wm. F. Pinar (Ed.), Scottsdale, AZ: Gorsuch, Scarisbrick Publishers, pp. 402-416.

Apple, Michael. (1982). *Education and Power* , Boston: Routledge & Kegan Paul.

Apple, Michael, and Landon Beyer (Eds.). (1988). *The Curriculum: Problems, Politics, and Possibilities*, Albany, NY: SUNY Press.

Apple, Michael, and Leslie Roman. (1990). "Is Naturalism a Move Away from Positivism?: Materialist and Feminist Approaches to Subjectivity in Ethnographic Research." In *Qualitative Inquiry in Education*, E. Eisner and A. Peshkin (Eds.), New York: Teachers College Press.

Aronowitz, Stanley. (1988). "Postmodernism and Politics." In A. Ross (Ed.), *Universal Abandon*, Minneapolis: Univ. of Minnesota Press.

Banks, James A. (1991). *Teaching Strategies for Ethnic Studies* (5th Ed.). Boston: Allyn and Bacon.

Barritt, Loren, Ton Beekman, Hans Bleeker and Karel Mulderij. (1983). "The World Through Children's Eyes," *Phenomenology and Pedagogy*, Vol 1:2, pp. 140-161.

Bastian, Ann, Norm Fruchter, Marilyn Gittell, Colin Greer, and Kenneth Hoskins. (1988). *Choosing Equality*, Philadelphia:

Temple University Press.

Bell, Derrick. (1992). *Faces at the Bottom of the Well*, New York: Basic Books.

Berger, T. (1981). *Fragile Freedoms: Human Rights and Dissent in Canada.*, Toronto: Clarke, Irwin. Cited in Roger I. Simon. (1992). *Teaching Against the Grain: Texts for a Pedagogy of Possibility*, New York: Bergin & Garvey.

Berry, G., & J. Asamen. (1989). *Black Students*, Newbury Park, CA: Sage Publications.

Bloom, Alan. (1987). *The Closing of the American Mind*, New York: Simon and Schuster.

Boateng, Felix. (1990). "Combatting Deculturalization of the African American Child in the Public School; A Multicultural Approach." In *Going to School: the African American Experience*, K. Lomotey (Ed.), Albany, NY: SUNY Press.

Bowles, S., and Gintis, H. (1976). *Schooling in Capitalist America*, New York: Basic Books.

Buber, M. (1958). *I and Thou*, New York: Charles Scribner's Sons.

Bullough, Robert. (March 1989). "Teaching Is Nurturing: Metaphor in a Case Study of a Beginning Teacher." Presentation at AERA 1989 Conference.

Burbules, Nicholas, and Suzanne Rice. (November 1991). "Dialogue across Differences: Continuing the Conversation," *Harvard Educational Review*, 61:4.

Burnham, Walter. (November-December, 1983). "Post-Conservative America," *Socialist Review*, No. 72.

Cannella, Gaile, and Judith Reiff. (Fall 1994). "Preparing Teachers for Cultural Diversity: Constructivist Orientations," *Action in Teacher Education* (ATE journal), Vol. XVI, 3, pp. 37-45.

Carlson, Dennis. (1989). "Managing the Urban School Crisis: Recent Trends in Curricular Reform," *Journal of Education*, 171:3.

Carlson, Dennis. (April 1992a). "Constructing the Margins: Of Multicultural Education and Curriculum Accords," unpublished manuscript presented at AERA Annual Meeting, San Francisco.

Carlson, Dennis. (1992b). "Education as a Political Issue." In *Thirteen Questions: Reframing Education's Conversation*, J. Kincheloe and S. Steinberg (Eds.), New York: Peter Lang Publishing.

Carter, Judge Robert L. (Summer 1995). "The Unending Struggle for Equal Educational Opportunity." In *Teachers College Record*, 96:4, pp. 619-626.

Children's Defense Fund Report. (1990). *Latino Youths at the Crossroads*, Washington, D.C.

Comer, J., and N. Haynes. (1990). "Helping Black Children Succeed: The Significance of Social Factors." In *Going to School: the African American Experience*, K. Lomotey (Ed.), Albany, NY: SUNY Press.

Commission on Minority Participation in Education and American Life, *One-Third of a Nation*, Washington, D.C.: American Council on Education, 1988; cited in Banks, 1991.

Cone, James. (1970). *A Black Theology of Liberation*, New York: J.B. Lippincott Co.

Coontz, Stephanie. (March 1995). "The American Family and the Nostalgia Trap." Kappan Special Report, *Phi Delta Kappan*, pp. K1-K20.

Cornbleth, Catherine, and Dexter Waugh. (1995). *The Great Speckled Bird: Multicultural Politics and Educational Policymaking*, New York: St. Martin's Press.

Cox, Harvey. (1984). *Religion in the Secular City: Toward a Postmodern Theology*, New York: Simon & Schuster.

Crawford, Alan. (1980). *Thunder on the Right: The "New Right" and the Politics of Resentment*, New York: Pantheon Books.

Crichlow, Warren. (1990). "Multicultural Ways of Knowing: Implications for Practice," *Journal of Education*, 172:2.

Cummins, James. (1994). "From Coercive to Collaborative Relations of Power in the Teaching of Literacy." In *Literacy Across Languages and Cultures*, B. Ferdman, R. Weber, and A. Ramirez (Eds.), Albany, NY: SUNY Press. pp. 295-331.

Darder, Antonia. (1991). *Culture and Power in the Classroom: A Critical Foundation for Bicultural Education*, Westport, CT: Bergin & Garvey.

Densmore, Kathleen. (1995). "An Interpretation of Multicultural Education and Its Implications for School-Community Relationships." In *Educating for Diversity: An Anthology of Multicultural Voices*, Grant, Carl (Ed.), Boston: Allyn & Bacon.

Eagleton, Terry. (1991). *Ideology*, New York: Verso Press.

Eisenhart, M., and M. E. Graue. (1993). "Constructing Cultural Difference and Educational Achievement in Schools." In *Minority Education: Anthropological Perspectives*, E. Jacob and C. Jordan (Eds.), Norwood, NJ: Ablex Publishing Corp., pp. 165-180.

Eisner, Elliot. (April 1981). "On the Differences between Scientific and

Artistic Approaches to Qualitative Research," *Educational Researcher*.

Eisner, Elliot, and Alan Peshkin. (1990). *Qualitative Inquiry in Education*, New York: Teachers College Press.

Erickson, F. (1993). "Transformation and School Success: The Politics and Culture of Educational Achievement." In *Minority Education: Anthropological Perspectives*, E. Jacob and C. Jordan (Eds.), Norwood, NJ: Ablex Publishing Corp., 1993, pp. 27-52.

Farber, Kathleen, and William Armaline. (Spring 1994). "Examining Cultural Conflict in Urban Field Experiences through the Use of Reflective Thinking." *Teacher Education Quarterly*, pp. 59-76.

Ferguson, R., M. Gever, Trinh Minh-ha, and Cornel West. (1990). *Out There; Marginalization and Contemporary Cultures*, Cambridge, MA: The MIT Press.

Figueroa, R., and E. Garcia. (Fall 1994). "Issues in Testing Students from Culturally and Linguistically Diverse Backgrounds." *Multicultural Education*.

Fine, Michelle. (1986). "Why Urban Adolescents Drop Into and Out of Public School," *Teachers College Record*, 87, 393-409.

Fine, Michelle. (1991). *Framing Drop-Outs*, Albany, NY: SUNY Press.

Fordham, Signithia. (1988). "Racelessness as a Factor in Black Students' School Success," *Harvard Educational Review*, 58:1.

Fordham, Signithia. (1991). Peer-Proofing Academic Competition Among Black Adolescents: "Acting White" Black American Style. In *Empowerment Through Multicultural Education*, C. Sleeter (Ed.), New York: SUNY Press, 1991.

Fordham, S., and J. Ogbu. (1986). "Black Students' School Success: Coping with the 'Burden of Acting White,'" *Urban Review*, 18:3.

Fox, Matthew. (1990). *A Spirituality Named COMPASSION*, San Francisco, CA: HarperCollins Publishers.

Freire, Paulo. (1970). *Pedagogy of the Oppressed*, New York: Herder and Herder.

Gay, Geneva. (1995). "Mirror Images on Common Issues: Parallels Between Multicultural Education and Critical Pedagogy." In *Multicultural Education, Critical Pedagogy and the Politics of Discourse*, C. Sleeter and P. McLaren (Eds.), Albany, NY: SUNY Press, pp. 155-189.

Geertz, Clifford. (1983). *The Interpretation of Cultures*, New York: HarperCollins Publishers.

Gilbert, S., and G. Gay. (1994). "Improving the Success in School of Poor Black Children," in *Phi Delta Kappan*, 66, p. 133-137.

Gilmore P. (1985). "Gimme Room: School Resistance, Attitude and Access to Literacy," *Journal of Education* 167:1.

Giroux, Henry. (1983). *Theory & Resistance in Education*, Boston: Bergin & Garvey.

Giroux, Henry. (1988a). "Border Pedagogy in the Age of Postmodernism," *Journal of Education*, 170:3.

Giroux, Henry. (1988b). *Teachers As Intellectuals*, Boston, MA: Bergin & Garvey.

Giroux, Henry. (1990). "Rethinking the Boundaries of Educational Discourse: Modernism, Postmodernism and Feminism," *College Literature*, 17: 2/3. Reprinted in *Postmodernism, Feminism, and Cultural Politics: Redrawing Educational Boundaries*, H. Giroux (Ed.), Albany, NY: SUNY Press, 1991.

Giroux, Henry (Ed.). (1991a). *Postmodernism, Feminism and Cultural Politics*. Albany, NY: SUNY Press.

Giroux, Henry. (1991b). Postmodernism as Border Pedagogy: Redefining the Boundaries of Race and Ethnicity. In *Postmodernism, Feminism, and Cultural Politics: Redrawing Educational Boundaries*, H. Giroux (Ed.), Albany, NY: SUNY Press, pp. 217-256.

Giroux, Henry. (1992). *Border Crossings: Cultural Workers and the Politics of Education*, New York: Routledge.

Giroux, Henry. (1995). "The Politics of Insurgent Multiculturalism in the Era of the Los Angeles Uprising." In *Critical Multiculturalism: Uncommon Voices in a Common Struggle*, B. Kanpol and P. McLaren (Eds.), Westport, CT: Bergin & Garvey.

Glasgow, Douglas. (1980). *The Black Underclass*, San Francisco: Jossey-Bass Publishers.

Gollnick, Donna, and Philip Chinn (1990). *Multicultural Education in a Pluralistic Society* (3d ed.), New York: Macmillan Publishing Co.

Goodlad, John. (1984). *A Place Called School*, New York: McGraw-Hill.

Gordon, Beverly. (1990). "The Necessity of African-American Epistemology for Educational Theory and Practice," *Journal of Education*, 172:3.

Gordon, Beverly. (1992). "The Marginalized Discourse of Minority Intellectual Thought in Traditional Writings on Teaching." In

Research & Multicultural Education: From the Margins to the Mainstream, Carl A. Grant (Ed.), Washington, D.C.: Falmer Press, 1992.

Grant, Carl A. (Ed.). (1992). *Research & Multicultural Education: From the Margins to the Mainstream*, Washington, D.C.: Falmer Press.

Grant, Carl A. (Fall 1994). "Best Practices in Teacher Preparation for Urban Schools," *Action in Teacher Education* (ATE Journal), XVI:3, pp. 1-18.

Grant, Carl A. (Ed.). (1995). *Educating for Diversity: An Anthology of Multicultural Voices*, Boston: Allyn & Bacon.

Grant, Carl A., and Susan Millar. (1992). "Research and Multicultural Education: Barriers, Needs and Boundaries." In *Research & Multicultural Education: From the Margins to the Mainstream*, Carl A. Grant (Ed.), Washington, D.C.: Falmer Press.

Greene, Maxine. (1978). "The Lived World," *Landscapes of Learning*, New York: Teachers College Press, pp. 213-224.

Greene, Maxine. (1992). Untitled article in *Thirteen Questions; Reframing Education's Conversation*, Joe L. Kincheloe and Shirley Steinberg (Eds.), New York: Peter Lang, 1992.

Greene, Maxine. (1993a). "The Passions of Pluralism Multiculturalism and the Expanding Community," *Educational Researcher*, Jan.-Feb. 1993, pp. 13-18.

Greene, Maxine. (1993b). "Diversity and Inclusion: Toward a Curriculum for Human Beings," *Teachers College Record*, 93:2, Winter, 1993, pp. 211-221.

Grossman, Herbert. (1995). *Teaching in a Diverse Society*, Boston: Allyn and Bacon.

Grubb, H. J. (1986). "The Black Prole and Whitespeak: Black English from an Orwellian Perspective," *Race and Class* 27:3, pp. 67-80.

Grumet, Madeline. (1992). "The Curriculum; What Are the Basics and Are We Teaching Them?" In *Thirteen Questions; Reframing Education's Conversation*, Joe L. Kincheloe and Shirley Steinberg (Ed.), New York: Peter Lang.

Haberman, Martin. (1989). "More Minority Teachers," *Phi Delta Kappan*, 70, pp. 771-776.

Haberman, Martin. (1992). "The Pedagogy of Poverty versus Good Teaching," *Phi Delta Kappan*, 73, pp. 290-294.

Habermas, Jurgen. (1979). *Communication and the Evolution of Society*, Boston: Beacon Press.

Habermas, Jurgen. (1987). *The Philosophic Discourse of Modernity*, Cambridge, MA: M.I.T. Press.

Hacker, Andrew. (1992). *Two Nations; Black and White, Separate, Hostile, Unequal*, New York: Charles Scribner's Sons, Macmillan Publishing Co.

Haymes, Stephen. (1995). *Race, Culture and the City: A Pedagogy for Black Urban Struggle*, Albany, NY: SUNY Press.

Heath, Shirley, and Milbrey McLaughlin (Eds.). (1993). *Identity & Inner-City Youth: Beyond Ethnicity and Gender*, New York: Teachers College Press.

Heschel, Abraham. (1962). *The Prophets*, Philadelphia: Jewish Publication Society.

Heschel, Abraham. (1965). *Who Is Man?*, Stanford, CA: Stanford University Press.

Hessong, R. & T. Weeks. (1991). *Introduction to the Foundations of Education* (2nd ed.), New York: Macmillan Publishing Company.

Hirsch, E.D. (1987). *Cultural Literacy: What Every American Needs to Know*, Boston: Houghton Mifflin, 1987.

Hood, S., and L. Parker. (1994). "Minority Students Informing the Faculty: Implications for Racial Diversity and the Future of Teacher Education," *Journal of Teacher Education*, 45, 3, May-June 1994, pp. 164-171.

hooks, bell. (1989). *Talking Back: Thinking Feminist, Thinking Black*, Boston: South End Press.

hooks, bell. (1990). *Yearning; Race, Gender and Cultural Politics*, Boston: South End Press, 1990.

hooks, bell. (1992). *Black Looks: Race and Representation*, Boston: South End Press.

hooks, bell, and Cornel West. (1991). *Breaking Bread; Insurgent Black Intellectual Life*, Boston: South End Press.

Horkheimer, Max, and Theodor Adorno. (1972). *Dialectic of Enlightenment*, New York: Herder and Herder.

Husserl, E. (1970). *The Crisis of European Sciences and Transcendental Phenomenology*, Evanston, IL: Northwestern Univ. Press.

Jaimes, M. Annette (Ed.). (1992). *The State of Native America*, Boston: South End Press.

Jaynes, G. D., and R. Williams (Eds.). (1989). *A Common Destiny: Blacks and American Society*, Washington, D.C.: National Academy Press.

Kanpol, Barry. (1992). *Towards a Theory and Practice of Teacher Cultural Politics: Continuing the Postmodern Debate*, Norwood, NJ: Ablex Publishing Co.

Kanpol, Barry. (Spring 1992). "Postmodernism in Education Revisited: Similarities within Differences and the Democratic Imaginary," *Educational Theory*, 42:2.

Kanpol, Barry, and Peter McLaren (Eds.). (1995). *Critical Multiculturalism: Uncommon Voices in a Common Struggle*. Westport, CT: Bergin & Garvey.

Kanter, L., and Kanter, M. (1976). *Assertive Discipline: A Take Charge Approach for Today's Educator*, Santa Monica, CA: Kanter & Assoc.

Karier, Clarence. (1986). *The Individual, Society, and Education: A History of American Educational Ideas* (2d ed.). Chicago: Univ. of Illinois Press.

Kincheloe, Joe L., and Shirley Steinberg (Eds.). (1992). *Thirteen Questions; Reframing Education's Conversation*, New York: Peter Lang.

King, Joyce E., and Thomasyne L. Wilson. (1990). "Being the Soul-Freeing Substance: A Legacy of Hope in Afro Humanity," *Journal of Education*, 172:2.

King, S. H. (1993). "The Limited Presence of African-American Teachers," *Review of Educational Research*, 63, pp. 115-149.

Kliebard, Herbert M. (1992). *Forging the American Curriculum; Essays in Curriculum History and Theory*, New York: Routledge, Chapman & Hall, Inc.

Kozol, Jonathan. (1991). *Savage Inequalities; Children in America's Schools*, New York: Crown Publishers.

Ladson-Billings, Gloria, and Annette Henry. (1990). "Blurring the Borders: Voices of Liberatory Pedagogy in the United States and Canada," *Journal of Education*, 172:2.

Lather, Patti. (1986). "Research as Praxis," *Harvard Educational Review*, Vol. 56:3, pp. 257-277.

Lather, Patti. (1989). "Postmodernism and the Politics of Enlightenment," *Educational Foundations*, pp. 7-28.

Lather, Patti. (1991). *Getting Smart: Feminist Research and Pedagogy within the Postmodern*, New York: Routledge.

Levine-Rasky, Cynthia. (1995). "Disturbing the Subject of Educational Discourse," *Journal of Thought*, 30:1, pp. 7-18.

Levinson, Bradley A. (1992). "Ogbu's Anthropology and the Critical

Ethnography of Education: A Reciprocal Interrogation," *Qualitative Studies in Education*, 5:3, pp. 205-225.

Liston, Daniel, and Kenneth Zeichner. (1987). "Critical Pedagogy and Teacher Education," *Journal of Education*, 169, pp. 117-143.

Liston, Daniel, and Kenneth Zeichner. (1991). *Teacher Education and the Social Conditions of Schooling*, New York: Routledge.

Lomotey, K. (Ed.). (1990). *Going to School: The African American Experience*, Albany, NY: SUNY Press.

Lorde, Audre. (1990). "Age, Race, Class, and Sex: Women Defining Difference." In *Out There: Marginalization and Contemporary Cultures*, Russell Ferguson, Martha Gever, Trinh Minh-ha, and Cornel West (Eds.), Cambridge, MA: The MIT Press.

Lyons, Nona. (1983). "Two Perspectives: On Self, Relationships, and Morality," *Harvard Educational Review*, 53:2, pp. 125-143.

Macedo, Donaldo. (1995). "Literacy for Stupification: The Pedagogy of Big Lies." In *Multicultural Education, Critical Pedagogy and the Politics of Discourse*, C. Sleeter and P. McLaren (Eds.), Albany, NY: SUNY Press.

Marable, M. (1992). *The Crisis of Color and Democracy*, Monroe, ME: Common Courage Press.

Marable, M. (1983). *How Capitalism Underdeveloped Black America*, Boston: South End Press.

Martusewicz, Rebecca, and William Reynolds (Eds.). (1994). *Inside/Out: Contemporary Critical Perspectives in Education*, New York: St. Martin's Press.

Massey, Douglas, and Nancy Denton. (1993). *American Apartheid: Segregation and the Making of the Underclass*, Cambridge, MA: Harvard University Press.

McCarthy, Cameron. (1990). "Multicultural Education, Minority Identities, Textbooks, and the Challenge of Curriculum Reform," *Journal of Education*, 172:2.

McCarthy, Cameron. (1992). *Race and Curriculum: Social Inequality and the Theories and Politics of Difference in Contemporary Research on Schooling*, Washington, D.C.: Falmer Press.

McCarthy, Cameron, and Warren Crichlow (Eds.). (1993). *Race, Identity and Representation in Education*, New York: Routledge.

McLaren, Peter. (1988a). "Schooling the Postmodern Body: Critical Pedagogy and the Politics of Enfleshment," *Journal of Education*, 170:3.

McLaren, Peter. (1988b). "Broken Dreams, False Promises, and the

Decline of Public Schooling," *Journal of Education*, 170, No. 1, Boston Univ. Press, November, pp. 41-65.

McLaren, Peter. (1989). *Life in Schools: An Introduction to Critical Pedagogy in the Foundations of Education*, New York: Longman, Inc.

McLaren, Peter. (1991). "Critical Pedagogy: Constructing an Arch of Social Dreaming and a Doorway to Hope," *Journal of Education*, Vol. 173:1.

McLaren, Peter. (1992). "Critical Pedagogy, Multiculturalism and the Human Spirit; A Response to Kelly and Portelli," *Journal of Education*.

McLaren, Peter. (1995). "White Terror and Oppositional Agency: Towards a Critical Multiculturalism." In *Multicultural Education, Critical Pedagogy and the Politics of Discourse*, C. Sleeter and P. McLaren (Eds.), Albany, NY: SUNY Press.

McLaren, Peter, and Joe Kincheloe. (1992). "Critical Multiculturalism and Democratic Schooling: An Interview with Peter McLaren and Joe Kincheloe," *International Journal of Educational Reform*.

McNeil, L. M. (1986). *Contradictions of Control: School Structure and School Knowledge*, New York: Routledge & Kegan Paul.

Measor, Lynda. (1985). "Interviewing: A Strategy in Qualitative Research." In *Strategies of Educational Research*, R. Burger (Ed.), London: Falmer Press.

Miles, Mathew, and A. Michael Huberman. (1984). "Drawing Valid Meaning from Qualitative Data: Toward a Shared Craft," *Educational Researcher*.

Miller, Lamar. (1995). "Tracking the Progress of *Brown*," *Teachers College Record*, 96:4, Summer.

Mouffe, Chantal. (1988). "Radical Democracy: Modern or Postmodern." In *Universal Abandon*, A. Ross (Ed.), Minneapolis: Univ. of Minnesota Press.

National Coalition of Advocates for Students (1988). "Barriers to Excellence: Our Children at Risk," cited in McLaren, P. (1988a), *Journal of Education*, 170:3.

Nieto, Sonia. (1994). "Lessons from Students on Creating a Chance to Dream," *Harvard Educational Review*, 64:4, pp. 392-426.

Nieto, Sonia. (1995) *Affirming Diversity: The Sociopolitical Context of Multicultural Education* (2nd Ed.), New York: Longman Publishing.

Nieto, Sonia. (1995). "From Brown Heroes and Holidays to

Assimilationist Agendas: Reconsidering the Critiques of Multicultural Education." In *Multicultural Education, Critical Pedagogy and the Politics of Discourse*, C. Sleeter and P. McLaren (Eds.), Albany, NY: SUNY Press, 1995.

Ogbu, John. (1978). *Minority Education and Caste: The American System in Cross-Cultural Perspective*, New York: Academic Press.

Ogbu, John. (1983). "Minority Status and Schooling in Plural Societies," *Comparative Education Review*, 27:2, pp. 168-190.

Ogbu, John. (1988). "Class Stratification, Racial Stratification and Schooling." In *Race, Class and Schooling*, L. Weis (Ed.), New York: SUNY Press.

Ogbu, John U. (1989). "Minority Youth's School Success," Address for Conference Advancing Effective Teaching for At-Risk Youth, Johns Hopkins University, Baltimore, May, 1988; cited in *Black Students*, G. Berry and J. Asamen (Eds.), Newbury Park, NJ: Sage Publications, Inc., 1989.

Ogbu, John. (1990). "Literacy and Schooling in Subordinate Cultures: The Case of Black Americans." In *Going to School: the African American Experience*, K. Lomotey (Ed.), Albany: SUNY Press.

Ogbu, John. (1993). "Variability in Minority School Performance: A Problem in Search of an Explanation." In *Minority Education: Anthropological Perspectives*, E. Jacob and C. Jordan (Eds.), Norwood, NJ: Ablex Publishing Corp., pp. 83-112.

Omi, Michael, and Winant, Howard. (1986). *Racial Formation in the United States*, New York: Routledge & Kegan Paul.

Pang, Valerie, and Robertta Barba. (1995). "The Power of Culture: Building Culturally Affirming Instruction." In *Educating for Diversity: An Anthology of Multicultural Voices*, C. Grant (Ed.), Boston: Allyn & Bacon, pp. 341-357.

Peller, Gary. (1992). "Race Against Integration," *Tikkun*, 6:1.

Phelan, Patricia, and Ann Davidson (Eds.). (1993). *Renegotiating Cultural Diversity in American Schools*, New York: Teachers College Press.

Pinar, William (Ed.). (1988). *Contemporary Curriculum Studies*, Scottsdale, AZ: Gorsuch, Scarisbrick Publishers.

Popkewitz, T. S. (1987). "Ideology and Social Formation in Teacher Education." In *Critical Studies in Teacher Education*, T. S. Popkewitz (Ed.), London: Falmer Press, pp. 2-33.

Purpel, David. (1989). *The Moral and Spiritual Crisis in Education*, Boston: Bergin & Garvey Publishers, Inc.

Purpel, David. (1995). "Eyewitness to Higher Education: Confession and Indictment," *Taboo*, New York: Peter Lang Publishing, Vol. 1, pp. 185-202.

Purpel, David, and Svi Shapiro. (1995). *Beyond Liberation and Excellence: Towards a New Public Discourse for Education*, New York: Routledge.

Quantz, Richard, and T. O'Connor. (1988). "Writing Critical Ethnography: Dialogue, Multivoicedness, and Carnival in Cultural Texts," *Educational Theory*, No. 38, pp. 95-109.

Richardson, V., U. Casanova, P. Placier, and K. Guilfoyle. (1989). *School Children at Risk*, London: Falmer Press.

Roman, Leslie G. (1993). "White Is a Color! White Defensiveness, Postmodernism and Anti-racist Pedagogy." In *Race, Identity and Representation in Education*, C. McCarthy and W. Crichlow (Eds.), New York: Routledge.

Rosenau, Pauline. (1992). *Postmodernism and the Social Sciences*, Princeton, NJ: Princeton University Press.

Ryan, William. (1992). "Blaming the Victim." In *Race, Class & Gender in the United States*, P. Rothenberg (Ed.), New York: St. Martin's Press.

Schwartz, Ellen. (1992). "Multicultural Education: From a Compensatory to a Scholarly Foundation." In *Research & Multicultural Education: From the Margins to the Mainstream*, Carl A. Grant (Ed.), Washington, D.C.: Falmer Press.

Shapiro, Svi. (1990). *Between Capitalism and Democracy*, New York: Bergin & Garvey Publishing.

Shapiro, Svi. (1991). "Pedagogy in a Time of Uncertainty: Post-Modernism and the Struggle for Community," *Curriculum and Teaching*, Vol. 6:2.

Shapiro, Svi. (1992). "Educational Change and the Crisis of the Left: Towards a Post-Modern Educational Discourse." Reprinted in *Beyond Liberation and Excellence: Towards a New Public Discourse for Education*, D. Purpel and S. Shapiro (Eds.), New York: Routledge, 1995.

Shapiro, Svi. (1995). "Educational Change and the Crisis of the Left: Towards a Post-Modern Educational Discourse." In *Education, Democracy and the Politics of Difference*, B. Kanpol and P. McLaren (Eds.), Westport, CT: Bergin & Garvey.

Simon, Roger I. (1992). *Teaching Against the Grain: Texts for a Pedagogy of Possibility*, New York: Bergin & Garvey.

Sleeter, Christine E. (1989). "Multicultural Education as a Form of Resistance to Oppression," *Journal of Education*, 171:3.

Sleeter, Christine E. (Ed.). (1991). *Empowerment through Multicultural Education*, New York: SUNY Press.

Sleeter, Christine. E. (1993). "How White Teachers Construct Race." In *Race, Identity and Representation in Education*, C. McCarthy and W. Crichlow (Eds.), New York: Routledge.

Sleeter, Christine E. (1994). "Resisting Racial Awareness: How Teachers Understand the Social Order from Their Racial, Gender and Social Class Locations." In *Inside/Out: Contemporary Critical Perspectives in Education*, Rebecca Martusewicz and William Reynolds (Eds.), New York: St. Martin's Press, pp. 240-264.

Sleeter, Christine E., and Carl A. Grant. (1987). "An Analysis of Multicultural Education in the United States," *Harvard Educational Review*, 57:4, pp. 421-444.

Sleeter, Christine E., and Carl A. Grant. (1989). *Turning on Learning: Five Approaches for Multicultural Teaching Plans for Race, Class, Gender & Disability*, New York: Merrill-Macmillan Publishing Co., 1989.

Sleeter, Christine E., and Carl A. Grant. (1991). "Mapping Terrains of Power: Student Cultural Knowledge Versus Classroom Knowledge." In *Empowerment Through Multicultural Education*, C. Sleeter (Ed.), New York: SUNY Press.

Sleeter, Christine E., and Carl A. Grant. (1994). *Making Choices for Multicultural Education: Five Approaches for Race, Class, and Gender* (2d ed.), New York: Macmillan Publishing Co.

Sleeter, Christine E., and Peter McLaren (Eds.). (1995). *Multicultural Education, Critical Pedagogy and the Politics of Discourse*, Albany, NY: SUNY Press.

Solomon, R. (1988). "Black Cultural Forms in Schools: A Cross National Comparison." In *Race, Class and Schooling*, L. Weis (Ed.), Albany, NY: SUNY Press, 1988.

Solomon, R. (1992). *Black Resistance in High School*, Albany, NY: SUNY Press.

Soto, Lourdes. (1992). "Success Stories." In *Research & Multicultural Education: From the Margins to the Mainstream*, Carl A. Grant (Ed.), Washington, D.C.: Falmer Press.

Spring, Joel. (1990). *The American School; 1642-1990* (2d ed.), New York: Longman.

Steinberg, Shirley. (1995). "Critical Multiculturalism and Democratic

Schooling: An Interview with Peter McLaren and Joe Kincheloe." In *Multicultural Education, Critical Pedagogy and the Politics of Discourse*, C. Sleeter and P. McLaren (Eds.), Albany, NY: SUNY Press.

Tabb, William. (1970). *The Political Economy of the Black Ghetto*, New York: W.W. Norton. Cited in M. Marable, *How Capitalism Underdeveloped Black America*, Boston: South End Press, 1983.

Tiedt, Pamela, and Irus Tiedt. (1990). *Multicultural Teaching: A Handbook of Activities, Information and Resources* (3rd ed.), Boston: Allyn and Bacon.

Trueba, Henry. (1993). "Cultural Diversity and Conflict: The Role of Educational Anthropology in Healing Multicultural America." In Phelan, P. & A. Davidson (Eds.), *Renegotiating Cultural Diversity in American Schools*, New York: Teachers College Press.

Weiner, Lois. (1993). *Preparing Teachers for Urban Schools: Lessons from Thirty Years of School Reform*, New York: Teachers College Press.

Weis, Lois. (1988). *Class, Race, & Gender in American Education*, Albany, NY: SUNY Press.

Welch, Sharon. (1990). *A Feminist Ethic of Risk*, Minneapolis, MN: Fortress Press.

West, Cornel. (1990). "The New Cultural Politics of Difference." In *Out There; Marginalization and Contemporary Cultures*, Russell Ferguson, Russell, Martha Gever, Trinh Minh-ha, and Cornel West (Eds.), Cambridge, MA: The MIT Press.

West, Cornel. (1993). *Race Matters*, Boston: Beacon Press.

West, Cornel. (1993a). *Beyond Eurocentrism and Multiculturalism: Prophetic Thought in Postmodern Times* (2 vols.), Monroe, ME: Common Courage Press.

Wexler, Philip. (1987). *Social Analysis of Education: After the New Sociology*, New York: Routledge & Kegan Paul.

Wilson, William J. (1987). *The Truly Disadvantaged: the Inner City, the Underclass and Public Policy*, Chicago: Univ. of Chicago Press.

Wolcott, Harry. (1990). "On Seeking—And Rejecting—Validity in Qualitative Research." In *Qualitative Inquiry in Education*, E. Eisner and A. Peshkin (Eds.), New York: Teachers College Press.

Yeo, Fred. (1992). "The Inner-City School: A Conflict in Rhetoric," *Critical Pedagogy Networker*, Vol. 5:3.

Yeo, Fred. (1995). "Conflicts of Difference in an Inner City School:

Experiencing Border Crossings in the Ghetto." In *Critical Multiculturalism: Uncommon Voices in a Common Struggle*, B. Kanpol and Peter McLaren (Eds.), Westport, CT: Bergin & Garvey.

Yetman, N. (1985). *Majority and Minority: The Dynamics of Racial and Ethnic Relations* (4th ed), Boston: Allyn and Bacon.

Young, Lauren, and Susan Melnick. (1988). "Forsaken Lives, Abandoned Dreams; What Will Compel Us to Act?" *Harvard Educational Review*, 58:3.

Index

Subject Index